THE BUSY WOMAN'S GUIDE TO

High Energy

HAPPINESS

LOUISE THOMPSON

PENGUIN BOOKS

All the worksheets in this book are also available for
downloading at www.louisethompson.com

PENGUIN BOOKS
Published by the Penguin Group
Penguin Group (NZ), 67 Apollo Drive, Rosedale,
Auckland 0632, New Zealand (a division of Pearson New Zealand Ltd)

Penguin Books Ltd, Registered Offices: 80 Strand, London, WC2R 0RL, England

First published by Penguin Group (NZ), 2014
10 9 8 7 6 5 4 3

Designed, illustrated and typeset by Jenny Haslimeier, © Penguin Group (NZ)
Illustration on pages 3, 20, 42, 74, 130,164 and 234 based on image from
iStockphoto.com
Prepress by Image Centre Ltd
Printed in China by RR Donnelley Asia Printing Solutions Ltd

ISBN 978-0-143-57064-6

A catalogue record for this book is available from the National Library of New Zealand.

www.penguin.co.nz

Case studies are based on real people but some names have been changed to
protect privacy.

Every effort has been made to ensure that the information contained in this book
is accurate. However, neither the publisher nor the author is engaged in rendering
professional advice or services to the individual reader. The ideas and suggestions
contained in this book are not intended as a substitute for consulting with your
physician. All matters regarding your health require medical supervision. Neither the
author nor the publisher shall be liable or responsible for any loss or damage allegedly
arising from any information or suggestion in this book.

CONTENTS

FOREWORD

Many books are written to be read once and enjoyed for their momentary pleasure. Then there are those books that have the potential to make a real impact on your life. This is one of those books. Although designed to help you step by step through recovery from adrenal fatigue and similar states of depletion, it is really a book of self-discovery; an exploration of what exhausted you in the first place and how to find your own path back to not just the person you were before you became tired, but to a person able to experience life with the fullest health and vitality. In short, it is a guide to personal transformation, written from the trenches by one who went from a fast and overly full life in the news media business to almost total incapacitation and then back to health, albeit living a very different lifestyle.

Like the thousands of people I saw in my decades of active practice and likely millions more out there, Louise Thompson gave her all to her career and demanding life, and when she crashed, she found little help in the doctor's office. That is where this book comes in. If you are willing to look in the mirror – really look to see what is actually there – and commit to changing your life so that it can take you to a level of energy you never thought possible, this is a book that can help you do it. This is a book about confronting yourself, in a gentle, loving way, and not letting yourself get away with the usual mental tricks and dodges that stand in the way of an energetic, happy life. It does not allow you to wallow in self-pity or hold on to excuses.

Louise's book takes what she has learned from her own harrowing journey and combines it with her professional life-coaching wisdom to produce a true self-help manual. It is not for sissies! Centred on the mental game of transformative healing, this book will make you look inside yourself and discover what you really want, what is holding you back, and how to turn your life around. Along the way, it provides information on the critical roles that lifestyle, diet, nutrition and the proper dietary supplements can play in recovery from stress and depleted conditions. She also includes what I believe to be a critical piece often missing from self-help books: how important finding spiritual connection is in reclaiming a fully experienced, healthy life.

This book could only be written by someone who has taken every single difficult step of the journey herself. Louise had to overcome tremendous odds, persist when there was no hope, and keep searching for answers when the medical profession told her there was nothing wrong with her. Fortunately for Louise and for you, she persevered and found her way out of sickness into health. With a desire to share her story and those of others as inspirations, she provides many resources and insights to help you find your own way. This is a gentle boot camp for recovery. It will help you discover how prioritisation of values can lead you either on a continuation down the slippery path or into a new level of health. It is all about what you truly value.

So many people suffer unnecessarily from chronic illness, adrenal fatigue being one of them, for which there is help but the help seems hard to find. Much of the problem comes from looking for help in all the wrong places. When it comes to chronic illness, the medical profession is only equipped to offer temporary symptomatic relief. Medical doctors never study health, they only study disease. They cannot direct you back to health in a way this book does, because they have no paradigm for health. The prescription for health has been left for others, and, as you know if you have struggled with your own health issues, there is sometimes no shortage of well-meaning people who provide worthless information and advice, sometimes at a very high price. But this book is genuine. It comes from the lessons of experience, learned by someone who has the compassion and commitment to put what she has learned the hard way into a book that will ease the way to health for people willing to apply it. To any doubters of the tremendous value and truth in this book, I would simply ask, 'Have you tried doing what is written in the book?' Here's to your own personal journey back to health and happiness. And when you get there, share your story with others.

James L. Wilson, DC, ND, PhD
Author of *Adrenal Fatigue: The 21st Century Stress Syndrome*

WELCOME TO HIGH ENERGY HAPPINESS

We all just want to be happy, don't we? Well, the key to a happy life is creating an energetic one first. Everything starts with energy. Energy is the foundation on which the house of happiness rests. Striving for happiness without first addressing our energy levels is equivalent to building a house on sand.

Without energy, vitality and good health we have nothing. I know this first-hand. I am an ex-corporate executive turned life coach and yoga teacher who was bedridden with extreme fatigue for many months. I had just met the love of my life and I had much happy stuff going on, but I couldn't embrace it because I was so tired I couldn't even dress myself! I was 37. That's scary.

What was even scarier was that multiple health professionals had no idea what was wrong with me or how to get me well. All my blood tests came back as 'normal' despite the most soul-crushing tiredness. I was so far from 'normal' it was laughable! Inch by inch I had slid into this extreme fatigue; at one point I was just a bit run down, a few years later I was dragging myself through each day. I wish I could have read this book then. I could have turned things around completely and skipped the bedridden bit!

I have written this book in the hope that no one else has to go through what I did; that you will recognise the warning signals of tiredness that I ignored; that you can use the techniques here to build a solid foundation of high-energy practices – physical, mental and emotional – that will underpin the happiest life you can imagine.

Writing this book has made sense of my own experience. I went through it for a reason: so you don't have to! It's my mission to spread the word about how to live a high-energy life. Using the tools and techniques in this book, I hope that you will make simple changes to the way you think and behave so you never make the mistakes I did. We can all have a happy life lived with passion, purpose and energy. We just need to know how to generate energy and happiness from the inside.

I believe that tiredness and 'pushing through' have become normalised in our society in a way that is harmful (it's no coincidence that the number of coffee stores has increased as our levels of tiredness and stress have increased!). Feeling tired all the time is not normal at all, and it's not acceptable. It's something we can absolutely do something about, primarily by changing the way we think.

This book is a mind–body–spirit energy recovery programme and it's unique. It's how I got my energy back, and it's what I teach to my clients as they regain their mojo and create a life they love. It's a blend of life-coaching smarts and Eastern insight, which addresses destructive thought patterns that are draining your energy. We will essentially be upgrading your thought software from 'Beliefs and Thoughts 1.0' to a much more up-to-date, less buggy and smoother running operating system: 'Beliefs and Thoughts 2.0'! And we'll combine this with some Eastern wisdom: yogic techniques that are thousands of years old which liberate energy within the body. There will also be some simple food and diet tweaks (see page 142) that were a key component in my recovery.

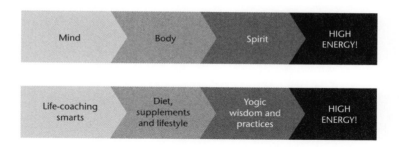

WHO IS THIS BOOK FOR?

If you find yourself saying 'I am so tired' all the time, then this book is for you. If life has become a grind some days, then this is for you. If you want to have a fuller, happier, more connected, vital life, then this is for you. If you have dark circles under your eyes that even concealer can't disguise, then this is for you. I know how you feel because I have been there (see My Story, page 14). But I also got myself back.

I am not a doctor and I am not a natural-health practitioner. I am a smart, high-achieving professional woman who got very, very tired indeed, just through living everyday life. I am not some sad 'loser' who couldn't handle the pressure, and it's not a sign of weakness to get fatigued. Having exhausted every option the medical profession had to understand my continual exhaustion, I figured out myself that I had adrenal fatigue, which doesn't show in blood tests because it's not what the standard tests are calibrated for. Adrenal fatigue is widely under-diagnosed: so many people are pushing through each day with another espresso, not realising there is something that can be done. I figured out a process to get my health and energy back. Now I have energy to burn! And you have the secrets I learned in your hands.

This is a toolkit you can use to get your energy and vitality back. I want you to feel extraordinary energy, so your partner and/or kids can barely keep up with you! I want spontaneous laughter, adventure and fun to fill your outrageously energetic life. Let's get started.

HOW TO USE THIS BOOK

This book is very much a toolkit. A huge kitbag stuffed full of all the mind, body and soul tools you need to restore your vitality, and empower your health and wellness.

I encourage you to *work* your way through this book. Creating a happy, energetic life is a participation sport rather than a spectator sport! You will get the most out of your journey by actually *doing* the exercises in this book, not just reading them. This will help you analyse your situation and understand the unique trigger points that create tiredness in your life. The path back is hidden in your own answers, so I encourage you to make a cup of herbal tea, find a quiet space, grab a pen and work through the answers that come up for you. Your road to vitality is in those answers.

I have created an online programme, which includes supporting audios, slide shows, interviews, videos and recipe books, as well as a forum of like-minded people to support your journey. It's an amazing and complete resource for wellness and energy. Some of the online resources are free – my gift to you – and some are paid-for resources. You can find this wealth of additional support for a life of maximum happiness at www.louisethompson.com.

These tools have been used by me and my clients. They work, if *you* work! I have seen so many men and women, grey with tiredness, stumble into my office and be transformed by their own diligent application of these tools. Seeing the beautiful butterflies they are emerge as they put these habits of energy into practice is a pleasure and a privilege. But it won't happen by magic; you need to do the work in the book, not just read it. The power is in the application.

Nothing in this programme is difficult. Nothing is complex. Nothing is going to take a degree in biology to understand. But it does take the decision to consistently choose yourself. Choose wellness. Choose to apply the tools. And choose a life that will rapidly unfold into the energetic one I know you deserve.

Our bodies are all different, and different readers are going to feel different levels of tiredness. I outline these on page 24 so you can benchmark where you are at.

Whatever your level of tiredness right now, this book is going to serve you enormously. I encourage you to implement every tool that resonates for you. All of them will boost your vitality and zest for life.

Here are some of the common signs that you may be heading towards burn-out:

- waking up feeling tired
- difficulty getting up in the morning
- craving salty or sugary snacks
- periodic bouts of low energy through the day (like a 3 p.m. post-lunch 'low')
- feeling the need to use coffee, fizzy drinks, wine, etc., to 'keep going'
- increased PMS symptoms

- ❆ getting colds and infections often, and finding they hang around for a long time
- ❆ feeling like everyday tasks are an effort and take longer, and you are generally less productive
- ❆ reduced sex drive
- ❆ decreased ability to handle stress, little things get to you more
- ❆ occasional dizziness on standing up
- ❆ loss of concentration, feeling 'foggy'
- ❆ feeling down, not loving life.

I would like you to think of this book like a cookbook. The recipes detailed here leave room for your own acts of deliberate choice; they are not a strict formula to adhere to. This is the best sort of cooking: follow a recipe for ideas and guidance but add your own initiative and creativity, and adapt and tweak it to what feels intuitively right for you. So, do that, make it your own.

Ten Truth Flashes of High Energy Happiness
I learned some fundamental truths as I recovered my energy, without which I would still be crying into my triple-strength espresso. These ten principles are the shortcut to high energy.

Truth Flash #1: You have to *prioritise* your energy levels. Only you can do that. There is nothing more important than this right now. It's your most important work in the world and is your foundation for a well-lived, happy life.

Truth Flash #2: Your body is an amazing miracle. It is a healing machine. It is your *job* to create the optimum conditions for it to *heal* itself.

Truth Flash #3: You must be prepared to choose to *think* differently and *do* differently in order to *feel* differently. It's not a passive programme; it works if you work!

Truth Flash #4: There is a zero-tolerance policy for whinging, moaning and generally feeling sorry for yourself. It brings others down, it brings you down. It brings your energy down. There is no room for a pity party here or in life!

Truth Flash #5: Consistency is key. How do people reach the top of Everest? One step at a time in the right direction. The same principle applies here. Choose consistently in favour of what you want. And what you want is to feel energetic and happy, right?

Truth Flash #6: Your physical body and your true emotional state are your *highest priority*. Now. Always. Forever. Put your own oxygen mask on first.

Truth Flash #7: You don't 'catch' continual tiredness, you give it to yourself. The great news about this is that you can take *responsibility* to heal yourself, too. It's a gift from which to learn and shape an awesome, energetic life.

Truth Flash #8: Emotions are messengers from our true, authentic self and they are not to be feared. Emotions are *energy in our body*. And we need to feel them and process them in the body.

Truth Flash #9: The only thing you *have* to do is breathe, and everything after that is a choice. 'Have to' is a limiting thought pattern that keeps you stuck.

Truth Flash #10: *Outrageous energy* is available to us all. We just need to be aware and consistently choose in favour of it. It's not a magic trick, it's a process.

You can download a pretty PDF of these Ten Truth Flashes to pin on your notice board or wall at home as a continual reminder of how to live with high energy, at www.louisethompson.com.

These Ten Truth Flashes will run throughout this book. Some of the tools are going to push you way outside your comfort zone. Go as far as feels right for you; listen to your intuition. As I say to my students in yoga class, we have to be prepared sometimes to feel a bit of stretch and mild discomfort as we lean into an asana . . . leaning into that discomfort, allowing ourselves to be comfortable with discomfort for a short time. Even *welcoming* discomfort for a moment or two. It's how we stretch and grow. So, be prepared to look at yourself closely and with honesty, and to move outside your comfort zone.

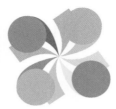

This book is primarily concerned with the mental side of the journey from fatigue to vitality. Looking at what is going on in your head is, I believe, the most powerful thing you can do to restore your energy levels. We are going to be talking a lot about the mind-body connection and building habits of High Energy Happiness for life. If you want more on the medical and physiological side of this area there are many people far more qualified than me to give that to you, so please consult your healthcare practitioner. This programme, however, has an absolutely unique perspective: I have first-hand experience, I know exactly how it feels to be tired all the time, and I know how it feels to heal using the techniques in this programme. This is not about theory; this is about practice and experience. It's every shortcut I know to get you buzzing with energy again.

We are going to work through the six sections of the programme together in this book:

1. **Understanding Energy and Fatigue – Why are you so damn tired?**

2. Empowerment – What can you do about it?
3. The Mind–Body Connection – Rewire outdated thinking patterns that keep you tired.
4. Honour Your Body – If you want to feel different you need to do different.
5. Energetic Action – twenty-two things to do, be, learn and see to live your happiest and most vital life.
6. Energy for Life – How to avoid relapse and to live a high-energy, happy life forever.

Ready? Let's do it!

MY STORY

If context is important to you, as it is to me, here you will find my story from start to finish, and how this book came to be. What I really want to explain is just how cumulative fatigue can be – that it's a slippery slope. That we can go from 'a bit run down' to 'tired all the time' to 'severely and chronically fatigued' if we don't stop and assess. When I look back at my story now, it actually seems completely bonkers that I allowed this to happen to myself, but there we are. I did! Wherever you are at right now, take a moment to pause and check in with your energy levels. Are they where you want them to be? My wish is that by reading this book you will recognise the warning signs of tiredness and fatigue and do something about them right away.

I write this now as someone who trains hard three or four times a week, will party until the wee hours, has trekked to Machu Picchu in Peru, and has a thriving practice as yoga teacher, wellness life coach and writer. I have a big, fat, full, fun life!

I wanted to start with those statements because a couple of years ago I had such severe adrenal fatigue that I couldn't dress myself. That's how bad it was. My blood pressure was 80/49. You do not need to be a doctor to know that's bad. My hair was literally falling out by the handful. I had a permanent headache, felt sick almost all the time and I was soul-crushingly tired. I lived in a world beyond tired. I had to leave my six-figure-salary job in media as I couldn't even crawl as far as the couch, let alone the office. I was bedridden. I was 37. I had less life in me than my 100-year-old grandmother.

It wasn't always that way, of course. The descent into extreme fatigue was so gradual I didn't even notice it happening. I didn't know what the warning signs were, and then when they became more and more obvious I pushed my body on (and on and on and on!) to do what I felt I needed to do to perform in my job, keep my friends and family happy, and so on.

Looking back now, I know it had started years and years before. I have always worked in newspapers (the *Financial Times* Group in London and the *New Zealand Herald* in Auckland) and loved the adrenaline rush of multiple daily deadlines. In print they are drop-dead deadlines: when the press has to roll, it has to roll, and you just have to have things done. I loved the rush of seeing my work in print.

I moved quickly up the ladder, running big commercial departments. Great teams, great times. We worked really hard, and we partied even harder. This was media in London in the 1990s: burning the candle at both ends was at the top of the job description. I thrived on it. My body seemed to love it, too. I felt great!

After six years of this lifestyle, however, I started to get sick. A lot. I lost my voice dozens of times. Any bug that was going round the office I got worse than anyone else. I got really bad headaches for days on end that painkillers wouldn't relieve. My doctor sent me for a brain scan in case I had a tumour. He suggested Prozac. I took it for three days; it made me feel so weird that I stopped. I struggled on. I partied on. I didn't know it then (and my doctors certainly didn't know) but that was the first stages of adrenal fatigue.

After nine years of working and partying hard, a reunion with my best friend from school, Holly, saved the day. She was going to travel round the world. And I just knew I was meant to go with her. So, I hung up my stilettos, bought myself a rucksack and kissed my life goodbye for a year.

Without knowing it I had rescued myself from descending into full-on adrenal fatigue. That year away from the pressures of my London life was the most amazing thing I could have done for my body. From trekking in New Zealand to watching the sun rise over Ayers Rock in Australia, riding elephants in Thailand, gently drifting down the Mekong river in Laos, meandering through the temples of Vietnam and Cambodia, the deserted beaches of Fiji and Malaysia – no timetable, no deadlines, no stresses, no struggles – my body healed itself. It got the rest and the lifestyle changes it needed to repair by accident. I was very lucky.

Fast forward a few years and life was very different. I had emigrated to New Zealand. I had gone back to work in a succession of high-pressure senior media roles. I had a broken engagement. I had started my own yoga business on the side. It was manageable, and I was doing okay health-wise. But my life was fuelled by strong coffee, and I had constant headaches and was taking thirty to forty ibuprofen a week. I felt on edge all the time and wasn't sleeping well. My memory, which had always been good, was mysteriously deserting me. There were periods when I would just completely crash. I would be in bed for a week, or even two. I would drag myself to the doctor every time to find out what was behind these collapses. They would run all sorts of tests, but never find anything. They offered me antidepressants with the unsaid suggestion that maybe this fatigue was all in my head. It was beyond frustrating. I knew there was something very wrong with me. But no one, it seemed, could help. So, the cycle continued . . . headaches, tiredness, coffee, ibuprofen, rush, rush, bad sleep, racing mind, nausea, headache . . . collapse . . . recover . . . rinse and repeat.

I stumbled onto the concept of adrenal fatigue on the web at this time. I asked my doctor about it, as all the symptoms seemed to fit. He was very dismissive that it actually existed. I pushed. I pushed a little more. Adrenal fatigue sounded right to me. He wasn't interested. In the end I changed doctors. My new doctor referred me to one of the leading endocrinologists in New Zealand. He did even more tests. I pushed him to test my adrenal gland function. Collecting all my pee over a 24-hour period was one particularly memorable test! He said quite categorically that adrenal fatigue didn't exist. And he could find nothing wrong with me. Basically, he told me to harden up and just get on with my life. I was shocked. I was a woman in my thirties who felt awful almost all the time and kept repeatedly collapsing, and yet he had nothing to offer me. His dismissive attitude had me reeling. If he was the best in the country, then where could I turn? I knew it was not normal to feel so exhausted, and to keep shutting down so completely every few months.

After the last appointment with this leading endocrinologist I remember thinking that there was no hope for me. This man, after all, was the expert. Maybe I should try and tough it out, harden up, like he said? Maybe it was all in my head? I felt like I was going mad.

I struggled on. I took on a promotion, bought a house, took on another promotion; life was busy, work was busy. I had a lot on: I was still teaching yoga, running my own business, plus I had started an intensive nine-month training programme to be a Martha Beck Accredited Life Coach, the first one in New Zealand. I also met my future husband at this time. It was, in short, one hell of a year!

My body was not doing well. I was now taking up to fifty ibuprofen a week, but nothing seemed to relieve the permanent headache I felt. I was sleeping badly. I was struggling to manage my blood sugar with daily bouts of hypoglycaemia and dizziness where my hands would shake as my blood sugar plummeted. I felt sick much of the time. The doctors were sympathetic but had nothing for me.

At this time I got a small cut on my right calf, a minor thing, but it would not heal. It was not infected, the wound just wouldn't close. It just stayed open for weeks and weeks. My adrenals were so fatigued that I actually had no wound-healing ability.

One day in January 2009, I collapsed at my desk. I just couldn't go on. I looked grey. I could barely stand. My PA called a taxi to take me home as I couldn't drive. I crawled to my bed. And there I remained for the next few months. I never set foot in the office again. My body had made the decision. I was out of there.

The following months passed in a blur. I was in bed but I couldn't even hold my head up to read. I couldn't eat. It was just too much effort, plus I felt nauseous all the time. I crawled to the bathroom on hands and knees. I slept on and off, but sleep didn't make me feel any better – I was just as exhausted when I woke from a sixteen-hour sleep as I was before it. I was never even bored. How weird is that? My brain didn't seem to have the capacity for boredom. I just sort of existed. It was a very odd time. Any light hurt my eyes, so I spent the whole time in semi-darkness like a nocturnal creature. I was half-woman, half-koala. The only noise I could tolerate was my beautiful, gentle husband-to-be quietly reading to me. He would read me a few chapters each evening of Bill Bryson's *Notes from a Small Island*. Life became small indeed.

There were improvements over time as my body got the rest it needed, but they were micro-improvements. Nevertheless we celebrated these small victories. Crawling to the sofa. Victory. Washing my hair in the shower. Victory. Progress was excruciatingly slow.

I was referred to another specialist at the hospital. More tests. No answers. He was, at least, a lovely and compassionate man. But he still had no answers! Other than to reassure me that tests showed I didn't have cancer/MS/heart disease/etc., he had nothing to offer me. He was mystified. All the tests said I was fine. He said I was the 'healthiest sick person' he had ever seen.

It was this last non-diagnosis when I was so clearly ill that led me to a conclusion that set me back on the path to wellness. As I lay there in bed I had an epiphany: *no one*, whatever their qualifications, knew what my body felt like better than me. And no one had to live with it in the way I had to. The solution had to come from me. I had been asking doctors what was wrong for over a decade. They clearly just did not know. I had to take control of my own recovery, or there would be no recovery. The answers did not lie outside me in medical science, they lay within me.

This blinding realisation was a real turning point. I remembered the information I had seen on adrenal fatigue years earlier and I felt a glimmer of hope – maybe that was the way to go? I logged back on. I had even more symptoms to compare now. I contacted the staff at www.adrenalfatigue.co.nz and they referred me to a local naturopath. I got a questionnaire from her (see Appendix, page 247) and filled it in. I was at the highest end of 'severe adrenal fatigue' on the scale. I started taking Dr Wilson's supplement programme immediately.

Four or five weeks later I noticed I had started to improve. I kept taking Dr Wilson's supplements and I could feel my body starting to slowly heal. I started to be able to dress myself most days, the nausea started to diminish and I managed to eat a little more. I set myself little targets to keep my body moving. I would try to walk to the mailbox at the end of our drive, for example. It was baby steps forward. But it was definitely forward.

With this foundation of the targeted supplements healing my body, I had enough energy to start to reflect on how I had got myself to such a desperate place. It became very clear to me that recovery lay not just in the supplement programme but in addressing the beliefs and thought patterns that had led me to make the lifestyle decisions I had made over the previous years. The beliefs that 'I must work hard to be successful' and 'I must keep others happy at the expense of my own needs' had led me to push myself way too hard over the years. I knew that recovery was not just a physiological process of putting the supplements *in*, but also a clearing *out* of unhealthy beliefs and thought patterns.

I joined a number of online support groups for people with chronic fatigue syndrome and adrenal fatigue. I was shocked to find that many of these people had been suffering for not just years but decades. Literally decades of these people's lives had disappeared in a fog of fatigue and exhaustion. I knew that that would not be me. It would not be me. I had just too much life to be lived. I had just met the love of my life who was nursing me back towards health with incredible patience and love, and I wanted to be well to live the life together that we both wanted.

I think that this was one of the big reasons why I recovered and many others suffer for so many years. My belief was so strong that recovery was not just a possibility, it was a certainty, and I was going to make it happen. I had a life waiting for me. This became one of the first stepping stones in the recovery programme I developed. This unique series of tools and techniques frees you mentally from fatigue, to be healthier and happier, and complements the fantastic work that Dr Wilson's supplements do to heal you physiologically from within. That's what this book and the online programme at www.louisethompson.com are all about.

The more I methodically worked through a series of life-coaching techniques to free my mind, the better I got. And the better I got, the more mental work I could do and the more I could start moving my body. It was slow but I was moving forward, mentally and physically. My husband was absolutely amazing. His support, gentleness and compassion throughout my recovery were absolutely critical.

Eighteen months later I declared myself well! It had been one hell of a journey. I had learned a huge amount about myself and had made some positive choices in terms of how I wanted my life to be in future. I kissed goodbye to corporate life forever and dedicated myself to being a full-time wellbeing professional: a yoga teacher and wellness life coach, helping people from fatigue to wellness to create a life they love.

I learned so much on that journey and figured out a whole load of shortcuts to wellness. I also made it my mission to work with people *before* they got to that critical place of fatigue; wherever possible I want to help them turn it around from 'run down' rather than right down the path of serious fatigue. This book is just as much for those feeling run down or exhausted as it is for those with severe adrenal fatigue or chronic fatigue syndrome.

I have been amazed at the huge number of people who have beaten a path to my door to work through the programme I offer. So many smart and amazing men and women just dragging themselves through each day. Seeing them transform so quickly, far faster than I did, has been just the most amazing experience, and their experiences and mine have formed the foundation of the programme that has now become the tried and tested High Energy Happiness formula that you hold in your hands.

Chapter 1

Understanding Energy and Fatigue

It's time to take responsibility. Full responsibility for your health, your energy, your body. Take ownership, it's real . . . and you have the power to fix it.

ARE YOU A BOILED FROG?

There is an anecdote about boiling a frog that I kind of like. It's from the 1800s when experiments of this type were much in vogue. The premise is that if you put a frog in a pan of cold water and then heat it up very, very slowly, the frog won't notice the incremental change in temperature and, instead of leaping out to save its own life, will in fact sit there until it boils to death.

There is much scientific dispute about the veracity of this principle; however, I don't care because I love the analogy. For many years *I was that frog*! I was getting more and more tired, but I couldn't see how bad it was because it happened incrementally. Little by little, degree by degree, my body was packing up and my soul was being crushed.

I see so many clients who have a job/health situation or relationship/living arrangement which, on the face of it, looks completely untenable. It is remarkable that they remain where they are. They are exhausted and miserable beyond measure. And yet they will say 'it's fine, really', and it is, because it's only 0.005 per cent worse than it was yesterday, so it's really not that bad.

Sometimes a reality check is in order. If someone else had to take over your relationship, job or health situation, would they want to trade places with you? If 'quite obviously not' is the answer, something is clearly not right. You may be living a 'boiled frog' existence in part of your life. If the situation is unacceptable to someone else and they would change it straight away, they are a frog who can feel the heat. They have come in from the cold and can accurately and objectively assess the temperature of the environment and take evasive action.

Have a look at what you are putting up with. No one likes to be a boiled frog but it's so easy to become one. Take a temperature check on your energy levels. Step back and look with perspective. What's the real temperature? What's the temperature difference from cold, not the difference from what it was yesterday? Is it a comfortable temperature for you? Is it a temperature you can happily stay in long-term or does it need to change?

Fatigue is very much like this boiled frog thing. It creeps up on us, creep, creep, creep. We put up with it, until it becomes normalised. We think it's just how life is, how we are going to move through life now. Tired, just pushing through each day to get to the end. Not having much fun but, you know, getting stuff done. Hanging in there.

I am here to say that there is so much more happiness, fun and vitality available to us than that! But moving towards it starts with a temperature check, a reality check. Don't be that frog.

THE SEVEN STAGES OF FATIGUE

I want you to assess where you are at right now. Maybe you are just a little tired now and then, maybe you are so exhausted that every single day is a grind you struggle through. Tiredness is a normal thing to feel. In response to activity the body gets tired to prompt us to rest. It's just one of those essential body regulation systems, like if we are not well hydrated the body will get thirsty to prompt us to drink. That's all normal. Tiredness is not normal, however, when it's relentless.

So, let's set a benchmark for you for later comparison.

ENERGY LEVELS

What is your energy level in general at the moment? Rate it out of 10 (10 being full of energy and 1 being low energy most of the time).

1   2   3   4   5   6   7   8   9   10

When was the last time you felt full of energy? ....
....
....
What were you doing? ....
....
....

Now, let's rate where you are on the fatigue scale. This isn't an exact science – our bodies are all different and, as I have said, I am neither a scientist nor a doctor. However, through my experience I have observed a definite pattern, a very clear set of stages from tiredness through to severe fatigue. Have a good read through. Where do you currently sit on this scale?

THE SEVEN STAGES OF FATIGUE

Stage 0: Situation Normal

You feel great. Don't even think about your energy levels. Doing lots of stuff. Tired by the evening, some nights more than others depending on what you've been doing. Go to bed. Wake up feeling refreshed. Energy levels are just not an issue or a concern.

Is this you? **YES/NO**

Stage 1: Inspired

Interestingly, this stage still feels pretty good! You are coasting on the adrenaline rush of the job or life in general. Busy, busy, social, work, events, things. Buzzing from one thing to the next with lots of energy and enthusiasm. However, you find it harder to wind down afterwards and are aware that there is very little downtime built into life. But it's not a problem – life is there to be lived!

Is this you? **YES/NO**

Stage 2: Wired

Life is still busy, of course, and may even still be pretty fabulous. However, you are starting to use a few wee extras to prop up the old energy levels as you are feeling quite tired now and again, and maybe not sleeping so well. You might be describing this as feeling a little 'run down'. Might be craving energy drinks, wine, coffee, ciggies, carbs (bread, bagels, sweet stuff, crackers, salty things) to prop up energy levels. Coffee. More coffee. Life is becoming a rollercoaster of good energy days and bad energy days.

Is this you? **YES/NO**

Stage 3: Pushing Through, Bouncing Back

Hmm . . . well, this really is pushing through the daily grind. Everything is more of an effort than usual. You have more bad energy days than good and it is an effort to stay focused on work. Social stuff seems never-ending but is still fun. Stage 3 is the real 'yo-yo' stage. After a long weekend chilling, or a couple of nights in, you feel better and bounce right back. You might be starting to experience intermittent sickness, headaches, nausea, and so on. You have a niggling feeling something is wrong. You have probably consulted the doctor to check it out.

Is this you? **YES/NO**

Stage 4: Hauling Ass

Everything is a $&%&*@# effort, from going to work to meeting a friend for a drink. Personally, I literally felt like I was hauling my ass around from the time I woke up, fantasising about when I could go to bed at the end of the day. You are constantly pushing yourself to get things done. The To Do list seems like your nemesis. You may have headaches, nausea, fuzzy thinking and feel dizzy. Life is one never-ending effort and chore-athon. If it wasn't for coffee nothing would happen. You are really pushing the doctor now – something is not right, surely? He/she still says that the tests show nothing is wrong. Little things are far more irritating than usual, and you are trying your hardest not to be crabby with pretty much everyone.

Is this you? **YES/NO**

Stage 5: Breaking Down

You go to bed at night and wake up feeling like you have just done an 18-hour day. Sleep doesn't relieve the tiredness. Nothing relieves the tiredness. You are suffering from dizziness, cuts not healing, reduced sex drive, increased PMS, continual fatigue, headaches, nausea . . . your body is just shutting down. All the blood tests say that you have no problem. How can that be? Even the coffee isn't kick-starting you any more. You don't want to go to work, go out, have sex, have fun. You just want to hide from the world until you feel better.

Is this you? **YES/NO**

Stage 6: Bedridden

You are bedridden or couchridden. Maybe you are on leave from work. Maybe you quit. Maybe, like me, you collapsed and never went back. Either way your body has made a decision and you can't push through any more. You are just exhausted beyond measure. But you may, weirdly, look perfectly okay, which makes it very hard for others to support you or sympathise. You are giving a koala a run for its money and sleeping or snoozing all night and almost all day. Things look, frankly, pretty grim.

Is this you? **YES/NO**

Okay, so see where you sit on this scale. You must be on it, or you would never have picked up this book! It can be well worth asking your partner or a friend where they think you are on the scale, as their perception might be more objective than your own.

The thing to note here is that each stage is progressive. Sorry to say, but things can actually get a whole lot worse. If I had known when I was at Stage 3 (Pushing Through, Bouncing Back) that the next and inevitable steps for me were Hauling Ass (Stage 4) and eventually being Bedridden (Stage 6), I would have taken it a lot more seriously than I took my need to get my To Do list done, the boardroom impressed, the latest movie seen and my roots touched up! Like I say, good to know.

So, this is the time to get committed, if you haven't already. This book (and the accompanying online programme) gives you all the tools you need to turn your fatigue around. There are Action Steps with every chapter to help you. As the fabulous straight-talking business coach Marie Forleo says: 'Turn insight into action. Insight without action is worthless.' She couldn't be more right. Use this insight, this reality check, to power you forward. It will be so worth it! Hold a picture in your mind of the person you want to be, bursting with energy. You can be her – you just need to get committed.

ACTION STEP 1: REALITY CHECK

I am currently at Stage .... on the fatigue scale. This has been going on for .... months/years. I am now aware that this tiredness can actually be progressive. I don't want that for me. I am a smart and fabulous individual, and I am committed to turning this thing round *right now*! I am committed to actioning the following programme to restore my vitality and energy, and create my happiest life.

ACTION STEP 2: CREATE A DELICIOUS VISION OF THE FUTURE

Write down some things you want to do/be/see/learn/have when you have your mojo not just back but better than back. Create a delicious vision of the life that awaits you to inspire you to take action.

When I am bursting with energy I will ....
....
....
I will also ....
....
as well as ....
....
I would like to go ....
....
and ....
....
I can see my energetic self having ....
....
as well as learning ....
....
People will say ....
....
about me, and I will love my relationship with ....
....
In short, I will be ....
....

Sounds good! Hold that vision in your mind as we move forward.

ACTION STEP 3: COMMIT

What are you prepared to do to have a delicious life filled with happiness, built on a foundation of vitality and energy? Anything? Whatever it takes?

What if I told you that there was an operation you could have that would magically fix your energy levels? Would you do it? Hell, yes. Even if there was a long post-op recovery? Still yes? What if I told you there was a pharmaceutical drug you could take that would improve your energy levels permanently? Would you take it? Uh-huh. What if it had horrible side effects? Would you still take it? Maybe? Well, here's the thing. None of these things currently exist. They are all external forces of healing, anyway. The real healing, the natural energy boost that works, doesn't involve a hideous surgery or filling yourself full of drugs. It's an inside job. Healing from the inside out. You don't get to abdicate the responsibility to a doctor, or a chemist or pharmacologist, or a surgeon. You get to manage and run your own recovery. Kind of cool, right?

Where do you sign up? Right here.

I, ..., am committed to working through the tools and implementing the ones that resonate with me in order to restore my energy levels. I am ready! Let's go.

Today's date ....

THE SCIENCE BIT

Right, so this is where I briefly explain the science bit behind fatigue. There are many places where you can read all the detail, and if that's your bag, please do go for it. (Start with Dr Wilson's excellent resource www.adrenalfatigue.org and take it from there.)

This is a different kind of book. While it is light on the science, it is heavy on actionable tools to move you towards energy and vitality. You're busy and you are tired. I don't want this book to be one that you never actually read and use because it's too daunting. I want this book to be your Energy Bible, your constant companion as you regain your vitality one chapter at a time. Okay. The Science Bit. We are going in!

Adrenal Fatigue

You have two adrenal glands. They are about the size of a big juicy grape and they sit on top of your kidneys, one on the left side of the body, one on the right. The adrenal glands are powerhouses of the endocrine (glandular) system. They are responsible for dozens of complex reactions in the body, such as playing a part in the regulation of blood sugar and blood pressure. Pretty important stuff. Below is a table that illustrates the functions of the hormones of the adrenal glands.

Hormone	What does it do for us?
Adrenaline (epinephrine); noradrenaline (norepinephrine)	Responds to real or perceived threats with the fight or flight response
DHEA; pregnenolone; progesterone; estrogens; testosterones; androstenedione	Antioxidant; tissue repair; sex hormone; balancer of cortisol; anti-aging function
Cortisol	Blood-sugar regulation; anti-inflammatory actions; immune response modification; heart and blood vessel toning; central nervous system stimulation; stress reaction normalisation
Aldosterone	Regulation of sodium, potassium and fluid volume

Source: page 259 of *Adrenal Fatigue: The 21st Century Stress Syndrome* by Dr James L. Wilson.

Fight or Flight

Your adrenal glands are primarily responsible for releasing various hormones in response to stress. The stress response, or fight or flight response, involves the production of a cocktail of corticosteroids, such as cortisol, and catecholamines, such as adrenaline (or epinephrine for those of you Stateside) and noradrenaline (or norepinephrine). You've heard of those, right?

Okay, so as animals, as mammals, we are programmed to respond to stress with the fight or flight response. This potent chemical cocktail gets released into the body within nanoseconds of a perceived threat. Read that again. In response to a *perceived* threat. Perceived. *The threat does not need to be real.* It can be real, or it can be imagined. Our adrenal glands don't know the difference.

Lion crashing through the undergrowth about to eat you	=	**Adrenal response to stress (real threat)**
Email popping into your inbox from your boss, that you haven't even read yet, but you think might be commenting negatively on the report you just delivered	=	**Adrenal response to stress (perceived threat)**

Note: whether it's a lion or an email, the adrenal glands respond the same way.

Now, when life was more full of lions than emails, this was an excellent survival adaptation of the body. It kept us safe. It made us run to the cave. It only got triggered a couple of times a week. And we *ran* to the cave. That physical activity burned off the adrenal hormone cocktail in the body. It's not called 'fight or flight' for nothing; that physical response is very important. Our cavewoman forebears did not get adrenal fatigue.

Fast forward to now. We receive bazillions of texts and emails every day. We have the world news (invariably horror-filled) in our faces at all times. We have people getting very wound up at us over a meeting time or a client approval like it's a matter of life and death. Our lives are crammed full with potentially (or imaginary) threatening events. We are also so much more sedentary. We do not run a lap of the office to burn off the adrenaline every time we get a shitty email (or what we *think* might be a shitty email) from a client. So the hormones stay circulating in our system and do not get quickly broken down by the body as they are designed to be.

That fight or flight button is getting pressed dozens, maybe hundreds, of times a day. And it's just not built to do that. Go back to the image of your adrenals sitting like juicy grapes, one on top of each kidney. Well, due to this chronic over-stimulation, now visualise your adrenals more like a pair of shrivelled-up raisins. They have worked so much harder than they were ever built to do that they have become completely run down and depleted.

They are mission critical, our adrenal glands. They are such powerhouses and they affect so many different functions in our body that this chronic depletion is felt all over the body. It's a survival response, remember, so it's naturally extremely powerful. The continual headaches I had were due to the fight or flight response pulling blood from the brain to the muscles so I could fight or flee. The diminishing sex drive? What animal is thinking about sex when it is in a state of permanent panic? And so on.

Being in a continual state of fight or flight is clearly not good for us, and the long-term effects on the body can be both catastrophic and cumulative, as you saw in the Seven Stages of Fatigue.

So, what's the opposite of fight or flight? Because that's where we want to be, isn't it? Well, that is called 'rest and digest'. Funny how we rarely hear or read about this when in fact we are meant to spend the majority of our time in this state! Fight or flight is sexy; rest and digest, not so much.

Nervous System

The autonomic (unconscious) nervous system comes with two settings, sympathetic and parasympathetic. Think of it like a light switch. The light is either ON or it's OFF. It can't be both at the same time. It's exactly the same with the nervous system. Either we are in sympathetic dominance (fight or flight: light switch on) or we are in parasympathetic dominance (rest and digest: light switch off). It can't be both.

Sympathetic Nervous System Dominance	Parasympathetic Nervous System Dominance
Fight or flight	Rest and digest
Light switch ON	Light switch OFF

I believe that with adrenal fatigue we create disordered and unconscious habits of thought that lead to us remaining in an almost continual state of fight or flight. Or, to put it another way, it's like our body is stuck with the light switch almost permanently on and it has forgotten how to switch it off. Teaching the body to relearn this skill is at the heart of what I want to share with you.

Here's the other thing to know: the immune system is suppressed while you are in fight or flight. You can't heal properly when you are in this mode (like the cut on my leg that wouldn't heal). Recovery depends on you being in rest and digest far more often, so that your adrenals and body can heal and restore your energy levels.

So how do you get your energy back? It's very simple. By consistently addressing two main principles:

1. Reducing the activity of your overworked adrenals with clever life-coaching techniques. This will reduce your stress levels and stop you being in a state of fight and flight so often.
2. Increasing your time in a state of rest and digest with some accessible yogic practices and Eastern wisdom that create the perfect environment for energy recovery.

Both these things allow your body and mind to heal from the inside out. Energy restored. Ba-da-bing.

WHAT IS WRONG WITH ME?

Right, I can hear you all say, I am with you on the science bit, it makes perfect sense to me. My adrenals are like two shrivelled raisins as I have inadvertently been in a state of fight or flight too often and for too long. I understand that because the adrenals are powerful glands that affect functions all over the body, this state makes me feel like crap in a myriad of different ways. This seems so straightforward. Why, then, is my doctor telling me I am fine?

It's a damn fine question, and I have to say this issue drove me almost to the point of insanity. Let's spend a little time looking at symptoms and testing so you can understand why before we move on. I highly recommend you also complete Dr Wilson's comprehensive Adrenal Fatigue Questionnaire (see page 247, or download a copy from www.louisethompson.com). We are not going to spend time discussing symptoms after this point (you can do that with your health professional). We are going to focus on the mental causes of physiological stress and how to deal with that to move you swiftly back to a life of vitality. Let's dive into fatigue symptoms now.

MY CURRENT HEALTH

Describe your current state of health below, listing your symptoms.

I feel ....

....

and ....
....
and ....
....
My body also feels ....
....
My mind/head feels ....
....
It seems to be worse when ....
....
Another thing I have noticed my body doing that it didn't used to is
....
Something I have noticed my body no longer seems able to do is
....
I have also noticed I feel ....
....
I am particularly tired when ....
....
I bought this book because ....
....

Acknowledge that it is *not in your head*! Read that list . . . this is real . . . it's happening to your body. Feeling tired all the time is not normal. You know how you feel better than anybody, including your doctor. Own it. Now let's do something about it.

Consult a Medical Professional

Let's talk about the medical profession for a moment. I want to make it clear that I am a massive fan of Western medicine. If you have an accident or a classifiable disease, your doctor or hospital should be your first port of call. I recently had a tumour in my ankle and I went in for MRIs and surgery to remove it, pronto! But with these more subtle autoimmune disorders, like adrenal fatigue, some practitioners are just not that good at seeing what's wrong. Even so, the medical profession should always still be who you discuss it with first.

If you are anything like my clients, you will already have been to the doctor numerous times (and/or a number of specialists and consultants) and have had numerous tests done that have come up negative. If you have not seen a doctor, however, then this is a non-negotiable: you *must* go check out your fatigue with your primary healthcare practitioner. Fatigue can be an indicator of some seriously scary conditions and they need to be eliminated before you start on your High Energy Happiness programme. One client of mine actually had a brain tumour and I have seen several suffering from Hashimoto's thyroiditis. So go get yourself checked. Insist upon it. Get a full check-up and blood work done. Take the list of symptoms you have just written with you. *Get a second opinion.* Confirm for your own peace of mind that there is nothing terminally wrong with you. It may be that you have something that is easily diagnosed and treated, like anaemia, which also causes tiredness.

In particular, ask your health professional to check adrenal function and thyroid function. State this clearly. You are the patient, the customer, you want answers; you are more than likely paying for your medical treatment and you want answers to your questions as well as the questions the doctor wants to ask. You are tired and not in the mood for confrontation. You can state this, too.

Do not be surprised if the doctor comes back to you saying your tests are 'normal', they can find nothing wrong. Remember the specialist at the hospital actually told me I was the 'healthiest sick person' he had ever seen. Take this frustration as a positive . . . what it means is that there is nothing terminally wrong with you that requires medical intervention. That's great!

The real bummer here is that blood tests do not definitively show adrenal fatigue, not like if you had, say, anaemia. The reason for this is the way the tests on various hormones, in particular cortisol, are measured. The 'normal' range is so large that even if your production of a number of critically important hormones reduced by half (i.e. enough to make you feel like absolute crap) then it would still fall in the 'normal' range, just lower down. The problem here is that the range of what is 'normal' for the entire population of the world may not be 'normal' for you. But, as you won't know what your 'normal' values are (because we only have tests when we are sick), you will have no individual benchmark levels to compare against and the doctor who is comparing you against the population range will find you 'normal'. Even if every cell in your body knows you are *not feeling normal!*

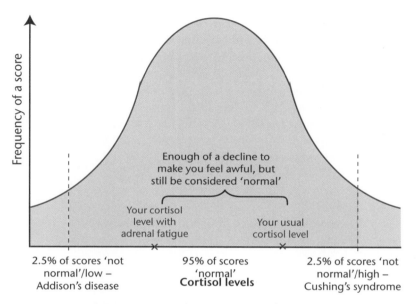

Enough of a decline to make you feel awful, but still be considered 'normal'

Your cortisol level with adrenal fatigue

Your usual cortisol level

2.5% of scores 'not normal'/low – Addison's disease

95% of scores 'normal'
Cortisol levels

2.5% of scores 'not normal'/high – Cushing's syndrome

Source: adapted from the graph of 'The Normal Bell Curve' on page 88 of *Adrenal Fatigue: The 21st Century Syndrome* by Dr James L. Wilson.

Taking Responsibility

For the purposes of moving forward here I am going to assume you have been to the doctor, maybe even got a second opinion, and have had a whole heap of tests done. They have all come back negative, and the doctor has little to offer you. Celebrate these negative tests. Awesome! There is nothing terribly wrong. That means you can get on with getting your mojo back.

So it's a relief to know where you sit on the adrenal fatigue scale, right? I know I felt enormously relieved when I found my score was at the severe end of the fatigue scale. When you know what's wrong with you, you can begin to deal with it. But, just to be clear, this final relief of having a label for what's wrong is not an excuse to throw a Pity Party for one. Uh-uh, no way. That's not the sort of attitude that is going to bring your energy back.

This is the time to stop looking *outside of yourself* for the answer to your fatigue. The answer does not lie in a doctor's office or an operation or a drug, *it lies within you.* Your body is an amazing healing machine. All you have to do is create the correct conditions for the body to heal itself. And that is just what you are going to do.

It's time to take responsibility. Full responsibility for your health, your energy, your body. Take ownership, it's real . . . and you have the power to fix it. Trust yourself and your capacity to beat this thing yourself. This is it. I believe you. I believe in you. And I believe you can get yourself well and bursting with energy and zest for life once again if you follow the steps I outline.

ACTION STEPS: TAKE RESPONSIBILITY

1. **Consult your healthcare practitioner (again). Get tested. Rule out other causes of fatigue.**
2. **Fill in Dr Wilson's Adrenal Fatigue Questionnaire (page 247).**
3. **Take responsibility. This is your time to step up, stop looking for answers externally, and realise the answer to your energy crisis lies within. Commit to actioning the tools in this programme to create the correct conditions for your body to heal itself.**

YOUR ENERGY HISTORY

Let's look at your energy over time. You might be tempted to skip this stage, but *don't*. It's going to give you super-valuable information and insight. You just committed to your healing journey, right? Well, this is part of it! Most of the exercises and tools are really short – this is by far the longest one. But, take your time, commit, and start working your way through.

Mark on the grids opposite for each year of your life (or as many years back as you can remember!) a score out of 10 for how satisfied (10 being super-satisfied, 1 being really unhappy) you were that year with your *energy levels*. You might be surprised what you uncover. Work through the grids, and then through the analysis exercise.

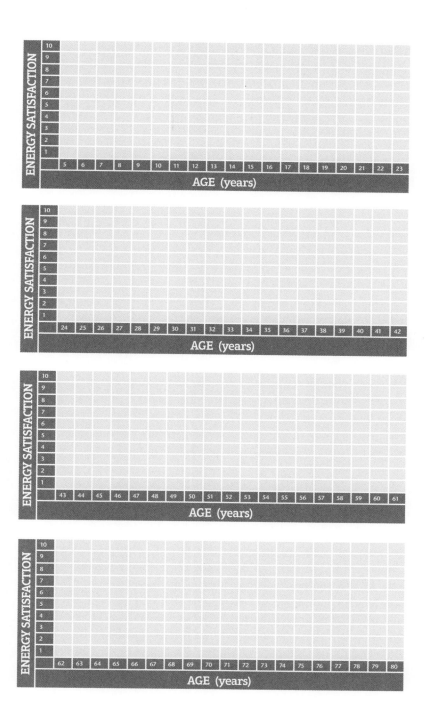

ENERGY TIMELINE ANALYSIS: PART 1

1. What age were you when you had the **least** energy? ....
   What was going on in the following areas of your life?

※ Career ....
   ....

※ Health, exercise and diet...
   ....

※ Love-life...
   ....

※ Friends and family...
   ....

※ Kids ....
   ....

※ Money ....
   ....

※ Home or living environment ....
   ....

※ Hobbies and fun ....
   ....

2. Repeat this exercise for your second-lowest energy time and
   your third-lowest energy time and make notes here.
   ....
   ....
   ....
   ....
   ....

3. What are the common patterns or themes you can see?
   ....
   ....
   ....
   ....
   ....

4. What is your personal low-energy equation?

For example, I have the **lowest** energy when I am working in a high-pressure job that I don't enjoy, when I am not expressing myself honestly in a relationship and when my home is a mess.

i.e. stressful job + hate job + low emotional expression
+ messy house = low energy

What is your low-energy equation?

.... + ... + ...

+ .... = low energy

5. Thinking back, what were your most common thought patterns at this time?

For example, I have to be the perfect partner, I need to have a high-powered career so I can be financially independent, etc. Note these thoughts down; they are very important to be aware of. We will come back to them later in the book.

....

....

....

ENERGY TIMELINE ANALYSIS: PART 2

1. What age were you when you had the most energy?...........

What was going on in the following areas of your life?

✵ Career ....

....

✵ Health, exercise and diet..

....

✵ Love-life..

....

✵ Friends and family...

....

✵ Kids ....

....

✵ Money ....

....

✵ Home or living environment...

....

✵ Hobbies and fun ....

....

2. Repeat this exercise for your second-highest energy time and your third-highest energy time and make notes here.

....

....

....

....

3. What are the common patterns or themes you can see?

....

....

....

....

....

....

4. What is your personal high-energy equation?

For example, I have the **highest** energy when I am travelling overseas, in a loving connected relationship where I am 100 per cent myself and when I have multiple creative outlets.

i.e. travel + connected relationship + creative outlets = high energy

What is your high-energy equation?

.... + ... + ...

+ .... = high energy

5. Thinking back, what were your most common thought patterns at this time?

For example, it's important I make time to paint, I feel free outdoors, I can be 100 per cent myself around Bob, I love this work, I feel I am making a difference, etc. Note these thoughts down; they are very important to be aware of. We will come back to them later in the book.

....

....

....

....

....

....

Good job! I know that was a lot to do right there (and I promise you all the other questionnaires in the other chapters are much more speedy), but I know it will have been illuminating for you, and it will form the foundation of your progress back to energy.

What are the three biggest things you learned from this exercise on your energy history?

1. ....

....

....

....

2. ....

....

....

....

3. ....

....

....

....

Chapter 2
Empowerment

*When you start getting honest with yourself and
making empowered choices from a fully conscious place,
your unconscious and your body won't have to step in
and try to do it for you.*

PRIORITY CLARITY

You may have an energy problem right now, but I can assure you it started as a priority problem. Let me tell you why.

Your body is the *moving temple of your soul*. Now I am a yoga teacher so I will hit you with the odd bit of woo-woo, but don't be scared. Embrace it, it's an ancient piece of wisdom and it's important.

Your body is the moving temple of your soul. That makes it pretty important. Kind of a priority, wouldn't you say? However, the moving temple of your soul lets its needs be known quietly – *in whispers*. The other parts of your life shout a whole lot louder so they naturally get more attention. Getting that report finished for the boss: LOUD. Getting the kids to bed: LOUD. Cleaning the house before the in-laws come to dinner: LOUD.

The Squeaky Wheel

It's known as the 'squeaky wheel effect'. While there are four wheels on the pram/car/trolley/cart/wheely thing of your choice, you only hear the squeaky one. So which wheel gets the oil and attention? The squeaky one, of course. It's the same in business: the manager who is always going on about the lack of staff (or whatever) gets more than their share when the time comes to increase numbers, even though it is a company-wide problem. The client who is an absolute pain in the ass gets more than they pay for just because they make such a nuisance of themselves, even though there are far nicer clients who may have paid more and who should be getting the better service. At the end of the day, the squeaky wheel wins.

The same kind of thing happens in your brain. You do know, on some level, that self-care, taking care of the 'moving temple of your soul', is jolly important. But it just doesn't shout as loud as the other things in life: clients, kids, partner, housework, job, family and friends. They are far louder so that's where your attention goes and that's where your priority goes. They are the squeaky wheel.

Until now. When you get really tired and it starts to impact on your life in a serious way (around Stage 3 or 4 on my fatigue scale on pages 24–26), then suddenly your body becomes the squeaky wheel. That's why you were drawn to this book.

Continual tiredness is a tangible sign that you have a priority disorder in your life – that you are putting too many squeaky wheels before your own wellbeing, and that you are trying to keep too many other people happy before you take care of what *you* really need.

I learned this the hard way: I put everything before the needs of my body. My work, keeping my boss happy, staff and clients happy, making sure the house was tidy, going out and socialising even when I was dog-tired because I didn't want to let anyone down, running my own business on the side and teaching yoga classes in the evenings. Exercise was number 342 on my To Do list, right after items number 341 and 340 'look after self' and 'rest'.

While bedridden, I had a lot of time to ponder the error of my ways. I had clearly neglected my moving temple of the soul and it was letting me know in the clearest possible terms. It had finally become the squeaky wheel and trumped all the other issues.

Prioritise

So, what I realised was this: my body needed to be number 1 on my To Do list, because without it *I had nothing*. Being bedridden is no joke. It was a dark time. And yet I can see quite clearly that all the millions of tiny choices I had made previously, prioritising everything else before my body, had led me to that place. The great irony being, of course, that now I couldn't do anything for anyone, including myself. I had nothing to give because I had neglected to give to myself first.

This was a big error. And the bottom line is that *everything* else can wait. It's the classic scenario of putting on your own oxygen mask on a crashing plane before you help your children: if you don't take care of yourself first then you may not be in any condition to later take care of the people and things you care about. It's Truth Flash #6: Your physical body and your true emotional state are your *highest priority*. Now. Always. Forever.

Learning that President Obama exercises every day (forty-five minutes minimum) was a real light-bulb moment for me. He makes it a top priority because it's vital he stay fit and healthy. How on earth could I think I was too busy to look after my body and find time to eat well and exercise regularly? Was I actually saying I was busier than the leader of the Western free world? Kind of embarrassing, right?!

So, there you have it: energy dips come from a million tiny choices to not prioritise our energy and wellbeing. They can seem like such small, inconsequential choices, but over time they have a big impact.

ACTION STEPS: PRIORITY CLARITY

1. What are you too busy to do right now for your own self-care?

For example, I'm too busy to . . .

- ❀ go to a yoga class
- ❀ listen to an eight-minute meditation audio
- ❀ have a twenty-minute hot bubble bath
- ❀ put my feet up and just rest for a few minutes
- ❀ exercise
- ❀ eat well.

What are you too busy to do for your own self-care?

a. I'm too busy to ....

b. I'm too busy to ....

c. I'm too busy to ....

2. What is a habit of wellness that you know would help your energy levels?

....

....

....

3. How long would it take?

For example, an eight-minute meditation audio daily or a one-hour yoga class twice a week.

....

....

4. Get honest, what are you choosing to make a priority instead?

I am too busy making a priority of ....

....

....

and ....

> ....
> ....
> and ....
> ....
> ....
> to take care of my wellbeing.
> **5. Then answer this: Do you have more to do than Barack Obama?
> YES/NO**

Right. So it's not a time issue. It's a priority issue. Here's the good thing. You get to set the priorities for *you*. You get to prioritise the moving temple of your soul. I'm going to show you how to do it.

DO YOU LIKE HAVING A PROBLEM?

This question tends to annoy some of my clients. But that's okay. I am not here to be liked (although that's always nice!), I am here to challenge and guide them to get well as quickly as possible. This is an essential question, and it may annoy you, too! I can live with that, because asking this question, and being deeply honest with yourself about the answer, are key steps towards constructing your life of happiness and energy.

Ready? Here is the question: Do you, in fact, *like* having a problem? What benefits are you getting from feeling so tired?

I said you wouldn't like it. I am sure you are shouting at me right now. *There is nothing good about feeling tired all the time! How rude of you to even suggest that there might be. What an insult!*

Bear with me and I'll give you an example from my own journey. When I finally got so sick that I collapsed at work and never went back, part of me felt *relieved*. It's fair to say that job was not really serving me any longer and I dreaded each day. It wasn't that the job or the place were bad, it was their fit with me that was the problem. And being so sick meant that I didn't have to go there any more. Genius! Brilliant, right? Despite the horror of being bedridden there was a definite hidden benefit. I didn't have to go to my sucky job any more. This was an unconscious benefit – I wasn't consciously choosing it, but it was a benefit nonetheless.

So, that's me being brutally honest. There was a pay-off to adrenal fatigue for me, big time. And there will be a pay-off for you, too. Maybe you are too tired to look after your sick, infuriating mother. Maybe you are really tired and that means you get lots of extra sympathy and attention from your usually inattentive and preoccupied family/boyfriend. Maybe, like me, it gets you time off from a job that crushes your spirit, without you having to do the hard thing and resign. Maybe it gets you out of sex with your husband whom you don't really love any more and, rather than front up for a divorce, the tiredness just lets you abdicate that responsibility.

Yes, I know we have only just started and it may seem as though I am being hard on you. But I am doing this because I care about you. I want you to have a life just bursting with joy and zing, and to do that and have that you need to be honest, really honest about what is really going on for you. This is tough love right here. What situation or relationship are you getting out of, or what attention are you getting, that is a secret, unconscious benefit of being so fatigued?

Go ahead. Think about it. This is *important*. Write it here.

ACTION STEP: TOUGH LOVE

A benefit I get from being continually fatigued is that I ....
....
....
The truth of this situation is I want to leave my (job/husband/country/
parenting group/whatever)...
....
Or, I want to ask ....
for ....
....

There. Well done. That wasn't so hard, right? Admitting it to yourself is really important. Because, the thing is, *your body already knows this truth*. It knows there is a situation (or more than one) in your life where either:

※   **there is something present that your inner, truest self just cannot tolerate; or**

❀ **there is something absent that your inner, truest self absolutely needs.**

Don't worry, you don't need to do anything about what you have just uncovered here (unless you want to). For now it's just enough to bring it into awareness. It's about being completely honest with yourself.

Have a good think while you are on a roll. Is there anything else that is secretly benefiting you from being so tired?

Another benefit I get from being continually fatigued is that I ....
....
....
....
....
The truth of this situation is I want to ....
....
....
....
....
Or, I want to ask ....
for ....
....
....
....
....
Is there anything else you are getting out of it? List it here.
....
....
....
....
....

Well done, you. Tough love, like I say, but that honesty is important. Your body already knows what you just shared above. It's been working silently on your behalf to try to change your situation by bringing you fatigue. When you start getting honest with yourself and making empowered choices from a fully conscious place, your unconscious and your body won't have to step in and try to do it for you.

ARE YOU SELLING YOUR HEALTH?

Well, this is another one of those hard questions that might well upset you! But, just like before, it's an important one to ask yourself. Every truth you uncover releases a little more fatigue and lets your energy start to bounce back in your body.

So, how much would you sell your health for? $100,000? $250,000? A million bucks? Ten million? Write a figure here.

I, ...

would sell my health for $ ....

Hmmm . . . no takers, right? Only an idiot would sell their health. Obviously. Well . . . let's look at this a little more deeply. I have to put my hand up here and say 'I sold my health'. I sold my health to a newspaper corporation in exchange for my good-but-not-amazing executive salary. I sold my health each time I wanted to resign but didn't because I wanted to leave only after I was mortgage-free. I effectively sold my health for the price of my outstanding mortgage debt. Which was about $150,000.

Now, of course I didn't realise this was what I was doing when I kept deferring that decision to quit and take better care of myself. In my head it sounded very sensible: Just three or four more years, the mortgage will be paid off and you will be free to do whatever you want. Actually what I had done was trade my energy, my health, my day-to-day existence, for the promise of $150,000. Not even the actual cash; the promise of it. How stupid a deal is that?

I sold my health for $150,000. Ridiculous. But I am willing to bet that I am not alone.

What have you sold your health for? The price of a cleaner once a fortnight to relieve you and give you some time to rest? Work it out, what's that in dollars? The price of working overtime to pay for the new car: what's that in dollars? The price of doing a huge amount of travel in order to keep your high-flying job?

Sometimes, people, it's just not worth the money. It's just not worth the trade. The key is to see it in the long-term, not on a daily basis. Each day I would think: 'This is okay, it's just another day, I can get through it.' Had I looked at the long-term reality of my health slipping away as I got more and more fatigued, I could have made a different deal.

This weird money/health trade-off comes up sometimes when clients look at the cost of Dr Wilson's supplements. 'They seem expensive, Louise,' they say. Really? *Really?* Compared with what?! When I compare the price of the supplement programme with the cost of me not being able to work for an entire year and the loss of a six-figure salary they seem ludicrously cheap. A few hundred bucks to save several hundred thousand? Best. Investment. Ever.

So have a think about it. Really think about it. Have you made some deals where you have sold your health? No money for supplements or the Zumba membership but you spend $200 every eight weeks on your hair. Come on. Your cut and colour is more important than your health?!

Start making some smart decisions. Be aware of the real trades you are making between money and health. Again you don't need to do anything right now, but being aware of the fact that you spend more on a daily soy latte than on your health is a good thing to know.

Have a look at the start of this section: what figure did you say you were prepared to sell your health and wellbeing for? Was it $10 million? $100 million? Nothing, there is no price that's worth it?

ACTION STEP: IDENTIFY HEALTH TRADES

It's time to get real. What trades are you making on your health? Define them here.

....

....

....

....

....

Still think you are getting a good deal?

THE POWER OF BELIEF

You don't catch tiredness, you give it to yourself. That's so important I am going to repeat it. You don't catch tiredness, *you give it to yourself.* Truth Flash #7.

You give it to yourself through thought patterns and beliefs that drive a state of continual stress and the lifestyle choices you make while in that state. This is, however, very good news. Because if you give it to yourself then that also means you can heal yourself.

And you can. If you believe you can. This is the time for a leap of faith. I want you to suspend the usual Western way of thinking, 'I'll believe it when I see it', and embrace the Eastern viewpoint, 'I'll believe it then I'll see it'. Why not? You have nothing to lose and your energy and vitality to gain.

Let me tell you a powerful story about the power of belief. Belief is mighty potent and it's a key ingredient for you to include in your vitality journey.

Mindset

The mind has such a powerful influence on the performance of the body, more so, I think, than the hours spent in a gym preparing. If you believe you can accomplish something, that knowledge can be far more powerful than the actual preparation. What you believe is possible is the greatest influence of all.

Consider this: when Roger Bannister broke what was widely considered to be an impossible barrier – the four-minute mile – on 6 May 1954, beliefs were challenged and changed. It must be possible because Bannister had done it. That change in mental consciousness and belief led to dozens of men breaking the four-minute mile in the following few years. What had changed? Certainly not training regimens or fancy kit in that short time period: it was entirely due to the change in belief of what was possible.

Have a think about anything that might be holding you back right now – the belief that you will always feel this tired, that nothing you have tried has worked, that you are just too busy to have a healthy life–work balance. See how that belief is holding you back far more than your body is. Commit to trying to challenge the impossible – you just never know what you might achieve or what you might inspire others to do.

Write down the beliefs you have about your health that might be holding you back right now. For example: I just have to put up with feeling this way. No one can help me feel better. I'm too busy for regular exercise. I don't have time to eat well all the time.

....

....

Understand that these are just beliefs . . . they are not necessarily the *truth*. Understand that by committing to this healing journey you are doing the equivalent of a brand-new sub-four-minute mile. Remember, beliefs like 'a sub-four-minute mile is not humanly possible' and even 'the world is flat' were once so commonly held that they were assumed to be fact. These are now things that we might even laugh at, they are so clearly false. You need to replace your old limiting beliefs with new positive ones. Here are some examples of healthier beliefs you may want to adopt:

- ※ I know I can have a really happy, high-energy life that comes from the choices I am empowered to make.
- ※ Everything I take action on from this programme is healing me from a place of fatigue.
- ※ My body is a healing machine! I am creating the optimum conditions for it to re-energise itself.
- ※ I trust in my body's innate wisdom. I can have a happy life built on a foundation of high energy and I am taking control of that healing journey.

ACTION STEP: EMPOWERING HEALTH BELIEFS

List some new empowering beliefs about your health here.

I believe ....

....

I know that ....

....

I am sure that if ....

....

I am ....

EMPOWERED CHOICE

Within this chapter lies one of the greatest secrets of the universe, a fundamental key to wellness and buckets of energy. Knowing this didn't change my life, but putting it into action did. And once you get into the swing of it, it gets easier and easier.

I want you to make a list right now – it won't take a minute – of all the things that are at the top of your To Do list over the next week or so.

List the first fifteen things that occur to you here.

MY TO DO LIST

1. I need to ....
....
....
....

2. I also need to ....
....
....
....

3. I absolutely must remember to ....
....
....

4. Sometime this week I have to ....
....
....

5. I must also really make sure I ....
....
....

6. I have to ....
....
....

7. And I have to ....
....
....

8. .... needs me to
....
....

9. And I have to do ....
....

for ....
....

10. ....
is making me ....
....

11. I should get ....
....
done, I've been really putting that off.
12. And I know I've been procrastinating but I really must ....
....
....

13. I said I would do/help with ....
....
but really I would rather ....
....
....
....

14. Other stuff To Do is ....
....
....
....
....

15. Finally, I need to ....
....
....
....
....

Gosh. What a busy bee you are! Okay, so now I am going to ask you to start watching your language. Not *that* sort of language; by all means, swear away. In my opinion, nothing can be more stress-relieving or funny than a well-timed, well-chosen cuss word or two. No, what I am talking about is your language around empowerment. Self-empowerment, to be precise.

I never cease to be amazed by how much of our power we give away. And by power I also mean energy. *Power is energy.* Power is *choice*. Once I realised this and started reclaiming my power of choice, lo and behold my energy started to return. It was almost magical.

Now it's one of the first tools I work my clients through. It's also one of the tools where I meet the most resistance. 'Yes, yes,' the client will say, 'in principle I get that *you* might have a choice, but you see, in *my* life it's different. My boss is so demanding that I really can't ask for annual leave, it really is the busy time of year for the business . . .' Enough with your Tale of Woe already! Here are a few of the ones I hear a lot. Do any of these sound familiar to you?

- ❀ I would love to make more time for me, but I can't because the children are so demanding.
- ❀ I want to say no to my boss about taking on extra work, but I can't.
- ❀ I can't commit to leaving work on time each day to see my kids because my job is so full-on and everyone works late.
- ❀ I can't join a yoga class in the evening because I have to babysit my grandson.
- ❀ I need to pick the kids up late from a party so I can't get an early night.
- ❀ I can't make time to rest because my husband needs me to make dinner each night.
- ❀ I want to quit my job, but I can't because then we wouldn't be able to pay the mortgage.
- ❀ I can't buy the supplements to get well because we don't have enough money.
- ❀ If my friends/family weren't so demanding I would make time for myself, but I absolutely have to go to the family barbecue this weekend because I promised I would.
- ❀ I'm exhausted, but I must just whip up six batches of cupcakes for the school PTA even though the mere thought of it makes me want to weep. I don't want to let anyone down.

Repeat to fade.

There is a reason I call them 'Tales of Woe', because that is what they are. Tales. Fairytales. Stories. Stories we have made the dangerous decision to treat as if they were truth.

Clients tell me that they are tired because they *have* to do this or that thing. Have to. They have so many things to do. What they don't realise is that it's the 'have tos' rather than the things themselves that are exhausting them.

The Secret

Here's the secret. The only thing you *have* to do is breathe. Everything after that is a choice (Truth Flash #9). Life becomes very different in a very short space of time once we truly grasp this fundamental truth.

I don't have to pay my electricity bill. Yes. Really. I don't *have* to pay my electricity bill. Really, I don't. I choose to pay my electricity bill because I like having light, heat and power. I could choose not to pay it, but I would rather not choose the consequences that go with that decision. When I get clear with the fact that it is my choice to pay, I find that my resentment at the bill melts away.

Go through every statement you made about why you can't improve your health or make time for yourself and substitute the word *choose* for any of the ubiquitous 'I should/I can't/I must/I need to/I have to'.

What I want you to realise is that 'I should/I can't/I must/I need to/I have to' are stories. Stories that you tell yourself over and over and over that keep you trapped in a place of disempowerment and fatigue. It's a language of disempowerment and fatigue.

How are they stories? Well, let me repeat the secret I told you earlier: The *only* thing anyone of us *has/must/needs* to do is breathe. Everything after that is a choice. What a revelation!

Right. So, let's see how this works in practice. I just love the power of this exercise. It truly is a life-changer. Take a look over the page at some examples of how this exercise works.

Disempowering Tale of Woe	Truth Using Choice	Empowering Truth of Energy and Ownership	Alternate Empowering Truth of Energy and Ownership
I can't make time to rest because my husband needs me to make dinner each night.	I am choosing to deny myself the rest I need rather than have a conversation with my husband about sharing the responsibilities of cooking or being more organised with making and freezing meals.	I am choosing to have a potentially uncomfortable conversation with my husband about him sharing more of the cooking as I am choosing to put my health first, and I know I need to rest.	I am choosing to speak up about my needs for rest, and stand in my truth. I hope my husband will support me, but I am clear I will follow through on my choice for rest regardless.
I would love to make more time for me, but I can't because the children are so demanding.	I am choosing not to make any time for myself by not prioritising investigating other alternatives for childcare.	I am choosing to make it a priority to have one afternoon to myself a week by scheduling a playdate/booking crèche spot/ regular time with Grandma.	I am choosing to prioritise the time I spend with my children rather than create time for myself right now. I feel no resentment as it's my choice.
I want to say no to Sally about taking on extra work, but I can't.	I am choosing to say yes to Sally and take on extra work that I do not want to fulfil rather than having a potentially uncomfortable conversation with Sally about my workload.	'Hi Sally, I do not have the capacity to take on this project. I have some options for you: either I can take it on and drop Project Pity and Project Party, or you can push the deadlines of delivery back on Projects Pity and Party. Or you can reassign this project to someone else. Please let me know what you decide.'	I am consciously choosing to say yes to Sally's request and work unpaid overtime for the next six weeks. I am going to consciously choose to book myself onto some assertiveness training/start looking for a new job as this is a choice that is not working for me.
I can't commit to leaving work on time each day to see my kids because my job is so full-on and my boss won't allow it.	I am choosing not to leave work on time each day to see my kids because I am choosing to avoid the fear of possible conflict/ feeling mildly uncomfortable at work when leaving on time.	'It's 5.30 p.m. I'm done for the day. Good night y'all.' 'Hi, kids!'	'Sorry, kids, I am choosing to get this project finished tonight, it's important. You guys are important, too, so this weekend I will not work and we will go to the beach together.'

Disempowering Tale of Woe	Truth Using Choice	Empowering Truth of Energy and Ownership	Alternate Empowering Truth of Energy and Ownership
I can't join a yoga class in the evening because I have to babysit my grandson.	I am choosing not to join a yoga class in the evening, which is really important to me, because I am choosing not to have a potentially uncomfortable conversation with my son about it.	'Honey, I really want to go to yoga one night a week. I would like for you to organise alternative childcare on Wednesday nights for your son.'	I am choosing to babysit my grandson on Wednesday nights. That is the best choice for me right now and I am super-happy about it.
I need to pick the kids up late from a party so I can't get an early night.	I am choosing not to get the rest I need rather than disappoint the kids or ask them to think of an alternative transport option.	'Hey, kids, I need you to speak to your friends' parents about a ride on Thursday. Or you need to catch the bus if you really want to be there.'	I am choosing to sometimes prioritise my own needs rather than always choosing in favour of what my children want.
I can't buy the supplements to improve my energy because we don't have enough money.	I am choosing not to buy the supplements to nourish my body to wellness because I am prioritising spending my money in other ways.	I am choosing to colour my hair at home this month even though I love the hairdressers, as taking these supplements is a priority for me right now.	I want to get my hair cut and coloured more than I want to be full of energy. I feel better about being a chic, tired person than an energetic, ungroomed one.
If my friends and family weren't so demanding I would make time for myself, but I absolutely have to go to the barbecue this weekend even though I am exhausted.	I am choosing to force myself to go to this event and deny myself the rest I need rather than have a potentially uncomfortable conversation with the host about declining.	'Hi, sweetie. I am so sorry to do this at short notice but I am not going to be able to make it this afternoon. Something has come up that I need to take care of. I hope you have an awesome time.'	My friend's party and her thinking well of me is more important than my health and my need for rest, and I am okay with that.
I'm exhausted, but I must just whip up six batches of cupcakes for the school PTA, even though the mere thought of it makes me want to weep. I don't want to let anyone down.	I am choosing to make cupcakes when I really need to just go lie down because my fear of being judged for shop-bought/no cakes is greater than the respect I have for my own body's needs right now.	'Look at these awesome cakes you can take, honey, straight out of the box. They will be yummy!'	On this occasion I am choosing to let myself down, and my body down, rather than let the PTA cupcake committee down. I shall think through the reality of the choices I am making before I commit next time.

INGRID'S STORY

I remember one client, Ingrid, looking at me wide-eyed and saying, 'You mean . . . what you are saying is that I can just choose what it is I want to do, and do it? And not feel bad about it? Really?' Yes, really. Ingrid was a persistently broke Pilates instructor in her mid-forties who spent all day as the 'beck-and-call girl' for her clients, and in the evening fulfilled the same role with her husband. Realising *she* could *choose*, rather than spend her days endlessly racing around trying to fulfil others' choices, was a revelation and a liberation. Once she got started she couldn't stop! One of her Tales of Woe was: 'I have to get up early to run sessions for private clients, which I hate because it's 5.30 a.m. and half the time the clients don't turn up, which I hate even more, but I have to be there because it's my job.' Tale of Woe. Not only woe but horribly victimy. Once she changed that into empowering language, she realised she was choosing to get up early without confirming she would be paid, because she was choosing to avoid asking the client for commitment out of fear of offending them. She was choosing to avoid potentially offending the client (who more than likely wouldn't be offended, anyway; it was after all a professional service they were choosing to book), and consequently she was also choosing to offend herself with a load of early starts for which she might not be paid! Once she realised she was choosing it, it actually seemed quite a mad choice to be making. Why the hell would anyone do that?! Dropping the 'have to' meant dropping the victim perspective, but the trade-off was huge.

Ingrid came in for her next session full of beans. 'Well, I said to the client that I wouldn't get up at 5.30 a.m. to train her unless she paid in advance to commit to the session. And she paid in advance, just like that! And I got up and I felt good about it, we had a great session. Another client said she couldn't commit and I said that's fine, that's your choice, but it means that I won't be getting up early to train you, and I had a lie-in and it felt great!' It was almost like the floodgates opened; once Ingrid realised that she did not need to keep playing the role of victim, that it was tiring, that she did not need permission from *anyone* to make choices for her life, she took that power and ran with it. Her career and her energy levels went through the roof.

The important thing to note here is that after you make your choice you just *move on*. Make the choice knowing that this is what is right for you. Choose it and move on, releasing any guilt around it. Choose the yoga class over babysitting, and fully enjoy that class and that time without thoughts of guilt. State your position and stand in your truth, with your boss, your client, your dad. You can't control their reaction, but you can honour yourself, and stand firm in your truth with clarity over your choices. Your highest purpose on this earth is to honour your authentic self, your true emotions and your physical body. You should never feel guilty about making that choice. Sure, someone else might not like your choice, but that is then *their* choice about how they react to it. It's not your responsibility. In Ingrid's example above, she gave the clients the choice: 'If it's an early session I need payment in advance if you are going to work with me.' Some clients chose to do so; they paid and either turned up or didn't. The clients who did not want to choose that were then free to find another instructor or train on their own or not train at all – whatever they chose. The point is that none of those subsequent choices were Ingrid's responsibility.

You may end up making exactly the *same choice*, and that's fine. You can still choose to work late every night rather than have one potentially uncomfortable conversation with your boss. But at least be honest with yourself about it. You don't have to do that, your boss isn't forcing you. You are choosing it. If that's what you want, that's fine, choose it and move forward with the energy of empowerment, even if it's not a choice that makes you happy.

I used to think: 'I don't like paying my taxes, because it's a whole heap of hard-earned money and it's a tedious process.' That is a disempowered position, and it fosters resentment. *Resentment depletes energy*. Because I now know that, and I want to boost not deplete my energy, I choose to think about my taxes in an empowered way: 'I don't have to pay taxes, but I still choose to do so. I choose to because I choose to run my own company and I choose not to go to prison for tax evasion.' That is the empowered truth. I don't feel so bad about the tax money any more, really it's run-my-own-company-and-stay-out-of-jail money that I am choosing to pay, which seems like a bargain! I also choose to have a fabulous bookkeeper come in and process it all for me to take the tedium out of it. No resentment and full energy!

ACTION STEP: EVERYTHING BEYOND BREATHING IS A CHOICE

Go back to page 54, where you filled in your To Do list. Go through it and rewrite it in empowered language, substituting the words 'choice' or 'I choose' for every must/have to/should. Then get clear: what are you actually choosing *between*? Are you still happy with that choice? Are there more options? Do you want to make a different choice? Do you want to make the same choice but *feel* differently about it?

Feel the resentment melt away as you empower yourself. As the resentment recedes, your energy will start to return.

Be vigilant. As you go through each and every day, be aware when you are slipping back into the language of the disempowered. Choose to be empowered and be conscious of the reality of the choices that you are really making. Do not hide behind have to/must/need to any longer. Literally, stop those words as they come out of your mouth. This is your life. These are your choices. Be aware of them. Make them and embrace the consequences.

Playing the role of victim is a cop-out. This is not what a generation of women fought for! You owe it to them and yourself to drop the victim mentality; stop giving all your power away. Start living life on your terms, your choices, your way.

SPRING CLEAN YOUR BELIEFS

Let's look at beliefs in a bit more depth. Belief systems are tightly packed clusters of thoughts that we have thought repeatedly about a particular area of life. For example, you will have a belief system for health, for family, for work ethic, for body image, for money and so on. These belief systems are very powerful; they are what drive our life. They can be healthy and supportive or unhealthy and unsupportive. What is interesting is that we very easily confuse a *belief* with *truth*. It's really important to be clear that *what you believe is not necessarily true*. It may *seem* true, but, well, it just might not be. Most of these beliefs are unconscious; they are operating below the surface like the operating system on your Mac or PC. You don't even realise it's there the majority of the time, it's just whizzing away in the background making your laptop function.

I like to visualise belief systems as bundles of fresh asparagus from the market. It's a bizarre analogy, but bear with me. When you try to pull out one stalk from the bundle it's really difficult, the asparagus are so tightly packed together. However, once you have loosened the tie and pulled out a few stalks, the whole bundle is easy to pull apart. It's the same with our belief systems. The first few thoughts we examine for truth will be hard to dislodge, but the more we do, the easier it gets.

Belief systems are bundles of thoughts

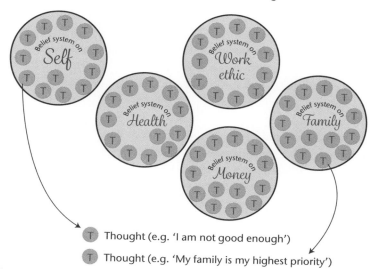

Belief systems are a mix of helpful, neutral and unhelpful thoughts. For example:

Belief system on health might include:
- It's important to eat well.
- I love to move my body.

Belief system on work ethic might include:
- I relax when the work is done.
- I must not let anyone else down.

Belief system on family might include:
- My family is my highest priority.
- I am deeply understood.

Belief system on myself might include:
- I am not good enough.
- I must do things perfectly.

It stands to reason that if beliefs are going to steer your life, you should have a good conscious, objective look at them. Right? I can guarantee you will have a number of beliefs that are good and healthy for you in the phase of life you are in now. You will also have a number of beliefs that are outdated, unhelpful, unhealthy or not even yours in the first place.

It's time to pull everything out of the cupboard. See what you have got and have a full spring clean. For many, this change is hard because they are so wedded to their old beliefs, beliefs such as 'I am powerless', 'Nothing I say makes a difference' or 'I'm not good enough'. So let's dig into this belief thing a bit deeper. Releasing old beliefs and consciously choosing energy-supporting beliefs is a key part of the recipe. And as it's your recipe you get to choose the beliefs for your particular flavour.

We form beliefs in reaction to circumstances. It can be a totally sensible reaction to what is going on in our lives at the time. For example, my family moved around a lot when I was a child, and I formed the beliefs (that were totally reasonable at the time) that: 'I must not have a different opinion to others and I must not stand out, no matter what, or people will not like me.' These were very helpful beliefs at the time, since they reduced the bullying I encountered as I blended chameleon-like into the background. A helpful belief for an eight-year-old perpetual 'new girl'. For sure. But helpful for a thirty-five-year-old woman running big businesses in media where the need to stand out and differentiate is key? Not so much. To move forward I needed a new healthy belief around standing out and about being able to share my own voice and opinions. A new belief I could *choose* in favour of, such as: 'If other people disagree, that's totally fine.'

When clients have trouble embracing the concept that everything in their lives is a choice, I know we are bumping up against some deeply held beliefs that are keeping them in a state of fatigue because they are confusing them with truth. So we rootle around until we find them, see if they are helpful and then choose new ones that support the life they have now.

It's fascinating work: your *beliefs* drive your thoughts, and your thoughts determine how you will behave – what you will choose in the moment, what you will do, what you will say. These choices, when made consistently, become habits. Our habits determine our happiness and energy levels as the balance of our lives reflects what we consistently do. So our beliefs are the deep driver, the operating system below the surface that drives the outcome of our lives.

This principle is why most diets don't work long-term. Why? Because they just try to change the person's behaviour at a habit level, without going down to the deep level of the beliefs that drive a habit of over-eating or under-exercising. They rely on willpower alone to create the change at a surface level. For long-term weight loss, effective action is better taken first by addressing that person's belief system around weight, body image, self-care and so on. So embracing this principle means you can really start rescuing your energy because you get to choose your *beliefs*, which drive all the tiny unconscious choices you make.

For example, my schoolgirl self formed a pattern like this:

Belief: 'I must not stand out, it is not safe.'

Thought: 'I must agree with whatever is said.'

Words and Actions and Choices: Chronic people-pleasing and approval-seeking. 'Let me do that for you.' 'I can do that.' 'I'll stay late and do it.'

Habits: People pleaser, working harder to gain approval, trying to make everything perfect so people will like me, working later and harder to deliver and gain praise.

Outcome: Fatigue and disconnection with my own needs and wants.

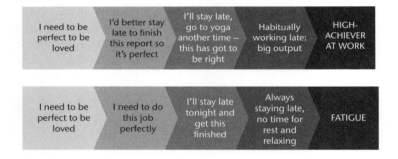

MADDY'S STORY

My client Maddy grew up in a very difficult home environment. Mental, physical and emotional abuse characterised her whole childhood. Nothing she did made a difference; she was stuck in this hell from a very young age. To cope, she stopped fighting, because fighting the injustice only made the abuse even worse. She concluded that nothing she did made any difference so she stopped the struggle and trained herself not to react to pain or show emotion. Maddy dedicated her life to protecting and caring for her siblings and alcoholic, depressed father as best she could in a hostile, impoverished environment. She eventually escaped this hell by getting pregnant at fifteen. Wanting a better life for her daughter, she managed to finish school via correspondence, get a job and move into a flat where she could provide a safe environment for her daughter, younger brother and younger sister. It's fair to say that this stage of her life, raising her daughter and siblings with no family support, was also tough. Fast forward to life at thirty-seven. Maddy is a grandmother and severely burnt out. Why? Because she is still running herself ragged looking after her teenagers and a grandchild and has a full-time job with a largely absent husband. Spending all her time putting everyone else first. Maddy felt she had no choice but to do what she was doing, taking on every responsibility without complaint.

When we looked at this more deeply, she could see that the beliefs she had formed in childhood to stay safe and keep the family together – 'I have to protect everyone' and 'I have no control over what happens to me' – were still running her life now. Her *situation* had changed, but her *beliefs* hadn't. The gap between her belief and the true reality of life was what was causing her fatigue. She was still trying to please anyone and everyone, just as she had tried to please her unpleasable mummy and daddy all those years ago. This prevented her from voicing her own needs, and ensured she absorbed more and more tasks.

Once this wonderful, strong survivor realised that she was operating with the old belief system, she agreed that it was time for an upgrade. Having lived her whole life for others and struggling with low self-esteem and worthlessness, Maddy didn't entertain ideas of who *she* was or what *she* wanted. Her beliefs were unhealthy and disempowering.

The truth was, as a thirty-seven-year-old these beliefs were no longer true. Maddy changed these beliefs to much truer, more empowering and healthy beliefs:

- ❊ 'Nothing I do makes a difference' became '*Everything* I do makes a difference!'
- ❊ 'I have no control over what happens to me' became 'I *do* control what happens to me – everything is my choice now'

She started small by making some modest changes and choices, and then as her energy and confidence increased she started to make larger ones. She was amazed that nothing bad happened.

As a consequence, she continued to grow and choose in favour of her new healthy beliefs. The change in Maddy was amazing. She is healthier and happier at thirty-seven than she can ever remember being in her life. Working with this amazing survivor was such a privilege and joy.

HARRIET'S STORY

Harriet had had a near-death experience ten years previously, which she had miraculously survived. She remembers lying on that hospital bed as she came round, thinking how incredible it was that she had survived and thinking that God must have saved her, that she was meant to live and take care of her husband and four small boys. She believed she had survived because her work was not yet done, she was alive to raise and care for her boys; she was not here for herself but for them. This belief ('I'm not here for me, I'm here for them') gave her the strength she needed to fight her way through recovery and to survive for her family.

Fast forward a decade or so and this gorgeous, loving woman's four boys – aged between eighteen and twenty-two – were all still living at home with her and her husband. Harriet was exhausted. She had a full-time job, did errands for friends, and cooked and cleaned for a houseful of 'her boys'. When I pointed out that this was a houseful of essentially grown *men*, not boys, she was astonished. Wow. They were indeed all truly self-sufficient, but she had never stood still long enough to notice! She was cooking and cleaning for them all like they were still young boys. Her entire life-purpose was built on the belief that she had been saved to be there for them. This belief was powerful, but again it was outdated – it was based on a different time and circumstance, and it was driving her into the depths of fatigue as she struggled to run her household and job to her exacting standards.

What was reality here? Once we examined her belief, 'I'm not here for me, I'm here for them', it seemed increasingly ridiculous and there was no wonder she was so exhausted! There was no balance, no room for *her* in that belief. The actual truth was she had done an amazing job raising her family, but they were all almost grown and now it *was* time for her! Time to do some of the things she wanted to do. Harriet embraced her new belief: 'I'm here for me, this is my time!'

We started slowly with a plan about *choice*. How about, to start with, the boys/grown men all got . . . shock horror . . . their own breakfasts? This pushed Harriet's buttons. 'But they won't be bothered and then they will be at college or work hungry,' she wailed, her maternal feathers very ruffled indeed. Well, yes, they will, I said, but that will be their choice, right? They will only need to choose that for a few days and then, for sure, they will choose to pop two slices of bread in the toaster for themselves each morning. I asked her to think about it, and to start small. Choose to ask them to get their own breakfast just one day a week so you can have the sleep-in you so desperately need.

At our next session I was just blown away by how Harriet had embraced this concept of owning her choice. It was like pushing over a row of dominoes. Once you push the first one down there is a glorious chain reaction. She had thought about it very deeply and realised that she was choosing to be fatigued by preparing all twenty-one meals for six people every week. And, yes, now she thought about it, they were grown men and they could make their own choices, too. She thought about it some more: actually, she loved breakfast time with her boys. That contact time at the start of the day was really precious to her and filled her with joy. What really was exhausting her was the preparation of the full family meal at the end of the day. She chose to keep making breakfasts, but to share the responsibility at dinner time. So Harriet prepared a roster and called a family meeting. She was nervous to bring this up, but she chose in favour of having the difficult discussion because she wanted to reduce the burden on her time and energy.

Harriet suggested that she would prepare dinner two nights of the week and each of the boys plus her husband would have one night a week. She was exhausted, needed some rest and relaxation time, and she needed her family to step up. She would prepare the menu plans and order the groceries to make it easy for them. Did that seem reasonable? Of course it was pretty hard for any of them to say that was unreasonable, so her plan was put into operation. It worked better than she could have imagined. Each boy cooked one night, with a sibling washing up. They loved feeling proud and doing something to help their mum, not to mention the life skills they were gaining, learning how to cook to impress future girlfriends. Harriet's husband's night to cook, Friday night, very quickly morphed into 'Takeaway Night', but that was all good, too! He chose to pay the money and get a takeaway rather than to cook himself. It was a good choice and the family embraced the variety on offer each Friday. Harriet just could not believe how much time and energy she got back. She could come home from work, go for a walk or to the gym, or simply run a long, hot bath, and know that dinner would be ready later and that she wouldn't need to clear up. On the nights she chose to cook, she loved it, *enjoyed it*, because it was her choice, not a chore. Just this one simple change in belief from 'I'm not here for me' to 'I'm here for me, this is my time' made a huge difference to the choices she made and, correspondingly, to her health and energy.

Interestingly, she didn't stop there. After Harriet saw how well it had worked once she chose and committed, she established cleaning and laundry rosters for the boys. She quit her energy-sucking job, started her own business, joined the gym and has a happy life full of choices she loves and honours. Harriet bounces with health and embodies the life of a fulfilled, energetic woman.

New Beliefs and Choices

Changing your beliefs is a matter of following the four-step Belief Realignment Technique:

1. **Awareness**. What are the beliefs that are driving your current choices?
2. **Analysis**. Are these beliefs valid in your current circumstances or are they outdated? Do they no longer apply?
3. **Release and Replace**. Release the old belief from outdated times. Choose a new belief that honours the *truth* of your circumstances *now*.
4. **Choice**. Remember you always have a choice. Choose in favour of your health and happiness.

There are more worksheets stepping you through the Belief Realignment Technique on other belief systems (e.g. relationships, body image, money) on my website, www.louisethompson.com.

ACTION STEP: BELIEF REALIGNMENT TECHNIQUE ON WORK ETHIC

Step 1: Awareness

Fill in the blanks with the first thought that comes into your head. Don't judge or edit. Whatever comes up for you is just fine.

1. Work means that I ....
....
2. I can't be perfectly happy until my work ....
....
3. What my work means to everybody is ....
....
4. Relaxation is ....
5. My priority is ....
6. If I don't work hard, then ....
....
7. People who don't work are ....
....
8. Work makes people ....
....
9. I wouldn't work so hard if ....
....
10. My dad thought work was ....
....
11. Work is ....
....
12. My mum always thought work would ....
....
13. In my family, work caused ....
....
14. Work equals ....
....

15. If I couldn't work, I ....

16. I'm afraid that if I didn't work I ....

17. Looking after other people is ....

18. People think I ....

19. Being tired means I ....

20. Resting means I am ....

21. If I had more money, I'd ....

22. Having money is not ....

23. In order to have more energy, I'd need to ....

24. Being busy means ....

25. When I have energy, I usually ....

26. If I weren't so busy, I'd ....

27. People think money ....

28. Keeping other people happy is ....

29. I must look after ....

30. People see me as ....

31. People will be upset if ....

32. My job is ....
33. People won't love me unless ....

34. There's always ....

Step 2: Analysis

Go back through the list. Some of these beliefs may well be healthy and life-enhancing. Perfect. Keep them. Identify which of these beliefs are no longer true for you (it might be quite a few). Understand that *everything* on this list is a *belief*; it is not the *truth*, even if you have believed it for years. For instance, I decided at an early age that 'To earn good money you must sacrifice' and 'Work is hard'. These learned beliefs set me up for two decades of working myself to the bone.

Now I believe that 'Work is easy and fun!' and 'Making money is easy when I am connected to my passion and helping people.' And do you know what? My new beliefs are so much lighter and my life is so much happier and healthier with them. I want that for you, too.

BELIEF REALIGNMENT TECHNIQUE					
Old belief	Is it helpful?	Is it true?	What is a new, healthier belief?	Do I want to keep this belief?	I could choose in favour of this by:
Example: 'Work is hard'	No	Possibly not	'Work is easy!'	Yes	Focusing on the aspects I enjoy, delegating what I don't

Step 3: Release and Replace

Acknowledge that a certain belief really supported you at a particular time in your life, but it's now outdated. Choose to let it go. It's like a dress you have kept for years that you once loved, but now, being objective, actually it's shabby, out of fashion and really isn't age-appropriate. Some clients like to make a little ceremony out of Letting Go; they write their old beliefs on paper and burn them so they can move on.

Step 4: Choose In Favour Of The New Belief

Write it down. Stick your new beliefs where you can see them: on the mirror when you clean your teeth, on your notice board at work. Drink in the new truth and start choosing it. Watch as your life and your energy miraculously start to change.

Chapter 3

The Mind–Body Connection

Our minds are not computers, our bodies are not machines. We are animals. Complex, evolved, highly sophisticated animals. Our mind and body are, of course, inextricably linked.

EAST MEETS WEST

I went to a number of talks and threw myself into research on fatigue while I was recovering. Fatigue is a problem that is on the increase worldwide, and there is a huge amount of important research delving into this area, and rightly so. So many amazing, gifted and highly qualified medical professionals searching for the one gene marker or depleted blood protein or rogue virus or whatever will nail it. I really, really hope that it's out there, and that they find it.

I spent time on different support forums for fatigue sufferers. So many questions about whether a particular food, test or pharmaceutical might make a difference. So many people suffering and for such a long time. And so much focus on a specific cause or cure. A magic bullet. Take this pill. Don't eat this thing. Do eat this thing. Maybe it's this virus.

The more I read the more it seemed to me that, enormously valuable though this work was, maybe there was another way of looking at it. That if it was a specific virus or gene that was responsible for this myriad of symptoms, maybe they would have already found it. Maybe, just maybe, it was possible that a black-and-white answer like that didn't exist. Maybe that linear Western medical approach might not be all we need in this instance.

I put my yoga teacher hat on and thought about it some more. Yoga has been described as a spiritual science. Did you know that? It's an ancient science of developing profound levels of understanding, compassion, freedom and health, extending back to before the beginnings of recorded history. It's a complex, interlocking system of ancient Eastern wisdom.

To see the connection between mind and body, not in the Western compartmentalised sense but in the Eastern sense, where mind and body are inextricably linked, is super-applicable when discussing tiredness and fatigue. In fact, 'yoga' derives from the ancient sanskrit word 'yuj' or 'yoke', meaning to unite or join together. One union to which it refers is the union of the mind and the body, connected through the breath. Yogic wisdom also talks a lot about 'prana'. Prana is our life force, it's pure energy, and it moves on the breath. Prana is a life force, the energy circulating the entire body through a complex network of energy channels called 'nadi'. Fatigue is an energy problem. A prana problem. Maybe there is something powerful in the mind–body connection that we can explore and address to improve energy levels?

The placebo effect is well documented, scientifically proven and the simplest way of illustrating the power of the mind–body connection. It's the highly replicable result of patients improving when they are given a dummy drug rather than the real drug. A large percentage of people heal because they believe in their mind that the drug is healing them; their body heals, even though they have been taking a sugar pill. It's the ultimate example of the power of the mind over the body, expressed in a logical Westernised experiment. Yogis have known this all along. What we do with our minds completely affects what happens in our body. I believe tiredness, exhaustion and fatigue are the archetype for this view. What we are thinking in our mind (perceived stress) relays directly into what we experience in the body (fatigue).

Our minds are not computers, our bodies are not machines. We are animals. Complex, evolved, highly sophisticated animals. Our mind and our body are, of course, inextricably linked. It stands to reason that what is going on with our mind can play out in our body as something like adrenal fatigue.

Think about it like this. If you went to a drive-through every day for breakfast, lunch and dinner you would expect that your body would put on fat, your cholesterol would rise, your blood pressure would rise and so on. It's not a surprise, it's a logical conclusion to a continual junk-food diet. What you put in your mouth absolutely affects how your body looks and how it feels.

I think it's the same with our minds and the thoughts we put in them. By continually feeding the mind 'junk-food' thoughts, we end up with a body that is fatigued. *Just as junk food leads to fat, junk-food thoughts lead to fatigue.* We are going to explore these different flavours of junk thoughts later in this chapter (see page 80).

I want to be completely clear, though, that just because I am advocating exploration of the mind–body connection in order to improve energy and happiness, I am not saying that the tiredness you feel is 'all in your mind' or that it's 'not real'. This is a very common problem I see with clients, who feel their doctor doesn't believe them because the blood tests don't show a particular marker; they get offered antidepressants and it is intimated that the fatigue is all in their mind and they are hypochondriacs. That is absolutely not the case, in my opinion. Feeling tired all the time, adrenal fatigue, chronic fatigue syndrome – they are all absolutely real. It is not all in your mind; it is, however, all in your mind–body connection. And you know what? That's excellent news, because that means we can address it. Now we know where to look.

ACTION STEP: REMAIN OPEN-MINDED

If this is all starting to feel a little woo-woo and out there, relax. Try to suspend the traditional Westernised viewpoint that we have to understand everything to see how it works. Sometimes we don't have to know, and we don't have to believe; it will still work anyway. Whether you naturally embrace the woo-woo or not, the exploration of the mind–body connection is a part of your journey to vitality. So commit right now to staying open-minded and curious.

BODY TALK

When we open up to the Eastern viewpoint of the inseparable relationship between mind and body, we can get better at listening to our body. If we listen, it has much wisdom to share. Fatigue is more than a medical symptom, it is a message from our body that all is not well on some level. Being open to expanding our view of how our body operates and exploring the mind–body connection is a fascinating and integral step on the road to High Energy Happiness.

I believe that exhaustion and tiredness are messages from our body in the same way that issues in our life can be messages from The Universe. Running low on energy is a whisper from our body that all is not well, and then if we progress down the scale of fatigue the whispers become shouts from the body with symptoms that we have to work harder and harder to ignore. Finally, collapsing as I did is the scream from mind and body that things in life are very far from okay and something needs to change. Continual tiredness is a message from your *body* and your *life*.

The body is amazing, it can do any number of things under

prolonged stress. I can now see how lucky I was that my amazing body chose adrenal fatigue as its messenger of relentless stress. It was an awful experience, but I am so glad that I did experience it the once. That one intense period of my life with soul-sucking fatigue taught me to value the messages my body was sending me. To listen to my body. To trust my body. Tuning into that inner wisdom was the turning point.

So, get quiet. Start to be aware of your body, and listen to its wise messages. It's a hotline to health. Sit quietly. Put your hand over your heart. Close your eyes. Be still. Breathe in and out through your nose, slowly, quietly. Be still. Now fill in the spaces below. Don't try too hard or fight or judge what comes up for you. Just write it down.

What is your body whispering to you right now? ....
....
....
What is your life whispering to you right now? ....
....
....
What is The Universe whispering to you right now? ....
....
....
What truth about your life have you been trying to avoid? ....
....
....

Your body has incredible wisdom. It's always trying to serve your best interests. In most cases that means to be happy and well and healthy and bouncy and all those good things. But if there is an intolerable situation, well, sometimes your body will take the reins.

Learning to listen to the wisdom of your body is a vital step in your recovery. Think about it. I know I spent a huge amount of time (and money) listening to the wisdom of numerous doctors, specialists and holistic practitioners, none of whom really helped me. It was only when I started to tune out from the *external wisdom* and tune into my *internal wisdom* that I started to make big strides in getting my energy back.

It's vital that you do the same. Listening when your body talks is one of the most vital tools you can learn for a happy, centred life.

THE TEN JUNK-FOOD THOUGHTS

There are common patterns of thought (the 'junk-food thoughts' that I referred to earlier) that I see repeatedly in my clients. These come from outdated or unhealthy beliefs. There are ten clear patterns of thought that I see. Some clients will exhibit almost all of these, some three or four. How many resonate with you? There is a section on each of the following:

1. **People Pleasers**
2. **Emotion Dodgers**
3. **Fondlers and Fleers**
4. **Integrity Avoiders**
5. **Perfectionists**
6. **I Am My Job**
7. **Adult Children**
8. **Adrenaline Junkies**
9. **Imposter Syndrome**
10. **I'm Not Good Enough**

These thought processes are like a PC's operating system; they are running continually in the background whether we are aware of them or not. How does that impact on your energy? Well, it's like this: I have an iPhone that I adore. When I first got it, however, I noticed that I was *forever* recharging it. The battery would run down so quickly I wouldn't even get a full day's use out of it. My husband's, though, seemed to be just fine on one battery charge for a couple of days. Why was that when we had the same make and model? As I complained one day about how quickly my iPhone would power down, my husband said, 'Are you definitely shutting the different apps down when you have finished using them?' Er . . . what? That would be a no then! It turns out that smart phones keep apps open in an 'intermediate state' so they will quickly start should users wish to return to them. So they are on in the background where you can't see them, taking up battery power even though they are not open or being used. How do you find out what's on in this intermediate state? You just double-click the 'home' button, and all the open apps show along the bottom row of the screen. How do you close them? Hold one down and they will all start to 'wiggle' with a little cross on them. Just close the ones you don't need open by pressing the cross. So I do this. Do you know how many apps I had open? Twenty-four! No wonder my phone never had any juice, it was keeping twenty-four apps running in the background all day, every day. Shutting them down increased the battery life of my phone by about 200 per cent just like that.

It's the same with low-energy thought patterns. They can be running, all the time, in the background, sucking the life force out of us without us being aware of it. These thought patterns are running behind the scenes, taking up so much juice that there is little left for us to use on the things we consciously choose.

We are going to look at each of these 'junk-food thoughts' so you can determine whether it's a programme you want to consciously shut down. It's really important to understand that these are styles and patterns of thought that we use habitually. They are not necessarily *truth*. Because we think them so often (sometimes for decades or all our lives) they feel like truth in our heads.

This is how it works in your head. Low-energy **beliefs** (e.g. 'I should be perfect' or 'I should keep everyone happy') lead to low-energy **thoughts** (e.g. 'I should get this report just perfect' or 'I should go to that party, I don't want to let her down'). These thoughts lead to **words and actions** (e.g. staying late at work to finish the report or dragging yourself to a function you don't really want to go to). These actions become **habits** (e.g. regularly overcommitting or not prioritising your own downtime) that determine a certain **outcome** (e.g. being fatigued). Low-energy beliefs and low-energy thought patterns drive the behaviours and lifestyle choices that create fatigue. It's actually amazingly simple.

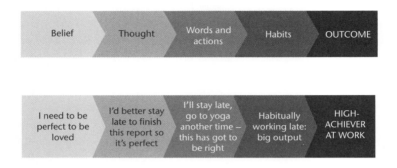

Our beliefs can drive a particular health and energy outcome, whether we are conscious of it or (as is typical) we are not. Of course you are tired. With those beliefs and thought patterns in your head, that is the only possible outcome! This chain of events is not just happening with regard to health – our deep beliefs direct all other areas of our lives, too.

POLLY'S STORY

I had a client who was seeing me for career advice. Polly was in her forties and flat broke, with few assets to speak of. She was an office manager, super-fit, a mad-keen runner. She was very frustrated about her lack of fiscal success at the stage she was at in life. Polly wasn't amused when I proposed that it was unlikely there was another financial possibility for her given her current beliefs around money: beliefs such as 'money makes people selfish' and 'money causes conflict in relationships'.

One day in session she mentioned a whole heap of stress that was coming up between her sister and her over

Christmas. The inevitable family drama! She was deeply envious of her sister's comfortable financial situation and felt that her sister didn't understand how hard it was for her to buy luxury presents. Interestingly, her sister really struggled with her weight and Polly felt very annoyed with the 'processed crap' that she was feeding her nieces. 'Why can't she just cook them healthy food? Take them out on their bikes for a ride, give them some exercise?' she said crossly. 'It's a disgrace.' I said that the unhealthy cooking and lack of family exercise was based on her sister's beliefs, which were clearly very different from Polly's own beliefs around exercise and healthy eating.

'Let's break it down,' I said. 'What do you believe about fitness and food?' 'Well, I believe it's the cornerstone of a happy life, that nourishing the body with food and exercise is a non-negotiable priority regardless of circumstance,' Polly replied, still annoyed. Okay, cool. 'What does your sister think?' 'Oh, she doesn't think about that at all, all she thinks about is money. She thinks money is really important, and that being able to buy what you need for your family shows that you love them. Oh!'

The penny dropped.

Polly could suddenly see that her sister had the financial outcome that her beliefs and thoughts dictated. A financially secure existence. She also had the weight and body of someone who had the beliefs she had about food and exercise. Polly had a runner's hard body, but her belief that money caused conflict and negative change meant that, of course, she had little money.

This was the biggest turning point for Polly. We worked on examining her beliefs around money, which ones were so old they didn't apply, which ones were not even hers but a previous partner's, which ones did not really serve her. She put together a whole new set of beliefs around money that resonated with the person she is today, and which serve her well. The following week she asked for her first raise in four years, sold a load of stuff to raise funds, consolidated all her debt and worked out a workable repayment plan. She never looked back.

So it is, of course, the same with energy as it is with money. If you have *low-energy levels* you have *low-energy thoughts*. In order to have high-energy behaviour we need high-energy beliefs and therefore thoughts.

What's also interesting to notice is the thinking styles I *never* see in my clients. I do not see people who are super-chilled and take life as it comes. I do not see happy-go-lucky surf bums. I have never had a client who is unambitious and a low-achiever. Usually they have many responsibilities, are ambitious, successful, smart, well liked and do a lot for others. They are also very tired. The beliefs that create their success are a double-edged sword because, when taken to extreme, they can lead directly to the twin outcome of fatigue.

But a lifetime feeling tired does not have to be our destiny. By bringing these thinking styles and deep beliefs into awareness we can modify them, lessen their impact, introduce healthier thought patterns and take our health and our energy to a whole new place.

How many of these ten inter-related thinking styles detailed in the following sections resonate for you?

People Pleasers

As children we are brought up to play nicely with others and are rewarded for doing so. Our very survival depends on being loved and liked – we are too young to take care of ourselves, so learning how to please others is a hard-wired and powerful skill of survival. However, as we grow, our dependence on others lessens, so we, in theory, should be less afraid of displeasing others and more secure in our ability to be our true selves whether others approve or not. Some people have made a living out of this. Simon Cowell, the ruthlessly honest judge of *American Idol* fame, thrives on the fact that he does not parrot the view of the masses: he disagrees, speaks his mind, gives his own opinion and to hell with the consequences.

Why do so many of us 'people please'? I know I was a people pleaser because I was an approval junkie. I thought that by doing/saying/being what I thought would please others I would gain their approval or love. The deep belief at work here is 'I must please others for them to love me' or a variation on that, such as 'If he/she disapproves, he/she will withdraw love or approval', 'I must be approved of to be a good person', 'If people like me, then I am good enough'.

People pleasing made me a pale shadow of the woman I really am. It also made me really tired, as I did not honour my own true needs to rest, recharge and do what made me happy.

Many of my clients also fall into the people pleaser trap. They come to me so we can sort out their life–work balance, and some kind of people pleaser belief usually lies at the heart of their unhappiness. At a deep, subconscious level they believe that they will guarantee themselves love and affection if they please others.

However, the truth is that when we try to please others by trying to fit with what we perceive their expectations of us to be, *we become less of ourselves*. Sometimes we give and give so much of ourselves to please others that we do not know our own needs and preferences any more, much less realise they are just as valid and important as anyone else's. This is a crying shame. Keeping that inner voice hidden takes up a whole heap of our energy.

What does people-pleasing look like?

It's a really insidious habit. And it comes in a whole heap of disguises. It's fascinating that some of the more hardcore people-pleasers I meet do not see themselves as people pleasers at all! It's such an ingrained thought process that they can't even objectively see it for what it is. These are the sorts of things people pleasers repeatedly say:

- I haven't got time to exercise/go to yoga/chill out and read a book by myself because I'm too busy.
- I just have to stay behind to get this proposal done, it's really important to the business. I'll miss the gym/drink with a friend just this once.
- I was late/missed my appointment/didn't catch up with that friend for lunch because a last-minute thing came up with work/the kids.
- I didn't really want to help with the PTA, but I just felt I had to.
- The whole weekend was just rushing from one kid activity to the next, I haven't even drawn breath!
- I have to call my mother every day or she gets upset.
- My friend/boyfriend really hurt my feelings (but I haven't told him as I don't want to make him cross).

People-pleasing is a *priority disorder*. It's the habit of *consistently* making others' needs and desires more important than your own. Know this: you were not put on this planet to be a pleasing machine. It's *okay* to say no to stuff. It's okay to *not* do what everyone else wants all the time.

Here's the thing. Either your needs count or *nobody's* needs count. Either you think that meeting people's needs is important (the kids getting to band practice, your mother getting her nightly phone call, your boss/client being happy with the report) or you don't. Because it stands to reason that if other people's needs are important, then *your needs must also be important*.

Your needs might be things like:

- **My body having sufficient time to rest and recharge**
- **Having a bit of quiet time to myself to rest/exercise/have a long, hot bath**
- **Making money doing something I love**
- **Having a fun night out with my friends**
- **Having a job that I actually enjoy, where I look forward to Monday mornings**
- **Feeling that it's okay to have some time on my own.**

Let me make this crystal-clear. I know you have an important job and a family to take care of. However, you have a higher responsibility than all those things: *Your first priority is your own physical body and your true emotional state*. Truth Flash #6. If other people's needs matter, your needs matter, too. So figure out what you need and start making some *prioritised choices*. For example:

- **Choose to leave work on time twice a week no matter what. If the task is that important someone else will find another way to get it done, or they will find it's not that important after all, and next time they will respect your time and ask you earlier.**
- **Tell the children they are coming on a bike ride/walk/ play on the beach with you so you get in your exercise commitment to yourself. Or pay for a babysitter or swap chores with a relative and make that exercise class. Do what it takes, but honour your commitment to yourself.**

❀ Block out some 'white time' at the weekend just for you. If the kids miss an activity, then they do. They will get over it. What they won't get over is having a tired, fatigued, unfulfilled and resentful parent.

❀ Tell your mother you will call her every other day or once a week or whatever fits into your schedule and energy commitment. Her reaction to that is her reaction. You can't control that. She may not be pleased. Or she might be fine. Either way, your higher priority is to your own physical body and true emotional state; pleasing your mother is below that priority. You cannot control her reaction. Let it go.

I need to add a note here about feeling selfish. This is not about encouraging you to abandon all your responsibilities. It is a call to reassess the *balance* of your needs with the needs of others. It is absolutely not selfish to prioritise your needs a proportion of the time – your needs matter, too.

ACTION STEP 1: SAY NO TO OTHER PEOPLE

Okay, it's an obvious one, but if you are going to stop people pleasing and reprioritise, then you are going to have to say no to some stuff. That's okay, it's usually other people's stuff.

It doesn't mean you are selfish. It means you are prioritising properly. You are prioritising your energy and your health. If it's that important to them, they will find another way.

Remember: you chose to read this book because you were sick and tired of feeling sick and tired, and I told you right back at the beginning that if you want to *feel* different you need to *do* different. So, this is you *doing different*.

Start small if you need to and build up your confidence, but do start.

Write a list here of fifteen things you 'have to' do this week (or use your To Do list from page 54). See how many of them you can say no to. If saying no is too hard, how many can you get off your To Do list by asking someone else to do them or by paying someone else to do them?

	To do	Just say no	Ask someone else	Pay someone else
Example	Make cakes for the fair	Just say no		
Example	Cook dinner		Takeaway Thai	
Example	Call Mother	Just say no		
Example	Clean the car			My son to do for $5
Example	Polish presentation	It's good enough as it is		
1				
2				
3				
4				
5				
6				
7				
8				
9				
10				
11				
12				
13				
14				
15				

ACTION STEP 2: SAY YES TO YOURSELF

Do something that is exclusively for you. Preferably something that feels really decadent, something luxurious, something that makes your soul sing. Here are some ideas:

1. Spend the whole day in bed watching movies.
2. Sit the kids in front of the TV while you do a pilates DVD in the bedroom.
3. Dial out for dinner and use paper plates so there is no washing up.
4. Go to bed at 8.30 p.m. and read a novel that has been on your bookshelf for the past three years.
5. Book tickets for a show and get all dressed up.
6. Go to the movies on your own and see a movie that no one else wants to see but you really do.
7. Call a friend and go play that game of golf you have been promising for months.

Whatever feels like *relief* or like *fun*, do it! This is about you pleasing you. If other people don't like it, that's their reaction and it's none of your business. They don't have to like it. The important thing is that on a number of levels it pleases you.

Visit www.louisethompson.com for a people pleaser meditation to help you say no to others and yes to yourself more easily until it becomes a habit.

ACTION STEP 3: INSPIRATION TO NOT BE A PLEASING MACHINE

A while ago I watched a Jonathon Ross interview with the incredibly talented singer Adele. It was an old interview from early 2011, when she was enjoying great success but just prior to being launched into the superstardom stratosphere. At this point, I had only ever heard her songs on the radio (and sung along enthusiastically but badly), but never even seen what she looked like let alone heard her speak.

Well. When I saw this interview, I was just blown away by her sheer authenticity. She shone. She was funny. She was a bit rude. She was 100 per cent, unapologetically, herself.

Adele is the antithesis of the manufactured pop star. She's not skinny with perfect teeth and a honed dance routine. She is just a north London girl with an astounding voice, raw song-writing ability and an incredible way of wearing her heart on her sleeve. She is quite literally What You See Is What You Get (WYSIWYG). I just loved her.

I think Adele is the poster-girl antidote to people pleasing. Her WYSIWYG will not appeal to everyone. She doesn't care. She is 100 per cent herself anyway. Is she on a diet? No. Is she speaking in politically correct sound bites? No. Has she put on a posh accent? No.

In fact, the less she tries to people please and the more she is herself, the more people love her. Not everyone. But the ones who love her, love her even more. I honestly think more of us could do with taking a leaf out of Adele's book.

Some people will not like that. But that's okay. We were not put on this planet to be pleasing machines. We were put here to be true to ourselves, and to let our own unique talents, needs and passions shine. To live our beautiful life to the full. We can only do that by being *more* of who we truly are, not less. More of who we are – absolutely and unapologetically.

Dare to be *more* of who you are this day. Say no to something. Do something unexpected that surprises or pisses off a few people but makes *your soul sing*.

That's your assignment. That's why you are here. And the people who really matter will love you more for it. Trust me.

Emotion Dodgers

I noticed an interesting phenomenon the more people I coached. Conversations would go something like this:

Me: Tell me how you feel about your mother saying that horrible thing/your boss rejecting that project you worked so hard on/ your husband working late.

Client: Oh, you know. You feel rejected, that she just doesn't approve of you no matter what you do/you feel disappointed they don't want to progress the project after you have put so much work in/you feel he doesn't want to help you out and you are hurt about that. It's disappointing but you just get on with it, you try to keep moving forward.

Interesting. You. You. You. Read it again.

Me: Tell me how you feel about your mother saying that horrible thing/your boss rejecting that project you worked so hard on/ your husband working late.

Client: Oh, you know. *You* feel rejected, that she just doesn't approve of *you* no matter what *you* do/*you* feel disappointed they don't want to progress the project after *you* have put so much work in/*you* feel he doesn't want to help *you* out and *you* are hurt about that. It's disappointing but *you* just get on with it, *you* try to keep moving forward.

See how the client repeatedly uses 'you' instead of 'I'? I am asking how *they* feel and they are answering as if it's *me* with the situation we are discussing. They answer as if the emotions are *general.* As if the emotions don't belong to them, they belong to 'you'.

'Honey,' I say, 'you are answering for me. I don't feel anything about your mother/project/husband.' I encourage them to answer for themselves; to *own* their own emotional reality. That means starting the sentence with 'I'. 'I feel . . . whatever.' I ask them the same question again, and get them to answer it actually owning their emotional response this time.

It's incredibly hard for many. They have spent so many years deliberately distancing themselves from the reality of their own feelings that they literally can't voice their own emotional reality. It takes practice to start owning it again. To be vigilant about how 'you' and 'I' are used in speech and to use it correctly.

Know this: language is extremely important. Do not underestimate this. The language you use sends a signal to your inner self. Either you are standing up for it or you are not. Either you are acknowledging it or you are not. Either you are listening to it or you are not. Stop hiding behind 'you'. Identify what it is you feel and *own it.* There is no feeling you can have that is not valid and true for you. The fact you feel it is enough. No one has to agree. You do not have to explain or validate it. Hell, you don't even need to tell anyone. You just need to be honest with your own true self and own it.

Emotion dodging chews through energy like nothing else. Those emotions are coming up because your true self has something to say. Have the courtesy to listen.

Pushing the emotion down hides it in your body, like in a deep freeze. It doesn't go away. It's cryogenically frozen in your tissues and psyche. And running that deep freeze takes a hell of a lot of energy. By choosing to actually own your true emotional state and *feel* it, you will need fewer power reserves to keep it all hidden, and your energy levels will start to recover.

ACTION STEP 1: IDENTIFY THE EMOTION

Okay, so *what* are you actually feeling? For someone who has been habitually dodging their emotions for a long time, sometimes a lifetime, that can be a big first step forward in itself. Many women were brought up to believe that it is somehow unfeminine to express 'negative emotions', especially anger. It's very common, and I see so many clients who believe that the only emotion they are allowed to express is 'positive'. This fake positivity, or 'Pollyanna' as I call it, does us no favours at all, because the real emotion is still there, lurking under the surface, leeching energy to keep it hidden. My massage therapist, Trish, describes it as 'issues in the tissues' – she can literally feel all that stored emotion in the knots in the muscles.

This thing about 'positive' and 'negative' emotions is bull anyway. Emotions are not positive or negative, they just *are*. They are valid in their very existence without being defined by a polarity. It's like the weather. Thunder is just as valid a weather state as sunshine. It's not a negative weather state. And we need rain as much as sun to make the world a habitable place. Both are equally important.

I agree with author and life coach Martha Beck's wise view that there are four emotions. She expands on this in her amazing book *Finding Your Own North Star: Claiming the Life You Were Meant to Live.* Basically, at any one time we are feeling one of four emotions:

※ **mad (anger . . . anything from mildly irritated to raging fury)**
※ **sad (sadness . . . ranging from upset to distraught)**

❀ **glad (joy . . . from contentment right through to ecstasy)**
❀ **scared (fear . . . from worried all the way to petrified)**

I instruct emotion dodgers to start getting in touch with their true emotions, without judgement. Just start noticing what you are truly feeling, just like you would notice the weather. Without judgement. Is it sunshine or snow? Is it annoyed or is it content? You don't have to do anything different yet if you don't want to, but at least start being honest with yourself. Ask yourself in the moment: What am I feeling right now? Am I mad, sad, glad or scared? It's one of the four. Put a label on it. Try to do this a dozen or more times a day. Buy a packet of stickers – green dots, red stars, whatever – and then put one on the bedroom mirror, one on the kettle, one on the dash of your car, one on your phone, one on your computer. Whenever you catch sight of a sticker as you move through your day, that's your reminder to ask yourself: What am I feeling right now? Am I mad, sad, glad or scared?

Give your feeling a label. See also if you can feel it in your body. The rush and tension of anger feels very different from, say, joy, which feels noticeably light in the body, which is different again to either sadness or fear. It's called a 'feeling' because that's how we process it, physically – we *feel* it in our body. So, go ahead. Feel it. Don't be afraid. There is no feeling so bad you can't stand it. Feel it and let it move through you. Release it. Feel your energy releasing back at the same time.

ACTION STEP 2: OWN YOUR 'I'

Once you have got better at defining exactly what emotion you are feeling, have a go at owning it fully. Transition from speaking in the second person, 'you, you, you', to speaking in the first person, 'I'. Own your 'I'. Have a practice here with something small. Start getting used to owning your own emotional response to events.

I am choosing to (walk the dog/email the CEO/go to the dry-cleaners)
....
today and I feel ....
....
about it.

Have a go at another one:

This lousy thing happened in the last month ....

....

and I feel ....

about it. I also feel ....

....

....

and would have preferred ....

....

....

to happen instead. I would have felt ....

....

....

about that.

And this one:

This awesome thing happened to me yesterday ....

....

....

....

(on my birthday/Christmas/in the queue for the bus) ....

....

It was a very cool thing. I felt ....

....

....

....

....

about it.

Get used to owning your emotions. They are all okay.

As you move through your day, all day, every day, be aware when you are saying 'you' when you actually mean 'I'. Use the green dot/ red star sticker reminders to cue you in. Correct yourself 100 times a day if necessary. It will get easier as you go. But it's crucial. You cannot start to process your emotional reality if you do not own it. Owning your emotional reality brings your energy back because you are no longer using up energy suppressing it.

To own it you simply say 'I'. This is you taking your power back. And your energy back. Do it. *You* are worth it!

ACTION STEP 3: LEAN IN

In the introduction to all my Beginner Yoga courses I outline to the new students how to look after their bodies, and I always say that 'we do not work with pain'. We do, however, ask them to move their body in a way it is designed to do, with tried and tested asanas that are thousands of years old. Their bodies may not have moved like this for decades, and it may feel odd, unusual or uncomfortable. But that's how we stretch and grow. When we breathe into that feeling of 'uncomfortable and odd', we start to relax. If it's truly painful, however, they should listen to their body, stop and practise an alternative asana.

What if life worked in the same way? What if as soon as something got painful we could just say stop and be given something easier?

We all spend life (both consciously and unconsciously) moving away from pain and towards pleasure. That's basic human nature. Some pain is avoidable, so we avoid it. Most sensible! Some pain, however, is just not – there is no easier option. We suffer great losses and disappointments that are going to be a part of our lives however much we wish they weren't. It's how we learn to deal with this sort of unavoidable pain that allows us to stretch and grow as people. There is a big difference between *moving through pain* and *dodging pain*. Pain is an essential part of the healing process if we will let it be so.

How we stretch and grow in the asana 'Warrior' is by leaning into the stretch, in a controlled way, in a safe environment, and each time it gets that little bit easier. Just a little. And the next time a little easier still. And then, we stop and we move on and we focus on another asana. Then, when it's time for Warrior in the next class, we once again lean into that stretch and again it's a little bit easier. Over time we can learn to be truly conscious while we are in it, to relax, breathe and appreciate it fully, regardless of the sensation our body is experiencing, knowing that it is doing good things for our bodies.

Leaning into unavoidable pain and grief is much the same process. If we try to avoid it, do not acknowledge it, try to deny its existence, it will always be there: a part of us that never gets any easier. We consume a huge amount of energy keeping it hidden. This may feel like the least painful option at the time, but in the long run, it's much harder. It's the hip surgery that will be needed down the line, which could have been prevented with regular stretching. If we are brave enough to acknowledge our pain and our losses, and lean into them, we will move through them more easily. The purpose of grief is to help heal our pain, so by leaning into it we allow the mechanism that Mother Nature gave us to do its slow but magical healing work. Did you know the chemical composition of tears is different when they are emotion-based tears rather than irritant-based tears (say, from chopping an onion)? It is suggested that this is a subtle healing mechanism of the body. How cool is that?!

You may find this concept of leaning into pain hard to grasp. I did: it's counterintuitive, after all. But it is invaluable in energy recovery when dealing with losses. Learning to lean into pain and loss in a controlled way in a safe environment, a little at a time, and to feel the feeling all the way through, to fully acknowledge it, to breathe, to experience it and then to take your focus elsewhere until the next time is important. And each time it gets a little easier. The healing work happens. Mother Nature is one smart lady.

What emotion have you been avoiding? Identify it and schedule some time to feel it. If it's anger, go punch some cushions. If it's grief, go play some sad songs and cry your way through. Let the emotion out, lean into the process and let Mother Nature in, and your energy will eventually rise. Getting real with your emotions is the path to living a life of vitality.

Fondlers and Fleers

As you know by now, it takes a whole heap of energy to suppress what we really feel in the moment. For example, when you are mad but you suck it up and smile sweetly, or that time you are on the verge of tears but blink it back and compose yourself, or the amount of upset that is hidden behind 'I'm fine'.

What it took me a very long time to realise is that emotional acknowledgement is vitally important to health. Note that I say 'emotional acknowledgement' not 'emotional expression'. I want to say that upfront. You don't have to change anything about how you act or behave or express emotion, not until you want to or feel that's the right course of action for you. You can keep the façade of 'I'm fine' for as long as you like. The point I am making is that even if outwardly you look the same, inwardly you must acknowledge what is truly, emotionally real for you. That is enough to get the healing process underway. Expression is better, but get there in a timeframe and an environment that feels appropriate for you.

Martha Beck describes the two ways we avoid acknowledging emotion in her extraordinary book *Steering by Starlight: The Science and Magic of Finding Your Destiny.* I have found her analysis to be absolutely true in my dealings with my clients, so instead of reinventing the wheel I am going to borrow her terminology here.

When life presents us with a stressful situation and there are two distinct coping strategies we use to avoid feeling what we feel, we will favour one coping strategy over the other.

So, Camp A is the 'story fondlers'. Story fondlers get 'stuck' in their story, usually a tale of woe of some sort. It's the friend who is forever moaning about how terrible her boss is or how she is undervalued. It's the colleague still going on about that awful break-up. Five. Years. Later. Story fondlers over-identify with their role in the story, and it becomes a disproportionately large part of their view of themselves. Being at the centre of the story, which is endlessly repeated long past the point where it has been cathartically useful, casts them in the lead role of 'poor undervalued employee' or 'cheated-on girlfriend who didn't deserve that'. If you look closely there is usually some sort of psychological pay-off that comes with this. Sympathy. Attention. And so on.

I once dated a serial story fondler. I have never met anyone who moaned so incessantly about his job. For the record, this job was in a shiny office of a Top 100 company where he was paid six figures a year for what seemed like pretty minimal responsibility. It seemed the cushiest number ever to me and our whole social circle. But to hear him, let's call him Bryan, talk about it you would think he was off to a particularly strict gulag each day. I was sympathetic at first: 'Oh, no. Your boss/policy review project/corporate entertainment budget does sound a nightmare. Here's an idea . . . you could do/ say/change *x*.' And the next day I'd have more sympathy and a few more constructive suggestions. And a few more the day after that to alleviate the clearly serious problems he had experienced that day at the gulag . . . I mean office. Amazingly, I listened to those never-ending Tales of Woe for over a year before I realised with startling clarity: he doesn't want to change anything! He likes it how it is! He likes, loves, talking about it! So, I stopped offering suggestions, but on and on he still went, completely identifying with the lead role of

'Chief Victim of Cushy $150K Job'. Needless to say we eventually split up. I couldn't take it any more. And, I'll tell you what, I bet he is still in that same job, still trotting out the same old story.

Okay, so that's a story fondler. Sure, it's a fairly extreme example, but on a lesser scale I am sure you know a few. Be honest . . . is the story fondler in your life actually *you*? When we get very tired and descend that pathway into burn-out there is a great story right there, isn't there? I have had some clients who have been fatigued for not just years but decades. Awful, awful. Such large portions of their life have gone by half-lived in a blur of exhaustion. But here's the thing: beware if you are story fondling your fatigue. You can spot story fondlers with watch-words like 'my' fatigue, 'my' tiredness. It's over-identification with the symptoms and it's story fondling. A comfort zone that allows the fondler to escape the processing of any painful emotions around their life (the stuff you will uncover in the integrity avoiders section, see page 100). They never have the time to *do* anything about their situation because they are so busy *talking* about it. Endless repetition of 'I'm so tired' doesn't achieve anything in terms of restoring your energy. It just makes you more tired and sucks the will to live out of those around you. Wouldn't you rather apply yourself to getting your energy back, make an awesome empowered life for yourself and elicit admiration, happiness and inspiration from those around you? The victim role doesn't suit you, honey. Time to upgrade right now.

We also have the flipside of the coin. The equal and opposite side of the coin that the other half of us gravitates towards in order to block what we are really feeling. This is Camp B: the 'fire fleers'. Fire fleers have a cunning plan to avoid painful thoughts and emotions. We shall block them out by drinking much wine and having an awesome time! Or smoking and gossiping! Or taking drugs and partying! Or madly exercising like a lunatic! Or frantically doing stuff for other people or stuff that doesn't even need to be done! Clean your pet walrus? With a toothbrush? This holiday weekend? Sure, I'd love to!

So fire fleeing seems a lot more fun than story fondling. Which it is, until it isn't. It's just as destructive as excessive story fondling, because not only do all our true emotions get buried under a sea of vodka tonics (and tequila shots! Let's do it! Who's in?!), but we also manage to avoid the reality of what we feel (bad marriage/job/money situation) the following day as we are so hungover. And the day after that we can go out and do it all again! Obviously, this can slip into some pretty scary places – drug addiction, alcoholism, workaholism – and I don't think it's any surprise that one of the indicators for adrenal fatigue is excessive exercise. As you can probably tell, I am a recovering fire fleer. And even when I am aware of it, it's still my modus operandi in situations of real stress. In my twenties, pretty much all I did was fire flee. It was more or less my career! I had so many emotions and thoughts I was trying to escape: 'Am I good enough to do this job? What if I get found out? Is my marriage in trouble? What will my family say if I get divorced in my twenties? Am I letting everybody down?' I lurched from fire fleeing session to hangover to fire fleeing to hangover on a daily basis. And it set me up for the slow decline into adrenal fatigue that was to follow.

You will recognise yourself as one or the other. It's not a bad thing, it's just how we are built. It's good to know what your natural coping style is, and why you do it. It's a way to avoid processing and feeling painful emotions or taking action that may lead to feeling painful emotions. So next time you feel the urge to fondle or flee, ask yourself: What truth am I avoiding here? Get honest.

ACTION STEP FOR STORY FONDLERS

Stop fondling. Stop referring to yourself as someone with fatigue. Stop labelling it 'my fatigue' like it's a favourite handbag. Stop talking about it full stop. Stop using it to elicit sympathy or attention or get stuff done for you. Stop talking and start *doing*. Do the exercises in this book. Start behaving differently in the world. Start changing stuff. Act like the energetic person you want to be. Change the job, the boyfriend or the living arrangement that's bothering you and move on.

ACTION STEP FOR FIRE FLEERS

Stop fleeing. Acknowledge that there is something going on and something you are avoiding. Stay still and *stop doing* and changing things for long enough to work out what you are feeling. Name the feeling. Are you mad, sad, glad or scared? And about what? Stop being a boozehound, smoking, taking drugs, working out like a maniac for long enough to actually figure out what's real for you. Feel that feeling in your body. Cry, be mad, whatever, it's all good. But *feel* it.

Integrity Avoiders

Many of my clients are burying a deep secret. A truth they don't want to admit to themselves. Their marriage is in trouble. Or they hate their job. Or motherhood is just not fulfilling them even though they love their kids. Or they are still dominated by keeping Mother happy even though they are forty-nine with a family of their own. Or they are secretly in love with someone else. Or they made a horrible mistake moving city. Whatever. This truth is there, underneath. It's like an undercurrent, a strong undercurrent, and the fight to not get dragged away by it is burning energy all the time.

One of the most energy-liberating psychological moves is to get honest. Stand in your truth. Own it. It may not be pretty, and it may be hard to acknowledge, but it is truth. Once you align with your truth, however hard it is, you are in integrity with your true self. When you are in alignment the energy-sucking stops. Recognition may be hard, but it is a route to reclaiming your energy.

For me, the deep truth I was avoiding was that I was in a job where I felt compelled to follow the company line, but I felt that line was increasingly at odds with my own values. I tried to hide this dissonance from myself because it would mean some painful decision-making and I was avoiding the inevitable confrontation that would ensue. So, I kept trying to bury this conflict. And I became more and more tired.

You can tell when you are out of integrity. Things feel 'off'. What you say is different to what you feel. There is a gap between the words you speak and the way you feel inside, and the lack of alignment will eat you up inside. I can look back and see that other low-energy times have also coincided with relationships where, deep down, I knew the relationship wasn't right. I would be saying and doing one thing – 'I want to stay with you. Let's make this work' – and yet buried below I was scared to admit to myself that actually it was a mistake. I got so dazzled by all the external reasons to stay together (nice man, we've sacrificed a lot to be together, I promised, etc.) that I tried to ignore the deep truth that we were not really a fit. That deliberate pushing down of deep truth is a number-one energy drain.

So, be honest, where are you out of integrity? Where are there gaps between what you say and what you feel? What are you trying very hard to keep buried? You can also look back at your Energy Timeline (page 38) for inspiration and common patterns.

ACTION STEP 1: GET CLEAN WITH YOURSELF

Get clean. Dig down and find the truth. Come on now, be brave. I'll hold your hand.

1. **A situation in my life where I am not being completely honest is** ....

....

....

I pretend that ....

....

....

when, in reality, deep down I feel that ....

....

....

....

2. **Another situation in my life where I am not being completely honest is** ....

....

....

....

....

I pretend that ....

....

....

when, in reality, deep down I feel that ....

....

....

....

3. Another situation in my life where I am not being completely honest is ....

....

I pretend that ....

....

....

....

when, in reality, deep down I feel that ....

....

....

....

Well done. These are hard things to admit. Allow yourself to sit with that truth. Don't force yourself to do anything right now. The awareness of integrity dissonance is a great first step.

ACTION STEP 2: GET CLEAN WITH A COMPASSIONATE WITNESS

You don't have to tell anyone about the above situations, if it doesn't yet feel right. Move at the speed that feels right for you. As with all tools in this book, I urge you to go with those that resonate the most with you. However, I have seen the healing power of this next step, so I put it here for you to consider.

Find a compassionate witness. Share your truth with someone. Talk to a close and discreet friend, or hire a compassionate and confidential witness, a coach like me or a therapist. Just talking through your truth and letting all those words that you have kept hidden tumble out can be remarkably healing in itself. Release that which is hidden and let your energy levels rise as you no longer require the same drain of energy 24/7 to keep it buried.

ACTION STEP 3: GET INTO INTEGRITY

Okay, so this is a bigger step, for sure. Take a baby step. What situation can you change that would feel more in alignment for you? Take a small step towards aligning what you say and do with what you feel.

There is a wonderful quote by one of my favourite authors, Tim Ferriss, in his life-changing book *The 4-Hour Work Week: Escape 9–5, Live Anywhere, and Join the New Rich*: 'Success in life is defined by the number of uncomfortable conversations you are willing to have.' I just love that, and think it's very true indeed. Uncomfortable conversations are a fact of life and a fact of personal growth. Sometimes it's a straight choice: have the uncomfortable conversation or choose to keep living with the energy drain of being out of integrity.

Your choice. Move at the pace that feels right to you, but move. Be brave. Remember: if you want to *feel* different you need to *do* different.

Perfectionists

Hands up if you are a perfectionist. Yep, I knew it. Almost every single client I have without exception is a perfectionist. The need to be all things to all people is just crippling to our energy reserves.

The trick to moving past perfectionism is to understand that it is simply a style of thinking that's not always helpful. It is not about a right or wrong way to do a thing, or about getting a job done 'properly'. It is simply a *style of thinking*, and there are different styles. And some styles take way more energy than others.

In 1968, at the Olympics in Mexico City, a chap called Dick Fosbury won the gold medal in the high jump by clearing the bar in a way never before seen at the Olympics. Until that point all athletes had used the straddle method to clear the bar. The Fosbury Flop, as it became known, changed that forever. This style of clearing the bar was more energy-efficient, allowed for a greater clearance, meant that slender-build athletes could compete (as it was no longer all about sheer strength of thigh muscle to push off) and knee injuries were massively reduced. All in all it was just a more efficient style that made for improved performance. Fosbury's new style changed the high jump forever.

This is how I want you to start thinking about perfectionism. It's a *style* of thinking that you have been using to get through life. It's like the straddle approach. It works, sure. You can clear the bar, sure. But it takes a lot of effort and it can get you injured.

It's time to upgrade your style. It's time to Fosbury Flop your thinking. I want you to float through life in a more effortless way, with energy to spare.

Perfectionism is so yesterday. It is outdated as well as actually impossible. Progress is the new black. This is your new mantra: 'progress, not perfection'. Striving for perfection is impossible. It. Does. Not. Exist. Call a ceasefire with yourself. Stop pushing yourself to reach a standard that is mythical and therefore impossible to reach and impossible to maintain. Perfectionism is simply a big stick with which to beat your self-esteem.

So give in. Surrender. Continuing to think like a perfectionist in this day and age is like trying to stop the tide coming in. It just can't be done. Seth Godin, the influential business blogger and author, says we are asking the wrong question when we aspire to perfect. The question is: when is it *good enough*? (Read what he says about it at http://sethgodin.typepad.com/seths_blog/2011/06/how-do-you-know-when-its-done.html). I now agree with him. Gone are the days when I will flog myself to get to 'perfect'. It's hard – sometimes I can fall back in wanting to 'straddle the bar' – but I know that it's in my best interests to go with 'good enough' most of the time. I'll publish my blog post when it's written rather than spending days polishing it like I would have done. I'll invite people to dinner even though the house isn't immaculate. I'll settle for a half-an-hour walk because although it's not as 'perfect' as an hour at the gym it's what I can make happen today.

Relaxing your grip on perfect will transform your energy levels. Perfect is really tiring. Progress is not.

ACTION STEP 1: DEFINE PERFECT

Okay, so what is it? What would day-to-day life look like if it was perfect? Define it. Be specific. What does perfect look like to you?

....

....

....

....

How nice. And how exhausting. Understand that nothing is ever as perfect as it looks. Accept that this version of perfect comes at just too high a price. Let's get something more real happening. Something achievable that feels like progress not perfection.

What would feel like a liveable, doable version of the above?

....

....

....

....

....

....

....

ACTION STEP 2: DON'T COMPARE

Don't compare your day-to-day life with someone else's showreel. You will lose.

Who do you know who has 'the perfect life'? Who behaves perfectly? List them:

1. ....

2. ....

3. ....

4. ....

How many did you get? Any? Know this: none of these people are perfect even if you may think they are or some aspect of their life is. From the outside other people look much shinier and more perfect than it feels for them on the inside. Right now someone is probably thinking some aspect of you or your life is perfect. What do they know, right?!

The trouble is, we compare our insides with someone else's outsides. We compare our day-to-day existence with their showreel, where their makeup is flawless and they have just stepped out of the salon. This comparison ensures we feel inadequate, which is perfect ammunition to push ourselves a little harder. Remember, fatigue is not something you catch, it's something you do to yourself. And it's exactly this sort of thinking that perpetuates it.

ACTION STEP 3: I LOVE THAT ABOUT ME!

There is a technique in psychology called 'reframing'. Basically, you take a situation that makes you feel bad and learn to think about it in a more positive way. Reframing sounds dull. I prefer the game of 'I love that about me'.

I read a blog post a few years back, written by a fellow Martha Beck life coach named Jeanette Maw, which really resonated with me (you can find Jeanette's blog at www.goodvibeblog.com). The gist was that she is really lax at picking up her voicemail messages, getting to them weeks later when there are dozens of really out-of-date messages. Her partner was nagging her to be more efficient and to clear her messages promptly. As someone who guiltily, inexplicably but consistently avoids my voicemail, I related instantly. Her response, though, was the exact opposite of mine. Whereas I would agree with my husband that, yes, I should get onto that and be more efficient, get it done, implement some 'perfect' system where I clear it twice a day, getting back to people promptly, Jeanette said, 'Are you kidding? I love that about me!' Instead of seeing the need to change to be more 'perfect' she saw it as a character trait, a loveable quirk. Why the hell would you want to change that?! Good point.

So, I had a look at the things I really wanted to be more perfect at:

- parallel parking
- reverse parking
- any kind of parking, actually
- baking cakes
- clearing my inbox each day
- finding my way somewhere without getting lost at least four times
- sorting out any kind of technical glitch
- planning stuff properly instead of just doing it immediately and doing it wrong ('How hard can it be?' is my mantra and the root of most of the best and worst decisions in my life).

Now I can see that these things that I resist are much better looked at not as evidence of my 'imperfection' but as a celebration of the uniqueness of me! Instead of feeling stupid that I can't park within a bus ride of the curb, I love that about me. It shows my vulnerable side instead of my usual fierce independence. I have limited spatial awareness and that's just fine. My ineptness is a source of amusement for me, my husband and friends, and I don't have to try to be perfect at it at all. God, that's a relief. It's so relaxing. And energising. I am officially utter crap at parking – and I love that about me!

So, what do you want to be more perfect at? List them here:

1. ....
2. ....
3. ....
4. ....
5. ....

Great. So, how about stopping trying to be perfect at those things? How about accepting that it's just not your bag? How about reframing it? 'I suck at ironing/navigating/computer knowledge/running – and I love that about me!' It's what makes you unique and special. Perfect is boring. And so 1985. Switch it up, baby.

I Am My Job

If ever there is a thinking style and belief set that breaks my heart in a client, then this is it. The 'I am my job' brigade. Reason being, I was a fully signed-up member of this club. Hell, I led that club. I was the goddamn poster girl for it. Frankly, this thinking style not only ruined my health but it cost me my first marriage. It also made me successful in a very cool profession, but, you know, that's a high price to pay for a broken marriage at thirty and being bedridden at thirty-seven.

Over-identification with what you perceive to be your primary role can be dangerous indeed. (Please note, I am absolutely including motherhood here – you would not believe how many exhausted mothers I work with.) It can lead us to make some very poor choices and to have some very distorted priorities.

When your status and your sense of self is completely wrapped up in what you do, the inevitable result is that you invest far too much time and energy in your job. There is an obvious consequence of this in terms of the balance of life, the quality of relationships, health, hobbies, fun and so on.

It's hard, though. I couldn't tell where Louise, Advertising Director, stopped and Louise, myself and I, began. All I could see was Louise, Advertising Director. Now it feels pretty sad to even type those words, but being honest with you is the best way I know to help you hold the mirror up to yourself and illuminate the patterns that are draining your energy.

Here's the thing. You are not your job. You *do* your job. You are *more* than your job. You, darling, are just you. Now that I am actually so much more in alignment with my job, I can see that I am not my job. I am myself and my work is part of my purpose, but it is certainly not all there is to me. It is a priority, but not *the* priority. My work is an extension of who I am; I am not my work.

Another thing. The 'I am my job' thinking style is not just for those in a corporate cubicle environment. I see it with self-employed small-business owners and also with full-time mothers. You are in the 'I am my job' brigade if things on the following list are common in your life:

- **'It's just not a good time for the business for me to be away right now.'**
- **You talk about the business like you are a couple: 'We are moving into Europe right now.'**
- **Your wardrobe is almost exclusively work wear.**
- **Whenever you treat yourself to awesome new shoes they are to wear to work.**
- **You work weekends regularly.**
- **You take the kids to a dozen after-school activities each week, but the last time you had a girls' night out was June 2009.**
- **You are so tired after your day that you have no energy or inclination to connect with your partner.**

Realise that this way of thinking is a fast train to exhaustion, and to an extremely poor balance in your life. Basing your identity on just one facet (there are eight facets – career, health, wealth, primary relationship, hobbies and fun, personal growth/spirituality, home environment, and family and friends) in life is very risky. It's a real 'all your eggs in one basket' approach. You might be made redundant. Your job might change. Your company might get bought out. Your kids will grow and not need you in the same way any more. If all your self-worth is vested in this one area of your life, you are storing up the mother of all emotional tempests to come.

BELINDA'S STORY

One especially awesome client springs to mind. Belinda had been working for the same company for nine years; she was one of the founding staff members. She joined the firm just after losing her father in a horrific car accident at twenty-two. It was a vulnerable time, and Belinda threw herself into her work to cope with the loss of her dad. She worked late, she worked early, she worked weekends. She was indispensable. She was needed so much by the business. She did every job that needed doing, from the marketing planning to fixing the server. She was absolutely, completely, totally and utterly spent when we had our first session. She looked grey, almost transparent, translucent, a bit weird, like a ghost. She looked at least forty years old. She was thirty-one.

Belinda just couldn't see herself as separate from the business. The owners of the business were her best friends. She could never take time off because there was always an important pitch or event to be delivered. She was on her knees with fatigue but she kept pushing herself on. She had no relationship, never went out with friends who were not from work, had no home of her own, no hobbies, her health was terrible, she ate on the run, she never cooked, all she did was work, just to get the business through the next busy time. She talked about the business in terms of 'we' all the time. The business was her friend, lover, her be-all and end-all, and it was all-consuming. She couldn't see how one-sided this relationship was. She was blinded by the belief that she was her job.

Working with Belinda to bring her back from the brink of absolute collapse was unbelievably challenging. She fought me every step of the way! It was maddening!

Belinda had given the business her twenties and her health, but still it was not enough. She was taken for granted, passed over for promotion, never respected with any equity or shares. Working through all the exercises in this programme to regain her health was a major challenge for her.

But she persisted. Her health was so bad she knew there really was no choice. So, forward we inched. And then with greater and greater momentum. I knew we had reached a major turning point when she stopped referring to work as 'we' and simply as 'work'. I cracked open the champagne that day!

These days there is a whole lot more to Belinda than her job. She looks vibrant and beautiful. Her blue eyes sparkle and her chic new bob suits her perfectly. She laughs constantly. She has a new house with some very cool flatmates. She dates. She has rediscovered her love of acting . . . she has been taking classes. She has an acting agent! She has a showreel! She is getting auditions and callbacks! She has a heap of new theatrical friends. She goes dancing for fitness and she loves it. She's taken a sabbatical and travelled to South America. She is a fascinating girl living life to the full. Who knew that girl was in there? I always knew she was in there, but, my God, we worked hard to uncover her. She proved that she could go back to work at the same place, in the same challenging environment, once she had the tools to cope at work while keeping her other passions alive. She's no longer 'trapped' by thinking that job is her only option – she now thinks about what's best for her and the lifestyle she wants. Now, if a good opportunity comes along, you can guarantee she'll make that change and take it!

Belinda had the courage to work through the limiting belief that she was her job. She found that she was much, much more than that. It has not just changed her health but her whole life. She really is an awesome woman with high energy, living an outrageously fun life.

So what about you?

ACTION STEP 1: TAKE AN INVENTORY

Rate your satisfaction (1 being this part of my life sucks and 10 being this part of my life totally rocks) in the different areas of your life, based on the wheel below (and check out my website for a fuller version of this tool). Have a look at the overall picture. How does the balance of your life look? Are you investing too much of your sense of identity in one area?

Life Satisfaction Scores

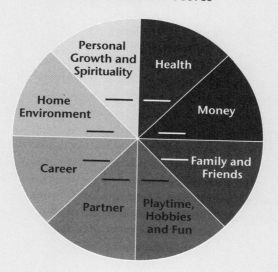

ACTION STEP 2: WHO ARE YOU?

If you take away your job, who are you? Complete the exercise below *without* mentioning your primary occupation. You may find this exercise hard, but please dig deep until you have at least three things in each category. You can list as many as you like, but no fewer than three.

What are you good at?

1. Physically? Practically? What can you build, create or fix? What can you do or achieve physically? What physical features do you have that are pleasing? ....

....

....

2. **Intellectually? Academically? What's easy to do or remember or learn or participate in? What comes easily to you?** ....
....
....
....

3. **Socially? What are your most connected relationships? Who are you when you are with these people? What do they see?** ...
....
....
....

4. **What else is fabulous about you?** ....
....
....
....

5. **What are your three greatest accomplishments?** ....
....
....
....

6. **What are your greatest strengths?** ....
....
....
....

7. **What makes you special?** ....
....
....
....

You are a fabulous human being with amazing and unique skills, qualities and characteristics that make you uniquely you, and you are so much more than your job or your valuable role in the family. Good to know, right?

ACTION STEP 3: TOO CLOSE TO SEE

Sometimes we are just too close to see what we are when we strip away our job. It's a great boost to ask others who care about you to name five characteristics they love about you. Ask over a coffee, over Sunday lunch, by email or your Facebook status, or create a quick one-question free survey on www.surveymonkey.com. Ask people to give five words that describe you. The answers may surprise you. You may resist this exercise due to a fear of 'putting yourself out there', but I promise you it is worth it. Take a moment to ask the people you know and love.

When you are done, make a collage of your words at the website www.wordle.net and display it in your office and your home. Use this as a reminder there is so much more to you than your job. This was mine:

ACTION STEP 4: BACK IT UP

This is one of my all-time favourite exercises. I use this a lot when I lead management training workshops and so on.

When you are next in a group (say five or more people), whether that's at Sunday lunch, the mothers' coffee group or in your team meeting, suggest this game as a team builder and bit of fun. It's super-easy and very revealing.

All you need is some A4 paper, some felt-tip pens and some sticky tape.

Give everyone a sheet of paper and a pen. Get each person to stick a piece of blank paper on the back of the person to their left so everyone has a sheet attached to their backs.

Then ask everyone to write down something positive about each person on their backs without telling them what it is. Just write one sentence – do not include your name. It's anonymous feedback. I always set up the exercise by stating that if you can't think of one positive thing to say, then that says much more about you than it does the person you are writing on! Also, it doesn't matter if you have only just met, you can still observe 'good manners' or 'great taste in shoes' or 'smiley'.

Everyone then moves around the room writing on each other's backs until everyone has a one-sentence positive message from each person on their piece of paper.

Next, take off your piece of paper and read it. If people would like to share, then be open to that. Also be open to those who want to keep it private.

I have found this to be unbelievably revealing. Seven or eight one-word statements usually have a really common theme. See what you learn from yours and what it says about you as a person – both in your primary role and as a person in general. What is the balance and overall theme of the statements? What can you learn from this snapshot?

ACTION STEP 5: BALANCE THE WHEEL

Okay, so if your wheel from Action Step 1 (page 111) is out of balance – and, let's face it, you wouldn't be reading this book if it wasn't – it's time to do something about it! Look at the two lowest categories from Action Step 1. What are they?

Lowest Category 1: ....
....
....
Lowest Category 2: ....
....
....

List here three small actions you could take, however tiny, to improve your scores in these categories this very week.

Lowest Category 1:

Action 1. ....
....
....
Action 2. ....
....
....
Action 3. ....
....
....

Lowest Category 2:

Action 1. ....
....
....
Action 2. ....
....
....
Action 3. ....
....
....

Do it! Do it, soldier. As I have said all along, if you want to *feel* different, you need to *do* different. There really is no time like the present and no one is going to do it for you. Bringing more balance to your life creates the right conditions for your body to create and release energy. Get to it!

ACTION STEP 6: CORPORATE REALITY CHECK

This is one specifically for those of you who are slaving away in a cubicle and still believe you are your job. Guess what? The corporate cares about you a lot less than you care about it. Sorry, my friend, but that is true. The business could make you redundant tomorrow without losing a beat, even though you have been there for donkey's years and are really important and have done great work. You are investing too much of yourself in a thing that isn't *your* thing. I know you think it's your thing. But it isn't. Not really. Are you a major shareholder? No. Well then it's not 'your' thing. It's someone else's thing. You, honey, are just the labour. I'm afraid that's the cold, hard truth of the matter.

But this doesn't mean you haven't got a 'thing'. You have. Your thing is *your life*! And guess what? It's been patiently waiting while you pour all your time, energy and attention into someone else's thing. Log out, walk out and call a friend. Start embracing that there is much more to life than the job. We just need to make space for it to flourish.

Adult Children

This thinking style is present in so many of my clients, and it really can be crippling in terms of the energy it zaps out of the body. What happens is we form some very strong beliefs, usually at a time of some trauma or perceived trauma in childhood, that help us cope with whatever is going on with us at the time. Because we form these beliefs young, they seem to crystallise as almost a part of us, and we carry them through into adulthood still playing them out in our everyday lives. However, what makes a great coping mechanism for an eight-year-old being bullied at school does not make a great coping strategy for an executive running a department.

SARAH'S STORY

Sarah had a childhood characterised by systematic neglect. She grew up believing that 'all emotions are fear'. Because she lived in a permanent state of fear, she had a limited concept that an emotion could be anything else. She was at the mercy of her parents while trying to protect her three younger siblings. The beliefs 'I must look after everyone else', 'It's my fault' and 'It's dangerous to feel any emotion', as well as 'Nothing I do makes any difference, I can't change my situation', were all firmly imprinted in her brain at a horribly young age, and reinforced time and time again. Sarah used a storm of 'perpetual doing' to distance herself from feeling fear – it was her coping style.

Fast forward to adulthood and Sarah, an incredibly smart woman, had made much of her life. She was a high-flying corporate accountant, literally high-flying between different international departments around the globe on a monthly basis. Sarah was also the main breadwinner for her husband and sister. She travelled incessantly, worked long hours and also did all the cleaning, housework, bill paying and so on. She expected it of herself to do everything for everyone. They expected it of her. She was beyond exhausted. Sarah had been descending into severe adrenal fatigue for years. This super-smart, funny woman had lost all her sparkle and could barely raise her voice above a whisper, she was so exhausted. She looked grey, old, tired, beaten: absolutely beaten by life. She was one of the strongest, most courageous women I had ever met.

When we looked at Sarah's life it was clear to see that the beliefs she had formed in childhood, that had kept her and her siblings safe, of sorts, were running her life still. She was still that terrified seven-year-old, but in a forty-three-year-old's body. Unpicking these beliefs one by one and seeing that they were outdated and no longer applied to her meant that adult Sarah could pick a whole new set of beliefs that were in accordance with who she really was and which supported the life-stage she was at. This was absolutely key to her recovery.

'All emotions are fear' was a belief that led to Sarah being a Grade-A emotion dodger. Sarah's 'Inner Lizard' (see page 132) was so loud she had actually thought it was her own voice! She had grown up with so much fear that she literally didn't know that she could feel other things, and that it was okay and safe to do so. Teaching her she could legitimately feel mad, sad and glad, as well as scared, was huge. The realisation that anger was something she could voice, and that she could set boundaries and define what was and was not okay for her, was enormous. Sarah didn't have to suck it all up, she was an adult now and she could make her own choices. Her 'I must look after everyone else' coping style of perpetual doing had left her exhausted. She was picking up way too many of the responsibilities of the other two adults in the house. Sure, being a supportive sister and wife is great, but doing the mothering role for them? Not so much. Learning that this wasn't her responsibility was mind-blowing for her and helped her to redistribute the balance of chores.

Sarah had long ago stopped voicing her needs because she had grown up thinking 'Nothing I do makes any difference'. It's what psychologists call 'learned helplessness', and I see it in varying degrees in many clients with adrenal fatigue. At some point in life they have learned that nothing they say or do makes a difference to the situation (which as a child it often doesn't), so it becomes a rule for life. It's crippling. Sarah was stuck in the claustrophobic, energy-sucking thought patterns of an Adult Child. Understanding that, as adults, what we do, say and choose *can make a difference* is absolutely critical. Her neglectful parents were no longer in her life. They had lost the power to control her. She was in control of her life now. She just had to see that and take it. Seeing Sarah blossom as she took back control of her energy boundaries was just thrilling. Today this smart, beautiful woman has the high-flying job but wears it lightly, on her own terms, alongside a full, rounded life.

MARCIA'S STORY

Marcia was another Adult Child. She had a very domineering mother, who clearly resented Marcia having any sort of life of her own even though she was now thirty. She was still her mother's errand girl with no life of her own, living at home, and had never even had a boyfriend. She had learned that there was absolutely no point having any emotion that did not coincide with her mother's. It was just too much trouble! Life revolved around keeping Mother happy. Or trying to. This woman was never happy no matter what Marcia did! This regime had strangled Marcia's true self at birth. The only emotions that were valid in that household were her mother's. So, over time, Marcia had stopped listening to her own emotions and thoughts, her own messengers. What was the point? The belief 'What I think or feel doesn't matter' became imprinted in Marcia and she lost all self-efficacy. It was as though she had been sort of frozen as a child, too – she even still dressed like a teenager. Her speech was also weirdly childlike. It was odd; she was odd, frankly. She had few friends, was bullied at work, and I had never met anyone with such low self-confidence. She broke my heart.

What was fascinating was watching the adult Marcia emerge from the wreckage. Once she understood that her mother was not God, that her word was not law and that she, Marcia, had her own thoughts and feelings, and that they were just as valid and equally important, it was like watching a caterpillar become a butterfly in time-lapse photography. It was truly a wonderful journey. She diligently worked through the exercises one by one, slow, plodding, methodical. The penny started to drop. Mother was not always right? Mother was *not* always right! What I think *does* matter? OMG! What I think matters! I am an adult? I get to make my own choices? Wow!

There was no stopping her. This gauche overgrown teenager blossomed into a beautiful independent thirty-year-old woman before my very eyes. Full of energy and life and sparkle. Marcia quit the job where she was routinely bullied. She set up her own business. Just like that! Her mother, of course, said it wouldn't work, but she did it anyway! And she loved it, and it did work. She got her first-ever boyfriend, and, as I type this, she is engaged to be married! Marcia is happier and more fulfilled than she ever has been. As she keeps telling me: 'I feel like I won the lottery. And I was the prize!' This internal transformation from Adult Child was no less startling on the outside. Gone were the baggy charity-shop T-shirts (her mother didn't believe in 'wasting money' on clothes), and in were skinny jeans, knee-high boots, cute tops and designer sunglasses! A new hair-do. She looked a million bucks. And she felt it, too. The transformation was so dramatic, it's hard to put it onto the page. I am so proud of her.

So, hanging on to outdated beliefs that may have helped you cope when you were eight are not so good now. You grow. Your beliefs can grow with you. They need to fit your life *now*. The fabulous, independent human you are *now*.

Now it's your turn. Time to get reflective. This might be a tough one, but remember there is no emotion so bad you can't go through it. It's time to look back. See if you have an echo of an Adult Child. What beliefs are you carrying from childhood that may not be serving you now, and are zapping your energy through emotion-dodging or pushing you into working and perpetual doing that exhausts you?

ACTION STEP 1: UNCOVER YOUR CHILDLIKE BELIEFS

When I was a child I knew that I must ....
....

When I was young safety meant ....
....

The young me thought happiness was ....
....

In my family anger was ....
....

My mother thought it was important to ....
....

My dad thought I was a good girl if ....
....

I remember thinking it was important to ....
....

I would be in trouble when ....
....

Now, see which of these deep beliefs may be driving unhelpful, energy-zapping behaviour today.

Believing ....
....

makes me do/say/behave/act ....

Believing ....
makes me do/say/behave/act ....

Believing ....
....
makes me do/say/behave/act ....

Believing ....
....
makes me do/say/behave/act ....

Believing ....
....
makes me do/say/behave/act ....

Believing ....
....
makes me do/say/behave/act ....

Believing ....
....
makes me do/say/behave/act ....

Believing ....
....
makes me do/say/behave/act ....

Believing ....
....
makes me do/say/behave/act ....

Wow. Okay, so you don't have to believe all that if you don't want to. Look at what is helpful and appropriate for this stage in your life. You may want to revise or completely change some of these beliefs to be in alignment with the grown-up, independent person you are now, and with the life you now lead.

Write some more helpful beliefs that are in alignment with the adult you right here:

I think that ....
....
and it's important to ....
....
I believe I ....
....

and I also believe ....

....

....

....

Now. Decide. You are an *adult*. Which of these sets of beliefs do you want driving your life? That's right. It's *your* choice.

ACTION STEP 2: DIGGING OUT BELIEFS

If you are finding this tough, then I highly recommend you check out the work of an amazing spiritual teacher called Byron Katie, who has a technique for analysing limiting beliefs that is nothing short of miraculous. It's called 'The Work' and you can find it at www.thework.com.

Adrenaline Junkie

There are a couple of definitions of an 'adrenaline junkie'. The first is the bungy-jumping, parachute-jumping kind; the thrill-seeker who is addicted to the intense rush from extreme sports. Having done a bungy jump, I can quite categorically say it was the best thing I am *never* doing again! Up on the platform, pre-jump, nothing but air beneath my feet, I can say without any equivocation that I experienced a level of fear that I had no idea existed within me. I was almost catatonic with fear.

I did it. And the rush lasted for three whole days. I remember feeling absolutely invincible. Bulletproof. Like cars would bounce off me if they hit me. The rush of adrenaline was so extreme. The fear was a level beyond terror and, although the rush after was one of the most incredible sensations of my life, I could *never* do it again. I am absolutely not a thrill-seeking adrenaline junkie! It's just too scary to be repeatable for me. Which is interesting, because I *am* an adrenaline junkie in an entirely different way. This is the second definition of adrenaline junkie: the pressure-seeking adrenaline junkie.

The pressure-seeker habitually creates stressful situations in life because they get a rush from performing under pressure, by getting away with it by the skin of their teeth, by feeling needed, wanted and indispensable. Pressure-seekers habitually create stress in their life because they like the feeling of adrenaline coursing through their veins. And they like the psychological pay-off of achieving against all odds or doing what seems impossible to others.

I would create perpetual 'I'm going to be late' situations in my life, getting a rush by trying to beat the clock and not be late for a client appointment or presentation. I would leave things to the last minute, procrastinate, but know that then I would pull an all-nighter to get the thing done, fuelled by adrenaline and coffee. I chose a profession that is deadline after deadline after deadline, trying to deliver what sometimes feels impossible. I set targets and budgets that were higher than necessary, I could have got away with something lower, but I wanted the kudos and glory of breaking records and I loved the thrill of living on the edge of success or failure. My personal and professional lives were constructed around a myriad of adrenaline-producing situations. I thought I had a busy, stressful life. I can now see that most of the stress in my life was actually self-created. At the time, I was self-congratulatory about just how well I handled pressure and thought on my feet. 'Not many people could do this,' I thought proudly. I was more than a little smug. They couldn't do it, because why the hell would they want to?! They could have performed at 95 per cent and done a great job rather than continually trying to give 110 per cent to match some sort of imaginary standard of achievement. I was addicted, quite literally, to the rush of pressure.

In fact, when I saw the final specialist at the hospital, the sweet and kindly doctor who said I was the 'healthiest sick person' he had ever seen, he said I was so ill that he couldn't believe how long I had carried on for. Most people would have given in way before, he said, when the symptoms were much less severe. They would have stopped, reassessed, gone on sick leave or stress leave. He said I was so strong, so committed, and while this was my greatest strength, my tenacity and determination were also probably my greatest weakness, as it had driven me to get as sick as I did. I think he was right.

It's been many years of trying to unlearn this behaviour and, to be honest, I still have a way to go on this one. I was addicted to stress, the rush, and I still have a compulsion to take on too much. It's a work in progress for me, but I know keeping a lid on this compulsive behaviour is key to me being happy and enjoying an energetic life. My adrenal glands are just not built to put up with what I was subjecting them to. The odd bungy jump, sure, because the body has much time for rest, recovery and replenishment in between. But not all day, every day, creating pressure and stress for myself. It's a relentless burden for the adrenals and it leads to burn-out.

I share this part of my story here so that if you are also a pressure-seeking adrenaline junkie it may give you pause to reflect. Can you dial it down a bit? Can you pack a little less into your day? Can you be okay with not being the best all the time? With doing an okay job rather than exemplary, just some of the time? Can you coast for a bit every now and again?

ACTION STEP: RECOGNISING YOUR ADRENALINE-JUNKIE BEHAVIOUR

Times when I intentionally create pressure and stress in my life are:

....
....
....
....
....
....
....
....

What could I choose to do differently here?

....
....
....
....
....
....
....
....
....
....

Imposter Syndrome

When someone asks me to speak at a conference or corporate seminar I occasionally get this inner freak-out that goes something like: 'Who am I to be doing that?! Maybe I'm not good enough', while I am saying, 'Sure, I'd love to!'

It's not a new thought. I used to have this undermining little voice in my ear in corporate life, too, whispering 'I'm not good enough' before a big presentation. Now, with the benefit of hindsight, I can see that I was really good at my job. Why was I worried and letting this insidious voice of doubt pull me off track?

Well, it's a voice that is particularly common in women and even has its own name, 'Imposter Syndrome'. Perhaps you can hear it sometimes, too? It is an inner fear of feeling a fraud in some way – that you are just about to be 'caught out' or 'found out'. It predisposes us to believe our *successes* are due to *external* factors, such as luck, and any *failures* are due to *internal* factors, such as our own abilities or skills.

I see this a lot in the workplace. Super-smart women not going for promotions that their much less capable male colleagues are sure they are a shoo-in for. Interestingly, it seems (in general) that men are more likely to think the opposite: they put failures down to external factors (bad luck; idiot client; market forces), and any successes down to their general awesomeness.

If a man is unhappy in his job he is more likely to say 'it's the job', and if a woman is unhappy in her job she is more likely to say 'it's me'. Men are generally also more likely to over-estimate their capacities and women to under-estimate. Interesting, right?

Clearly, Imposter Syndrome is seriously unhelpful. It's a killer for self-esteem and can hold us back from all manner of amazing opportunities. Coaching women to overcome this tendency and unleash their inner awesomeness is a deeply rewarding facet of my work. Self-doubt can be absolutely insidious; it robs us of our confidence and it robs us of our energy.

Below are Action Steps to nip those niggling feelings of being 'found out' in the bud.

ACTION STEP 1: NOTICE THE THOUGHT THAT PULLS YOU DOWN

Awareness is everything! Notice whether it's a thought that attributes your *success* to an *external* factor or your *failure* to something *internal*. Realise this thought is not necessarily true.

Write your thoughts about your successes, e.g. 'I just got lucky':

....

....

....

....

Does this attribute your success to something external? If yes, then try to find another reason you were successful that is due to something *internal*, e.g. 'I worked really hard and I had that brilliant idea about raising customer service that worked really well':

....

....

....

....

Try another one. Your thoughts about your successes:

....

....

....

....

Does this attribute your success to something external or internal? If external, find another reason you were successful that is due to something *internal*:

....

....

....

Write your thoughts about your failures, e.g. 'No wonder my marriage failed, I am so mean sometimes':

....

....

....

Does this attribute your failure to something internal? If yes, then try to find another reason things did not work out that is *external* to you, e.g. 'We both tried really hard but in the end we were just not a fit, we had grown apart':

....

....

....

....

....

....

ACTION STEP 2: RAVE REVIEWS

Be aware of all your successes. What have you done particularly well? Who rates you? What words of praise or emails of thanks can you reread? Focus on *hard evidence* of your skills and attributes. Make a 'Rave Reviews' book, collecting all the words of praise and encouragement you have received, either a virtual one in a web-based application such as www.evernote.com or get a big art book from an art store and paste in copies of letters, cards and words of praise you can remember. Add to this whenever you receive a compliment. Read it frequently, especially before first dates, interviews or a big pitch.

ACTION STEP 3: BELIEVE THE HYPE

If someone has asked you to do something or promoted you, then it's because they have no doubt you are up to it! Believe in their judgement – it may be far more accurate than your own. When you put yourself down you are undermining their good opinion, which is rude to say the least! Consider the possibility that they can see something special in you that you can't see yourself.

ACTION STEP 4: PLAY WITH THE BOYS

The funny thing about Imposter Syndrome is that it is much more prevalent in women than in men. Make some time to observe how the boys tend to roll: how they shrug off things that do not go well and how they fully own their successes. It's a much more confident way to live.

Which confident men in your life can you observe? Play a game at the next dinner party: ask three of the men how they became successful. Listen and learn from the responses. It's highly likely the man will say his success is due to his own self-efficacy. Listen, learn and see what turns of phrase you might want to adopt.

ACTION STEP 5: SEIZE THE DAY

Believe in yourself. Step up. Listen to the evidence of your awesomeness, not the sneaky imposter whispers. Read your Rave Reviews book to fire you up. Step into your own power. Go grab some new opportunities with both hands and rock it out!

What would you do if you knew you could not fail?

....

....

....

....

....

....

....

Now, go do that.

I'm Not Good Enough!

Newsflash! You are not, repeat *not*, perfect! I know – crushing, isn't it? The good news is neither is anyone else. However true you may know that to be intellectually, I bet that at certain times through the day/night/week there is a little voice quietly whispering in your ear that you are in some way falling short, not doing enough, not being enough – not good enough.

There is no belief as limiting, ubiquitous, insidious or energy-sapping as 'I'm not good enough'. If I had a dollar for every time I heard that come out of a client's mouth I would be writing this from my private yacht somewhere in the Bahamas. It is pretty much single-handedly responsible for stopping most people from living their happiest, most fulfilled and connected life.

- ※ 'I'd love to be a personal trainer/property developer/actress but I'm not good enough to make money from it.'
- ※ 'I get bored sometimes looking after the children. It's not what a good mother should feel. I'm not good enough for them, they deserve more.'
- ※ 'I'm excited about this promotion/project/job, but what if I can't do it? What if they find out I'm not good enough?'

So, let me say right here, 'good enough' is a myth. It's a mirage, an oasis in the desert, tantalisingly glimmering before us in perpetuity. If only we could actually reach it. We will never reach it! It's not real. *It doesn't exist!* Trying to reach the mirage of 'perfect' and 'good enough' is an exhausting and guaranteed fruitless mission that can dominate a lifetime.

Here's the thing: we are all works in progress. Happy, contented, energetic people with a lust for life know this. Relaxing the grip on 'good enough' allows us to risk more, try more, play more, rest more, laugh more. Happy people drop the struggle and accept themselves as fabulous, imperfect beings who are absolutely good enough. Imperfect rocks. Imperfect is reality. Imperfect is what makes us special and unique.

Ninety-nine per cent of us believe we are 'not good enough' on some level. The truth is that 100 per cent of us are entirely good enough. There is no such thing as perfect: there is only progress. Dare yourself to release the quest for perfection and embrace the relaxed reality of being a work in progress. Embrace the alternative view. Every time you hear that voice, 'I'm not good enough', turn it around. Say 'No more!' to that voice that robs you of your power and joy. Cry 'Enough! I *am* good!' and mean it.

So, gorgeous, let me whisper this truth in your ear: relax. You do enough. You have enough. You are enough.

ACTION STEP: STOP THE VOICE OF DOUBT

The next time you hear that voice of doubt whisper, 'I'm not good enough,' cut it dead in its tracks. Your new, empowering response is, 'Enough! I *am* good.'

Chapter 4

Honour Your Body

It's time for you to build a better relationship with your body.
After all, your body is the moving temple of your soul.

LIZARD BRAIN

Brace yourselves. We are going for another 'Science Bit'. I am going to give you the gist of some cool stuff about your brain. You can start using this info immediately to increase your energy. The concept of the 'Lizard Brain' is far from new and has been discussed ad infinitum not just by scientists but also by influential business blogger Seth Godin and, of course, life coach extraordinaire Martha Beck. However, I want to talk to you about this concept in an ultra-specific context: the role of your Lizard Brain in depleting your energy reserves.

Here we go. The basic idea behind the theory of evolution is that all the different species (including us!) have evolved from simple life forms. That all life is related to a common ancestor and complex creatures naturally evolve from more simplistic ancestors over time.

These early simple creatures had very simple brains that were tuned for one purpose only: keeping them alive so they could breed and continue the species. These primitive creatures (let's go with a visualisation of a little prehistoric lizard here – imagine it scuttling about) lived in very **scary** times: there was something that wanted to eat them around every corner. They also lived in very **scarce** times: they didn't have the option of popping into the nearest bakery when they were peckish, they needed to be constantly on the search for food, water, shelter and warmth in order to stay alive. Right, so a scary and scarce environment meant that their simple brains were always scanning for scary and scarce. Perfect.

Fast forward a bazillion years to the smart human creatures we have evolved into. We carry out all manner of complex and esoteric thought processes and behaviours in our sophisticated lives. And that's all before breakfast. Our environment has changed enormously from the prehistoric one. It's not a scary environment any more; we do not live in fear of marauding lions and tigers at every turn. It's really pretty **safe**. Even if you live in a rougher neighbourhood, it's still infinitely safer than when wild beasts lurked behind every corner, sizing you up as a tasty snack. Also, it's **abundant**. If you are hungry, you can buy something to eat. Even if you are a bit broke before the month's end, you will still have a roof over your head, even if it's at a friend's house. There is almost unlimited access to food, shelter, warmth, water. In short, we live in an almost limitlessly abundant time.

So, here's the thing. Hidden deep inside the brain, near the brainstem, is a part called the amygdala, otherwise known as the Lizard Brain. It's hard-wired to look for **scary** and **scarce** at every opportunity. Unfortunately, our environment has evolved faster than this bit of our brain. Our environment is now (by and large) **safe** and **abundant**. Do you see the problem?

The Inner Lizard

Our Lizard Brain, our Inner Lizard, is pre-programmed to look for scariness and scarcity in our environment at all times. It's how it keeps us safe; it thinks it is protecting us, alerting us to potential danger. Its sole purpose for being is to alert us to possible scariness or scarcity. But they rarely exist these days. So, instead of the Inner Lizard taking a nap and saying, 'Cool, my work here is pretty much done. I'll be in touch if you are about to be imminently run over by a bus. Until then carry on, enjoy that safe, abundant environment you've got there!', it is like a talkative four-year-old who has just discovered toilet humour and has to show it off at every opportunity. Our Inner Lizard, bless it, scans our environment for anything that is going on and turns it into an opportunity to share a made-up scary or scarcity thought. 'Oh, that email from your boss, I BET HE'S NOT HAPPY WITH YOU ABOUT THAT REPORT.' 'Oh, phone ringing, BET THAT'S SOMEONE COMPLAINING.' 'Watch what you say in that meeting, someone is always trying to PUT YOU DOWN.' 'He's very quiet right now; that must mean HE DOESN'T LOVE YOU!' And, so, on and on and on our Inner Lizard squawks.

Instead of talking about rampaging dinosaurs and inhospitable climes, our Inner Lizard uses our everyday equivalents to provide material to talk about. Inner Lizards are particularly partial to talking about a scarcity of **love, energy, time** and **money** as there is no genuine lack of food, water, shelter and warmth.

Do you hear a voice in your head saying:

- ❊ '**OH, NO. I don't have enough** *energy*!' (scarcity)
- ❊ '**OH, NO. I don't have enough** *time*!' (scarcity)
- ❊ '**OH, NO. I don't have enough** *money*!' (scarcity)
- ❊ '**OH, NO. He's being quiet, he doesn't** *love me*.' (scarcity)
- ❊ '**OH, NO. I might** *let that person* **down if I . . .**' (scarcity [lack of approval] and scary [they might attack me in some way])

> ❋ 'OH, NO. They are going to *find me out*' (scarcity [lack of approval] and scary [they might attack me in some way])
> ❋ 'OH, NO. They *don't really like me*' (scarcity [lack of approval] and scary [they might attack me in some way])

See how these thoughts are all *fear* based. They are about a fear of lacking something (scarcity) or a fear of some form of attack (scary/unsafe). Fear – whether it's real (i.e. a bus is actually about to run you over) or imagined ('OH, NO! He HATED what I said. He's going to be SO pissed off!') – creates the same physiological response that pushes our fight or flight response. This is meant to happen once a week, when we are physically in danger, not a hundred times a day, every time we receive an email and fear that it's bad news.

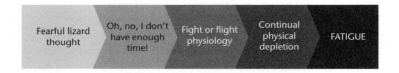

Have you ever heard those thoughts or variations on them? Of course you have. Did you think they were *true*? That you really don't have enough time, energy, love or money? Because that's just not the case, honey. That is like believing your four-year-old nephew is making a valid point when he says you are a 'poopoo head'. When a child says something like that do you say: a) 'Yes, yes, darling. Now off you go and play', or b) 'Yes, yes. You are so right, I AM a poopoo head! I must do something about that right now. Does everyone at work know? What can I change to deal with this poopoo head thing? This is such a worry to me, maybe there's some book I can read or course I can take . . .'

Obviously, you don't take the poopoo head thing seriously, do you? No, you just pat the kid on the head and send them off to play. You don't engage with that chatter. You know it's just nonsense. That's just what four-year-olds do. It's not real or true or serious.

The problem, though, and why it's so destructive, is that you don't see messages of scarcity or scariness as just idle chatter from your Inner Lizard. You think that voice is *real*, that voice is coming from you, that it *is you*, that you need to take it seriously. 'Oh, no. He doesn't love me' then becomes 'OH, NO. HE DOESN'T LOVE ME. Oh, my God. What can I do? Do I even love him? Is our marriage over? What will happen to the kids?', and on it goes. Hence the state of anxiety and continual physiological reaction over this perceived threat. But it's not real. It's just lizard chatter about lack and attack. It's just what lizards do.

Okay, so you can see how it works. You can see how destructive it is to listen and react to the voice of your Inner Lizard. Before we progress I am going to recap as this is such important stuff, and then we will move on to how to deal with it.

1. The amygdala is the bit of the brain that triggers the fight or flight response. Every time you believe your Inner Lizard, you generate the same physiological response as if you were just about to run for your life.

2. The Inner Lizard is not an accurate barometer of reality. It creates *fake fear*. How can you be sure? *Real fear* has a clear and present danger. You can see it, feel it, touch it. It's unquestionably there. And, oddly, we are actually usually pretty good at dealing with real fear. We jump out of the way of the bus in the nick of time. We hire a lawyer of our own. We take action. *Fake fear* is totally different. It's not real. You can't really get a grip on what it is you are lacking or needing to avoid. It is a generalised anxiety. It doesn't require immediate action. It can be hard to define what a useful action would be. Fake fear disappears under even the mildest scrutiny.

3. By continually pushing our body's fight or flight response every time we buy into one of these Inner Lizard chatters, we can make some catastrophically bad judgements in the real world. When we believe our Inner Lizard and don't stop to ask, 'Is that true? Is that fear even real? Is there any actual hard evidence for that view? So what? Does that even matter?', we act as if it's gospel. We pick a fight based on the Inner Lizard's suggestion that our boyfriend doesn't really love us. We get unnecessarily defensive with our boss when we believe the Inner Lizard that he is checking up on us because he doesn't rate our work.

In a hostel I stayed in once in Vietnam, there was a sign that said 'No News: No Shoes'. I can't tell you how much I loved that. It was the most relaxing and inspiring place ever. There is a lot to be said for 'No News: No Shoes' as a philosophy for life, most certainly when it comes to creating a life filled with energy.

Much of the news is shamelessly Lizardy. Broadcasters and publishers know that appealing to our Inner Lizard is a sure-fire way to get viewers and sell papers. How many sensationalised headlines have you seen designed to grab at your Inner Lizard? ('WEATHER BOMB HITS!' 'KILLER SHARK ON RAMPAGE!' 'HOUSE MARKET IN FREEFALL!') Often the reality once you get into the body copy of the article is much more tame ('forecast is pretty stormy for the next few days, not even that unusual for the time of year' or 'one shark attack reported, which is admittedly awful, but do you know we kill something like 100,000 times as many sharks per year as sharks kill us' or 'actually, that's not even an industry-wide stat, it's extrapolated from one realtor's March results'). It goes without saying that your Inner Lizard finds news that's designed to make you purchase or watch out of fear rigorously stimulating. By the time you read down and find it's not as bad as you thought, you have already pulled the trigger many times on your fight or flight response.

The biggest tragedy of the Inner Lizard is that not only can believing it be ruinously tiring, but it also causes us to play small in the world. The Inner Lizard is responsible for the businesses that never get launched despite a sound business plan ('You'll NEVER make any money') and relationships that falter despite promising beginnings ('WHY would he love you? He's better than you. He'll get tired of you'). The Inner Lizard turns us away from pursuing our dreams and hopes by whispering false messages of scariness and scarcity about love, money, time and energy. Its fake fear tells us to avoid risk, to play small. And the tragedy of it is that many of us do. It's time to tame your Inner Lizard. Not just for your health but for your life.

ACTION STEP 1: LISTEN

What does your Inner Lizard say to you? What do you not have enough of? What can't you trust?

What is the most common chatter? Look especially at the core modern-day themes of love, energy, time and money. List them here:

....

....

....

....

....

....

....

....

....

....

....

ACTION STEP 2: QUESTION

Be aware. Check whether the thought that pops into your mind from a place of scariness or scarcity is actually just your Inner Lizard chattering away. It's not *you*. It's not smart, capable *you*. Examine the thought consciously for validity before reacting to it.

Ask yourself:

* Is that true?
* Is that fear even real?
* Is that happening now?
* Is there any actual hard evidence that I can hold in my hands for that view?
* So what? Does that even matter? Really?
* What's the worst that can happen?
* Is that really that bad?

ACTION STEP 3: DESENSITISING AND DISCERNMENT

Be more selective in terms of the mind fodder you give to your Inner Lizard. Become a discerning consumer of media. By cutting back on the amount of Lizard food that goes in, your physiological reaction will change.

So, put your Lizard on a media diet. Trim down the number of publications you read and programmes you watch, especially the sensationalist stuff designed to push your fear response.

Learn some media discernment. There are some publishers and broadcasters who are more about fact, analysis and news than blatant Lizard-stimulating sensationalism. Work out who they are. Get the news in a way that leaves you informed but not in a state of physiological panic.

ACTION STEP 4: SEPARATION

This is a Martha Beck tool from her brilliant book *Steering by Starlight: The Science and Magic of Finding Your Destiny* and I just love it. It's the smartest way I have found to help clients separate that voice of scariness and scarcity in their heads from their own voice; to see their Inner Lizard as separate from themselves and as distinctly 'not me'.

What I want you to do, today, is buy yourself a visual representation of your Inner Lizard. It can be a ceramic ornament lizard, it can be a plastic children's toy lizard, it can be a sparkly brooch lizard, a lizard key ring. My clients turn up for 'show and tell' with all sorts of weird and wonderful physical embodiments of their Inner Lizards. I don't care where you get yours. Just do it. Seriously. Go do it. I'll wait.

Okay, good. So now I want you to name your Lizard. You will know what name suits it. My Lizard is called Lenny. It can be a boy Lizard or a girl Lizard. Again, you will know.

Now, I want you to be able to *talk to and make friends with your Lizard*. When you recognise a fake fear, scary or scarcity message from your Lizard, recognise it for what it is and lovingly tell your Lizard that there is no real drama, you've got it handled and he/she can go back to sleep. Over time the Lizard gets more and more relaxed and that continual descent into fight or flight will reduce. Energy goes up! You can even say these conversations out loud if you need to. I might say to Lenny, who is squawking away about me being late for something and how that means everyone will be disappointed in me and I am letting them down, 'Lenny, thanks for sharing, but you know, it's only half an hour and I'll text and let them know. It's fine, I've got this handled, go back to sleep.'

Do not skip this step. I know you will be tempted to, but don't. Having a physical representation of your Lizard is mission-critical to improving your energy levels and achieving a low-anxiety, happy life.

Buy. A. Lizard. Today. Or order one online. Today. In order to tame your Inner Lizard you need to name it. And to name it you gotta go find it so you can see it as separate from yourself, so you can see its voice is *not you*. Just trust me on this, okay?! My clients are routinely blown away by the power of this tool and the almost immediate reaction of their everyday stress levels.

EVELYN'S STORY

I have seen a wide range of Lizards in my time. One client even made a Lizard out of stripy socks and buttons. And one (I love this one most of all), a wonderful client called Evelyn, bought a rather expensive and beautiful Lizard ring. 'Wow,' I said, 'that is beautiful! But I am slightly surprised. We have established your Inner Lizard has a real thing about money. In fact, the whole reason you stayed in that job you hated for so long is because you believed your Lizard that you would have no money if you didn't. For the last six years you forced yourself to go to work each day and you believed your Lizard when she screamed, "You have no choice, Evie! You HAVE to work here! It's the *only* way you can pay your mortgage. There is nothing else you can earn good money doing. You HAVE to work here!"'

'You are right,' smiled Evie, 'I did believe all that, and it cost me so much in terms of my health and my happiness. So when I saw this ring I knew I had to have it. I need to see my Lizard [she called her Esmeralda] at all times to keep an eye on her! I saw the ring and I knew that would be on my finger every day. That Lizard has cost me so much, way more than this ring, this ring is the reminder of that and I will never let her run my life again.'

And do you know what? She hasn't. Evie quit her unfulfilling job after twenty long years in the industry. She retrained in her passion (and got a job paying just as much while she trained!), and now works with animals as well as running her small-holding. She rides daily, has an immeasurably better time with her husband and daughter, and she listens to her own voice for truth and guidance, not Esmeralda's. Her life is now run by love, not fear. She has more energy than she knows what to do with.

ACTION STEP 5: RACING BRAIN

If this one doesn't apply to you then skip it, but it's a common occurrence with around a third of my clients. If you sometimes wake up in the very early morning with 'racing brain', feeling noticeably panicky before you even get out of bed, then you need to be aware that your Inner Lizard has been rampaging during the night. You are in fight or flight response *when you are in bed!* There is no clear and present danger at the immediate moment. Understand that it's your Lizard running the show and setting a very bad tone for your day. So, talk to your Lizard, just as described above. Let him or her know there is nothing to be in a panic about, all is well and anything that comes up during the day you will handle; you are smart and capable. Tell him to please go rest and you will take care of things. Then fight the impulse to leap out of bed immediately. Lie there for another three minutes doing your yogic breathing technique (see page 154 or, even better, listen to the audio that you can download from my website, www.louisethompson.com). Calm your Inner Lizard and reset your physiology from fight or flight to rest and digest. Let the calm flow across your body. Start your day from this place of calm rather than the Lizard place of generalised anxiety. Make this a habit and see how much better you feel throughout the day.

You can also use this technique at bedtime to help you sleep.

Don't skip it. Trust me! This tool will instantly relieve the stress in your life. Find your Lizard. Name it. Tame it.

LIFESTYLE TWEAKS

We are focusing mainly on the mental causes of stress and therefore fatigue in this programme; however, we do have some basic body and diet housekeeping that we need to take care of, too. Taking the burden off your adrenal glands by, for example, balancing your blood sugar better through diet rather than relying on your adrenals to do it means they can devote themselves to rejuvenating.

This process of diet and lifestyle tweaks can become a full-time job if you let it, so we are going to keep it really simple.

> You can read more on diet, toxins, allergies, sensitivities and so on in Dr Wilson's excellent book *Adrenal Fatigue: The 21st Century Stress Syndrome.*

Many people may find a huge list of lifestyle instructions just too much – too daunting to implement. Especially when they are so tired in the first place! Hence I have a cheat sheet of my Top Twenty Dos and Don'ts. These are all simple, all doable. Start with five of them, integrate those into your life, then do five more, then another five until you are seamlessly living these principles. As your energy returns, it gets easier and easier to make these small changes. Don't try to do everything at once, but do start. Start today. Remember, if you want to *feel* different, you need to *do* different!

These simple dos and don'ts are designed to relieve the burden on your adrenal glands while they heal. Making these things a priority is a key part of your recovery. Remember our Truth Flash #1: you have to prioritise your recovery. Only you can do that. There is nothing more important than this right now. It's your most important work in the world.

> This cheat sheet is also available as a downloadable PDF for you at www.louisethompson.com so you can stick it on the fridge and check you are on track each day. My wellness partner in crime, Claire Turnbull, and I have also put together an easy and yummy recipe book, *Eat for Energy: Simple Strategies to Energise Your Diet,* that will give you *loads* of great ideas on how to integrate these small changes easily into your day-to-day life. Again, this is available at my website.

My Top Twenty Dos and Don'ts

Rest

1. **Breathe.** Make time each day to do yogic breathing (see page 154 for the full technique) a minimum of twice a day, three minutes a time. This will encourage your body out of 'fight or flight' and into 'rest and digest'. I recommend you do this when you wake up and when you go to bed.

2. **Prioritise time to rest when you are tired.** Nap when you can. This does not make you a loser or a lazy cow! It's essential self-care.

3. **Sleep more.** Go to bed earlier. Get up later. Be in bed by 10 p.m. With adrenal fatigue there is a late uplift thing that happens in terms of your cortisol levels that results in a second wind of energy that kicks in around 10.30 p.m. It is *essential* you are in bed, lights out, before this kicks in.

4. **Do slow, gentle exercise.** Stuff you enjoy. If you are tired then rest instead. Do not go hard out. If you are feeling overweight at the moment, park the anxiety around that, it really is the least of your problems. Work on restoring your energy as a priority and the weight will take care of itself later.

Diet

5. **Do *not* skip breakfast.** Breakfast *must* include protein (two eggs on a slice of wholegrain toast is perfect) to help regulate your blood sugar through the day. If you are pushed for time or usually skip breakfast, find an easy option like a low-carb, high-protein shake or snack bar. There are a lot of recipe suggestions and meal plans for supporting your adrenals in *Eat for Energy: Simple Strategies to Energise Your Diet*, which I have written with *Healthy Food Guide* nutritionist Claire Turnbull.

6. **Snack regularly.** Again, protein is good. Try to ease back on carbs as they produce spikes and dips in your blood sugar levels. An apple and a small slice of cheese, or a handful of almonds are perfect snacks. Be proactive today, go to the supermarket and stock up on this stuff so you have it handy. It's not hard and it's a foundation stone in your recovery. If you are too fatigued to do that, order online and get it delivered.

7. **Nuts and seeds are good for snacks:** sesame seeds, pumpkin seeds, sunflower seeds, flax seeds, cashews, almonds, Brazil nuts, walnuts, etc. A small handful is enough as a snack. Stock up. Buy some of those little zip-lock bags to store a mixture in so you grab a bag as a snack.

8. **_Do_ add salt to your meals** (unless specifically advised not to by your doctor). Salt naturally raises your blood pressure

and those who are adrenally fatigued generally have very low blood pressure.

9. **Cut back/out coffee and fizzy drinks.** Caffeine is *not good* for your adrenal recovery. I realise some of you will be weeping at this. It's often the hardest one, but it's just got to be done. You need to start seeing coffee as part of the problem of your low energy, not part of the solution. Wean yourself off gradually over a few weeks, but *do it*. Do this one *first*. It's an essential component of your recovery. You told me you were committed to getting your energy back, well I am telling you this is something you need to commit to. Not forever, but for now. There are some great alternatives: herbal teas, green tea, organic decaf coffee (always check decaf is 'Swiss water decaffeinated' to avoid introducing more toxins). If you are going to a café with friends, there are loads of other options. Choose one without moaning about it (remember Truth Flash #4: no whinging). Also, no caffeinated fizzy drinks. There are very few nos in this recovery programme, but caffeine is one of them.

10. **Eat fewer carbs, more protein, more veggies and fruit** (but go easy on fruit juice as it's so packed with sugar). Cut out as many processed carbs as you can and eat wholewheat or brown rice versions instead. Eating whole foods will stabilise blood sugar and provide a good stream of nutrients to boost your adrenals and the rest of your body.

11. **Choose the best quality you can afford:** free-range, organic, etc., to minimise toxic load on the body. Toxins mean the adrenals have to work harder, so give them a hand by choosing the best quality you can. I also think, without going too madly woo-woo here, it's an important principle to be eating ethically reared meat. This is something I am really passionate about. When you ingest meat that has been reared in a cruel manner with suffering, you are not putting good energy into your body. It's an energy of cruelty. The amount and accessibility of ethically reared meat is increasing every day; yes, you pay a little more, but isn't that worth it? It tastes better, too. Check out some farmers' markets – it's a cool day out.

12. **Cut back on junk food, cake, chocolate and alcohol.** I am not advocating complete misery and depravation: if you want a bit of chocolate, have a bit of chocolate, but try to make it top-quality rather than low-quality confectionery.

13. **Avoid anything you are allergic or sensitive to.** Personally, my body can't tolerate gluten at all so that's out, and also lots of perfumes and detergents bring me up in a rash. I have had clients with lactose intolerances, peanut allergies, allergies to tomatoes and all sorts. There seems to be a definite link between those with a predisposition to allergies and intolerances and those who are fatigued. I haven't figured out which comes first, the chicken or the egg. Are we predisposed to intolerances and allergies because we are fatigued, or are we predisposed to fatigue because we have intolerances and allergies so already have some sort of weakened immune function thing going on? Anything that inflames your immune system makes it harder for your adrenals to recover, so if you have sensitivities completely avoid the thing that you react to while you are working on this programme.

Pace of Life

14. **Eat slowly, don't rush.** Try to slow it down. Give your body time to digest what you are eating as it was designed to do. Put your knife and fork (or your sandwich) *down* between bites. Stuffing more food in while you are still chewing the last bite is gross. We are trying to promote 'rest and digest' not 'fight or flight', remember.

15. **Don't take on more activities than you need to do.** It's okay to say no! There are heaps of tools to help you set effective boundaries coming up for you in Chapter 5 (page 164) if you find you often feel guilty and are running yourself ragged looking after everyone else. Be gentle with yourself. Easier said than done, I know, but there are tools throughout this book to help you with this.

16. **Laugh a lot.** Seek out things that make you laugh. Laughing floods the body with all sorts of happy, healing hormones. Go to the movies, hang with funny friends who boost your mood, look on YouTube for funny videos, or get

friends' recommendations for books that made them laugh.

17. **Prioritise your recovery.** Your health is more important than your To Do list. I know I have said this before and I will be saying it again and again throughout this book. You have got to put your health first, choose that first. It's time to put the things above into action rather than attend the school PTA or stay late finishing that report. That's how people recover, they *choose consistently* in favour of what they want. Vitality and Energy. It's our Truth Flash #1.

18. **Make at least fifteen minutes of solitary time for yourself each day.** This is really important. I call it 'white time'. No phone, no email, no iPod, no TV, nothing but you and your breath and thoughts. You can be in the bath, meditating, out for a short stroll, or hiding in the wardrobe from the kids for all I care. But make time for fifteen minutes of non-giving-out of energy each day.

19. **Get some sunlight.** Natural sunlight is super valuable and healing. It positively affects hormone regulation and how well you sleep. Natural light needs to hit the back of the eye, so sunnies need to be off. Just ten to twenty minutes a day will enhance wellbeing and sleep.

20. **Enjoy the fact you are on your way to recovery!** This is not a glib last line; it's actually the most important of them all. I see my clients leave at the end of their first session and they are already looking and walking a little different, with a little more energy, a little more purpose. And that's because of hope. When you have been continually fatigued for months, years, even decades in some cases, and have exhausted every medical option, hope starts to die inside. So it's about empowerment, dropping that struggle for an external solution, and taking responsibility for creating the right conditions to create energy. It's a beautiful thing. Don't under-estimate the power of feeling empowered and the power of hope.

> ## ACTION STEP: MAKE CHANGE HAPPEN
> Print out the Lifestyle Cheat Sheet from www.louisethompson.com and start putting the above into action today. The Lifestyle Cheat Sheet is an easy checklist form for you to stay on track and easily integrate these lifestyle changes.

KICK-ASS SUPPLEMENTS

This section is most relevant for those who are continually tired, in Stage 3 or above of my Seven Stages of Fatigue. This is calling in the Big Hitter of energy recovery, a course of amazing supplements that aid the rest of your work in creating optimum energy levels. I don't believe supplements are the complete answer to healing fatigue, but I do believe they are an essential component to the journey. I think they are a critical foundation that helps create the optimum environment for outrageous energy to be born. I believe the body gets so depleted over years of reacting to constant real and perceived stress that the adrenal glands get to a point where, no matter how much good food you eat, you can't give them the intense dose of nutrients they need to heal themselves. I think it's faster and more complete to support their healing with a specific, top-quality supplement. Again, this isn't forever, just an intense burst to support your healing while you complete this programme.

Think back to when we did the first Science Bit: we visualised the adrenals that have gone from nice plump, shiny grapes to shrivelled-up raisins. To get them un-shrivelled and re-plumped up as fast and efficiently as possible, I suggest kick-ass supplements. I am also a really impatient person (my husband calls me 'The English Impatient' – ha!) and I like the speed of a targeted supplement. Yes, you can break it all down into individual components and do a whole heap of sourcing and mixing of herbs and minerals and whatnot (*Tired of Being Tired: Rescue. Repair. Rejuvenate* by Jesse Lynn Hanley and Nancy Deville has a whole heap of very smart and accessible detail on this). Personally, I am way too impatient for all that and, frankly, the state I was in, I was just too exhausted to implement it. The ease of taking simple supplements that include every single element my body needed to repair a few times a day was perfect for me. But, as I say all the way through this book, do what works for you.

Essential Components to Healing Fatigue

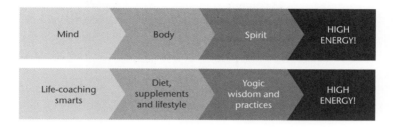

There is only one range of supplements I use and recommend, as it's what I used to recover. It's the Adrenal Fatigue Quartet by Dr Wilson, and it absolutely rocks. These supplements are absolutely the best on the market, in my opinion, and I have seen extraordinary results in people using them. Dr Wilson's medical pedigree is exemplary, and this range is his life's work. If you ask me, you simply cannot do better than this to support your body back to full energy.

I recommend you pay an extra fifty bucks or so to cover off your thyroid health as well. The thyroid is central to metabolic and energy levels. We are doing all this work on adrenal health and it would be frustrating to have energy levels held back by a low thyroid. Eighty per cent of people with adrenal fatigue also have issues with a weakened thyroid, as it's also exceptionally sensitive to the effects of stress. Signs and symptoms of an underactive thyroid include:

- ❀ **fatigue**
- ❀ **weight gain**
- ❀ **dry skin**
- ❀ **constipation**
- ❀ **intolerance to cold**
- ❀ **depression**
- ❀ **poor concentration and memory**
- ❀ **irregular periods.**

Another syptom is that the outside third of your eyebrows can start to thin. How bizarre is *that?* The outside of my eyebrows had become almost non-existent, so I added in Dr Wilson's 'Thyro Balance' thyroid drops to complement the adrenal supplements and, hey presto, my eyebrows started growing back. I suggest you add this into your dietary support; for an extra few dollars, it's more than worth it.

I am sure there are a whole heap of more important things that my thyroid is doing for me besides full eyebrows, but, hey, I liked seeing that visible marker of the change that was happening in my body. I could literally see it working! My clients are absolute advocates of this supplement range. The combination of the work we do and the proprietary blend of the exact quantities of minerals, vitamins and herbs your body needs is so powerful and creates accelerated healing. I used to get surprised when I got emails from clients saying 'I can't believe I feel so different already. I have been exhausted for five years and I already feel different after only three weeks! It's all working!' But now, to be honest, I expect it. By creating the right mental conditions and adding the right physical conditions, the body does what it is designed to do: it heals. Our bodies are *healing machines*, we just need to provide the right conditions. Truth Flash #2 right there.

The question I am usually asked is, 'How long will it take for the supplements to work?' That's a little like asking, 'How long is a piece of string?' In general, I have found that it depends on four factors:

1. how severe their level of fatigue is to start with
2. how long they have been fatigued
3. how old they are
4. how diligently they are applying the tools in the rest of the programme.

So I would expect a seventeen-year-old who had to quit school five months ago because she got so fatigued to bounce back faster than a fifty-five-year-old who has been fatigued for seven years, the last three severely. Generally, I see results in three to six weeks, often much faster. Usually the first sign of improvement is colour coming back into their face; they look fresher, younger, less grey. I have also had clients come in telling me they can feel the difference in their bodies and their energy levels within ten days of starting the programme.

As with most things in life, those who are diligent, who commit, who make the programme their priority, get their energy back the fastest and see results first. It really is the most extraordinary thing to observe. It thrills me to see a woman who was dragging herself to my office, just weeks before, bouncing in with a glow in her cheeks, feeling it working, being amazed and pleased and even more motivated to incorporate the other tools in the programme. It builds such momentum. Feeling the cells in your body respond, all the way to your eyebrow hairs!

ACTION STEP 1: COMPLETE THE QUESTIONNAIRE

If you haven't done so already, take Dr Wilson's comprehensive Adrenal Fatigue Questionnaire. You can find it in the Appendix on page 247, or at www.louisethompson.com.

ACTION STEP 2: USE SUPPLEMENTS

If you wish to order supplements, visit www.louisethompson.com for instructions or visit your local natural health practitioner. Find them through www.adrenalfatigue.co.nz. Targeted supplements are my preferred option as all the work has been done for me and the exact blend of what my body needs to heal is right there. All I have to do is remember to take them three times a day and that's it. Ba-da-bing.

ACTION STEP 3: MAKE YOUR OWN

If you are more of a DIY person and wish to create the precise blend of support your own body needs for accelerated healing and energy promotion, then start with the excellent book *Tired of Being Tired: Rescue. Repair. Rejuvenate* by Jesse Lynn Manley and Nancy Deville.

REFRAMING REST

Okay, here's the thing about resting, sleeping, napping. Listen up: when your body feels tired, it is not a marketing message from Starbucks that you need another trim latte. Feeling tired is a message from *your body* saying it needs to *rest*.

Rest is *phenomenally important* to adequate functioning of the human body. I know you are very busy, have heaps to do, people are relying on you, you are very important, etc. But consider these two facts:

1. **The human body can go for longer, much longer, without *food* than *sleep*. Yes, really.**
2. **Evildoers use *sleep deprivation* as a highly effective form of torture, that's how critical it is to normal functioning.**

Sleep is essential. Not just sleep but also rest. The doing of 'non-doing'. It's not 'wasted time', it's incredibly valuable time. You are *doing something when you are not doing something:* you are resting and recharging your body. And that's more essential than food.

If you want more energy, you need to really take these facts on board and reframe the way you think about rest.

You need to stop feeling so goddamn guilty about it! Do you feel guilty about eating lunch? No, you need to eat right. Well, there you go. Why should you feel guilty about having a rest, just stopping and chilling and taking five?

I am going to repeat myself, because this is so important. We are not machines. We are not people-pleasing doing machines. We are not put on this earth to be doing all the time. *We are human beings, not human doings!* We need to eat, to drink and to rest. It's just part of what makes us humans. Accept it and start *honouring* it.

Modern life perpetuates the myth that we are meant to be 'on' all the time. It's not true, and it's slowly killing us. As humans we require downtime in that same way my gorgeous three cats are champion nappers of the cat world. They don't apologise for napping – they just do it. Listen to your body. Feeling tired is an email from your body to say 'I need to have some rest now, please'. Listen up. Embrace the doing of non-doing.

ACTION STEP: TAKE A NAP

Next time you are tired, I want you to stop and rest and nap right there if you can. Leave the dishes unwashed – your body is more important than a clean house. Just go and nap on the couch for fifteen minutes. If you are at work, close the office door and just stop for a few minutes. If you can do so discreetly, close your eyes. If it's not possible, make a promise to yourself you will have some downtime when you get home, and stick to it. If it's the weekend, just go lie down for fifteen minutes and take a nap. Napping is glorious and recharging. Listen to your body, it's telling you what you need.

Detail your progress below.

Today I noticed my body felt tired when ....

....

....

....

....

and I chose to embrace the doing of non-doing and honoured my body by ....

....

....

....

YOGA NIDRA

Yoga nidra or 'yogi sleep' is one of the 'secret sauces' of my energy recovery programme. Am I the bendiest yoga teacher out there? Nope. Am I showing the most advanced asanas? No. Do I do the best final relaxation yoga nidra session? You bet I do.

Yoga nidra is an amazing, deeply restorative, guided relaxation session. It has been scientifically proven to reduce tension and anxiety, and to get us into that parasympathetic autonomic nervous system dominance (rest and digest) that we are after. It has even been used by soldiers suffering post-traumatic stress disorder. Yoga nidra is described as a spooky state of mind between wakefulness and sleep, or a conscious state of deep sleep. It is like sleeping but with awareness.

A number of swamis have said to me that ten minutes of yoga nidra equals several hours of actual sleep. I can't find any scientific proof of that, but based on what my students tell me I think there is something in that assessment.

The best way to do yoga nidra is to go to a yoga class. If you can find a class that is structured to allow for a generous and focused final relaxation yoga nidra session, it is absolutely the right option. The trouble I find is that for many classes the asanas (all the clever bendy postures) are the hero, and in many classes the yoga nidra component is lacklustre and utterly perfunctory. Frankly, this makes me sad and cross! I believe it is a waste of the biggest opportunity to make this healing practice accessible to millions of people every day of the week. It's a shame.

Yoga nidra is a guided meditative experience. The way I like to do it is in three distinct stages. First, giving you permission to relax (crucial); second, relaxing each part of the body in turn (so you are acutely aware of the difference in the body between tension and relaxation); and, third, engaging in a deep, soothing meditation to relax your mind (to take you to the spooky but delicious state of 'sleep with awareness'). I think yoga nidra is actually the *most* important part of the whole yogic experience. This is interesting, because when I took up yoga for the first time I thought the yoga nidra bit was stupid, pointless and a waste of time. What I have since learned is that the extent to which you think you don't need or don't have time for yoga nidra is directly proportional to just how much you do need it! It is soul food for mind, body and spirit.

At the end of the day, you can *read* about yoga nidra all you like, but you really need to *experience* it.

Check out the ten-minute yoga nidra audio for you to download from my website, www.louisethompson.com. You can use this to reinvigorate you during the day or to help you sleep at night. The more you play it, the more your body will learn to relax and the deeper you will go each time, flooding your body with healing.

ACTION STEP: TIME FOR YOGA NIDRA

Join a yoga class with a good yoga nidra session or commit to listening to my audio for ten minutes every day. Make yourself comfortable and enjoy the benefits of this deeply restorative ancient practice.

BREATH POWER

Right. Breathing. Really important to cover, even though I can see you yawning from here, and not just because you are tired. Learning about breathing is boring, right? Well, yes and no. I actually teach this in my yoga classes as well as to my clients, because it's another powerhouse secret to speed your recovery to Energyville.

We are all blessed with huge lung capacities that serve our bodies, but we generally only utilise about 30 per cent of them. We tend to breathe very shallowly, from the top of the chest up by the throat. This shallow breathing is symptomatic of being in the fight or flight response. It's a feedback loop that can keep stimulating itself: your body is breathing shallowly so it thinks it's in a state of panic or emergency, which in turn makes you breathe more shallowly, which reinforces the feeling of panic or emergency, which makes your breathing more shallow . . . and on and on we go.

Now, back in the first Science Bit we learned all about the difference between the sympathetic and the parasympathetic nervous systems (see page 31). Here is an additional factor to consider: when the body is in sympathetic dominance, it *can't heal* very well. The immune function is depressed as it is assuming you are currently fleeing a hungry lion. Immune healing is a *long-term response*. In reaction to a perceived or real threat, our fight or flight response pulls blood to the muscles and heart to effect a *short-term response*. It can deal with long-term healing later. Only when the body is safely in 'rest and digest' does it release the hormones in the quantities you need to effectively heal and mend your body.

Sympathetic Nervous System Dominance	Parasympathetic Nervous System Dominance
Fight or flight	Rest and digest
Light switch ON	Light switch OFF
Immune system depressed	Immune system boosted

It goes without saying that the more time we spend in rest and digest, the better. The faster we heal, the faster our energy levels improve.

Breathing is like a secret weapon here. It acts like a circuit-breaker to crash the body out of its fight or flight response. There are a number of yogic breathing techniques that flick that switch from ON to OFF.

The easiest way to do this is to learn a technique called 'yogic breathing'. It's a fabulous way to use all your lung capacity in a controlled way in what is called a 'three-part breath'.

You can download the yogic breathing audio (in the full programme) from www.louisethompson.com. Simply listen, close your eyes and follow the instructions.

YOGIC BREATHING

- Lie down somewhere quiet and comfortable.
- Place your right hand low down on your belly, by your abdomen.
- Place your left hand in the middle of your chest on your ribcage.
- If you had a third hand (which I know you don't), it would be up at the top of your chest, by your throat.
- Close your eyes (it's much easier to focus on the bodily sensations) and close your mouth. You are going to breathe through the nose only. It is a simple way to slow and deepen the breath as you simply cannot gasp for breath through the nose.
- You are going to inhale and exhale in three parts, consciously using your whole lung capacity. This will take you a few goes to get the hang of, but persist and focus, it will get easier, and in a minute or two you will find your rhythm.
- Inhale, letting the abdomen rise first.
- Then let the ribcage expand and lift.
- Finally let the top of the chest lift.
- Exhale, abdomen falls first.
- Ribcage falls.
- Chest falls.
- Inhale, abdomen rises first.
- Ribcage rises.

- ❀ **Chest rises.**
- ❀ **Exhale, abdomen falls first.**
- ❀ **Ribcage falls.**
- ❀ **Chest falls.**
- ❀ **Repeat, using your hands as bio-feedback to be aware of what is happening in your lungs. Breathe in this controlled, conscious manner for at least three minutes.**
- ❀ **Feel the waves of calm start to move through your body as you move into parasympathetic dominance.**

Please try to do at least three minutes of yogic breathing when you are still in bed in the morning to set a calm start to your day in 'rest and digest' mode, and again three minutes at night in bed. Every day. Make this a new habit. If you can do it more often, then do. Each time you reset the switch you are helping your body heal and restore.

My clients and yoga students are repeatedly amazed by how much this breathing technique helps them. They leave the session slightly sceptical about the value of breathing in this conscious manner, and return the following week converts to the power of the breath to calm the mind and body, help them sleep better and start their day from a more peaceful place. It's not hard; it just takes the decision to commit to three minutes twice a day, every day. I know many of you are going to resist doing this, so I encourage you to reread your commitment to yourself that you made at the start of the book (see page 28), to do whatever it takes to get your mojo back. I am asking you to commit to just six minutes each day. No excuses. You will be able to *feel* it working, and it feels delicious!

ACTION STEP: PRACTISE BREATHING

Practise your yogic breathing technique, either from the book or the guided audio. Commit to at least six minutes each day: three minutes when you wake up, three minutes when you are going to sleep.

This is *easily* one of the most powerful tools you can learn to improve your energy. It's using thousands of years of wisdom and it works – you can feel it working. Go do it.

ENERGY MANTRAS

In yoga we use mantras as a way of keeping the mind focused and present. Mantras work because we can hold *only one thought at a time* in our mind. When the mind wanders away and we find we are not actually meditating but thinking about getting the washing done or speaking to Mum, we pull the mind back to focus on our mantra, which *blocks the thought* about washing or Mum. A mantra is a short positive statement that gets repeated over and over in the mind. Repeated so often it becomes the default thought in the brain, calming the brain and allowing us to be present and peaceful.

You repeat the mantra with every count of your breath or each bead on a mala (which is sort of like a yogic rosary). This is how it goes in my mind: '(Inhale) I am whole and complete. (Exhale) I am whole and complete. (Inhale) I am whole and complete. (Exhale) I am . . . I wonder what I might make for dinner when I get home. Man that meeting went badly today— whoops! . . . (Inhale) I am whole and complete. (Exhale) I am whole and complete. (Inhale) I am whole and complete. (Exhale) I am whole and complete. Did I leave the iron on when I left? I hope I didn't, the house will be on fire by now— whoops! (Inhale) I am whole and complete. (Exhale) I am whole and complete . . .' and so on. The mind is like a naughty puppy; it continually runs away. The mantra is like a lead bringing it back to heel. The more you train it, the easier it gets.

Traditional mantras are in Sanskrit, which is the ancient language of yoga. For example, 'Om Namo Narayanaya' means 'Salutations to the god of harmony, balance, peace and inner-transformation'. I encourage my yoga students to also take an English-language mantra of their own choosing, which encompasses what they want to achieve out of their yoga practice. Mine, as you can see above, is 'I am whole and complete'. Students pick short, positive statements, such as 'I am healthy and calm' or 'I am at peace and all is well', as a mantra to help them remain present and calm the mind.

If you would like a Sanskrit mantra (they are very soothing), just ask your local yoga teacher or check out the worksheet of Sanskrit mantras at www.louisethompson.com.

So, how do mantras help you have more energy? Well, mantras are very powerful. That's why we are still talking about them thousands of years later. You get that endurance and longevity because it's a technique that works.

I like to use this mantra technique to help you manage your mind to have more energy. It's so powerful because we are thinking tens of thousands of thoughts a day, all day, every day. As you now know, some thoughts *give* us energy, and some thoughts *take* energy away. You don't have the choice to turn off your thoughts, but you do have the choice of what to think *about*. The mind is a question-answering and an evidence-finding machine. It's super-efficient. It's like Google. If you ask it 'What is the best way to make this cake?', it will come back with various suggestions of how to go about cake-making, based on stuff you've done, watched, learned and baked.

If you ask it 'Why am I so tired?', it will also come back with various answers and evidence. Those answers will make you feel even more tired. Answers like 'because you have had a long day' and 'actually you have a bit of a headache, too'.

To break this loop you need to ask your brain *different questions*. So, instead of asking 'Why have I accomplished so little today?', ask 'What's one good thing I have achieved today?' The former will give you evidence of tiredness, the latter evidence of positive accomplishment, however little that may be. Much more positive and energy-generating.

Another example, instead of asking 'Why is my whole body so damn tired?', ask 'What's one bit of my body that feels okay right now?' It might be just your pinky finger, but thinking 'My pinky finger feels great!' is much more energy-giving than 'Oh, my head hurts, my back is aching.' It's important to recognise that *your energy goes where your focus is*.

By thinking the same familiar, comfortable thoughts all the time we carve junk-food thought ruts in our brains, like the ruts a tractor makes in a field as it takes the same path again and again. This becomes the default track for your thoughts and leads you directly to Fatiguesville.

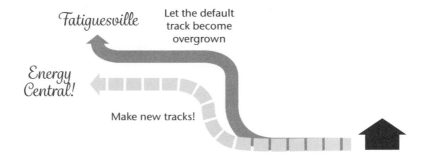

It takes both awareness and effort for the tractor to make a new track. However, by persisting and with repetition, this new track can become the new default. In the end it will become automatic. That is exactly what we are going to do with your brain. Cool, right?

TOP TEN FATIGUE PHRASES

First, write down your Top Ten Fatigue Phrases right here. These are the thoughts you think most often about your energy levels and your life. For example, I am so tired/my head aches/my whole body is so tired/I'll never make it through the day/why do I feel so awful, etc.

1. ....
2. ....
3. ....
4. ....
5. ....
6. ....
7. ....
8. ....
9. ....
10. ....

Notice how you feel in your body as you think all of those thoughts. More energy or less energy? Make no mistake about it: *these thoughts are keeping you tired.* Your brain is programmed to find evidence or answers for your questions and statements. So every time you think that thought, you reinforce it.

Also be aware that, in the case of extreme and continual fatigue, for many questions/statements *there are no answers*. No one really knows for sure (yet) what causes chronic fatigue syndrome or why it happened to you, etc. To be honest, there is no point repeatedly asking yourself these questions. The best medical minds in the world are beavering away, trying to figure out the answers. Asking yourself the same thing a thousand times a day is not going to get you the answer. It's a total waste of brain power and energy. So, ask yourself something that you *can* answer instead.

TOP TEN ENERGY-RESTORING PHRASES

Ask different questions: empowered and positive questions. What are some more energy-giving questions that you could ask yourself instead? For example, which bit of my body feels okay right now? What have I accomplished today? What can I do today to show my body I respect it? What would feel good right now?

1. ....
2. ....
3. ....
4. ....
5. ....
6. ....
7. ....
8. ....
9. ....
10. ....

Carving new thought ruts into your brain is time-consuming stuff. Your mind is used to travelling down the easy, well-cleared path that is your Top Ten Fatigue Phrases. You need to be very firm in deciding to start driving down the new path, and that is a choice you need to make dozens, even hundreds, of times a day. Whenever you hear yourself thinking those familiar thoughts you need to *choose to stop* thinking them. You cannot think two thoughts at once, so you simply need to replace the broken record with one of your new energy-giving questions. I say 'simply'; it's simple but it's not easy. However, this is essential work in creating a high-energy life and you need to start right now. This minute!

ACTION STEP: ENERGY MANTRAS

Develop one mantra that you can use to *block* low-energy thoughts. A great place to find your mantra is looking at your Top Ten Energy Restoring Phrases. Which one of those questions or statements resonates with you the most? Which feels the strongest? The most empowered? Use this as your energy mantra. For example:

- ❀ **'Every time I change a thought or take a supplement I am gaining energy.'**
- ❀ **'My body feels just great right now.'**
- ❀ **'My day is unfolding exactly as it should.'**
- ❀ **'I can choose whatever I wish for my life, and right now I choose peace.'**
- ❀ **'Resting right now is my most important work in the world.'**
- ❀ **'I love who I am.'**
- ❀ **'My life, my body, my choices, my way.'**
- ❀ **'I am safe and all is well.'**

Select your phrase and tweak it a bit if you need to so it's perfect. Then make it your energy mantra. Repeat it to yourself to block any low-energy thoughts or questions as you move through your day. You cannot repeat it too much.

My energy mantra is:

....

....

....

Write it out thirty times longhand to imprint it on your brain and to start making a new track. Do it daily until it becomes your new default.

GIVE YOUR BODY A VOICE

By now I hope you realise you live in an incredible miracle body! I hope you are now feeling super-empowered to be claiming back your rightful life of energy and happiness.

As a Westernised culture we are very quick to lay blame on our bodies for all sorts of things. You might hate your body for getting fat, for instance. But what choice did your body have? If you, the owner of your body, chose to overfeed it or feed it with junk food, then what option did your body have other than to store that food you forced into it?

To be angry at your body for not being as young and beautiful or as energetic or fit as you want is ridiculous. Your body has done all it can with the amount of exercise or self-care you have provided for it. It's not your body's fault. It can only do what it can with what you provide it.

I want you to start seeing your body as a treasured pet, not as the enemy. Think about how you speak to your cat or dog. We have three cats and they have the nicest life. They eat and sleep and get cuddled. They hear only words of praise and love and affection. They are the happiest, healthiest creatures. They are loved and spoiled rotten.

That is how you need to start treating your body – like a favourite pet. It's not the enemy. Being annoyed at it for having been fatigued and not able to carry on is ridiculous. That's *your* fault. Not your body's fault.

It's time for you to build a better relationship with your body. It's time to open up a different kind of dialogue and let go of the critical, blaming voice. Speak to it with love and affection. After all, your body is the moving temple of your soul.

ACTION STEP 1: LETTER TO YOUR BODY

This is one of the most powerful exercises I know. I'd like you to write a letter to your body. Let it know what you are thankful for, what you apologise for, and how you are going to work together as you move forward through life. Tell your body how you feel about what you have fed it, how you have cared for it, how much rest you have let it have, the thoughts you feed it with, how you speak to it, how you structure your life to look after it, how you have prioritised it, what you have expected from it and what promises you now want to make.

Here you go, here is the first line:

Dear body, this is me [your name] speaking. I have a few things I wanted to share with you. First, I wanted to say . . .

Copy this line out in your notebook or on your screen and complete the letter. Tell your body the truth about how you have treated it. Paint a picture of how it's going to be in future. This exercise has moved many clients to tears. I encourage you not to skip this step, but to put the book down now and write the letter. It's an incredibly healing and cathartic process. Don't move on until you have done this.

ACTION STEP 2: YOUR BODY'S REPLY

Done the previous exercise? Good job. Well, your body has great manners, and so having received your letter it's going to respond! Pull out a blank page and respond, letting your body do the talking. Start your letter like this:

Hello [your name], this is your body. Thank you for your letter, which must have been hard to write, and I appreciate you putting pen to paper. These are the things I need you to know in return . . .

As before, start a fresh page and complete.

Clients often say the exact same things about this Action Step. First, that it's hard to do the first few sentences but then it all just starts tumbling out. And second, that it is just so liberating! They are often quite shocked and ashamed when they look at the internal dialogue they have had with their abused but faithful body. They wouldn't treat anyone in their life that way, and if someone spoke to them like that they would leave/punch them. They are amazed at the blame they have laid at their body's door, and rebuilding that relationship of trust with their body is just amazing. And it all starts with these letters. So, get to it. Check out the following manifesto to give you some inspiration.

THE MANIFESTO OF HIGH ENERGY HAPPINESS

We all deserve to live an outrageously energetic and happy life.

If someone **drains you, walk away.**

Be grateful. This body will carry you through your life: it will take you to new places and lands, let you express your love and affection, earn your living, bear and raise your children. Does it not then deserve your love and gratitude?

If something is sucking your energy, stop it. **Stop blaming others for your energy or happiness levels.**

Embrace responsibility.

Everything after breathing is a choice.

Say hello to your body. Your one and only precious body. **It is the moving temple of your soul.**

Giving your body time and attention should not be last on your To Do list. Servicing your body is more important than servicing your car or washing the dishes.

Love your body.

Respect it. If you respect it, it will respect you in return.

Take joy from the pleasure and privilege of moving your body! **Walk. Jump. Run. Surf. Stretch. Dance.** Whatever movement pleases your soul.

Remember that **moving your body** regularly is not a chore but a **joy.** Imagine if you were paralysed and could not move.

Treat your body as you would a favourite pet. **Feed it well, groom it lovingly, let it rest when it is tired.**

Your body is always **on your side.** It always does its best for you.

If you think your body has let you down consider that the truth may be you are letting your body down with the choices you make.

Be patient: your body is not a machine but an animal in your care. It needs **time, patience and rewards** to learn new habits.

Continual tiredness is a message from your body to rest, not a marketing message from Starbucks to buy a latte.

If you are hungry for food, eat. If you are hungry for love or affection, **put the chocolate down and call a friend.** Never deprive or starve your body.

Stop with the self-hating body talk already! Talk to your body as if it were your closest friend. Share the kindness of word and generosity of spirit with your body, as you would with that friend.

You have but one body to carry you through this beautiful life. **Respect, love and honour how lucky you are.**

Stop comparing yourself with others. Be the best you that you can be. Every body is **unique & beautiful** in its own way. The celebrities in magazines are all airbrushed, anyway.

Chapter 5
Energetic Action

*It is not one choice or change that enables you to live a life of
High Energy Happiness – it is a million tiny ones.*

BLOCKERS AND BOOSTERS

By now I hope you are already implementing what you are learning and starting to feel the benefits in mind and body. The next section is all about building new habits of thought, plus practical things to do, learn and be. All of which are building blocks for a happy, balanced and energetic life.

This chapter is about setting energy boundaries. Prana boundaries. You have only so much mental, emotional, physical and spiritual energy to use in a day. It's a finite resource. Like time. There are twenty-four hours. No more, no less. The great news is you have infinite choice over what you choose to do with it.

We need to develop habits that *block* energy leaks (like the apps that are left running in the background) and *boost* and liberate energy. Things to stop doing. Things to start doing. Things to stop thinking. Things to start thinking. Feel more. Defer less. Be present. This is all about *action*.

On the following pages are twenty-two key actions for you to focus on to create your highly energetic and happy life.

PROTECT YOUR ENERGY BOUNDARIES

If you don't respect your time, then no one else will. If you don't respect your own energy boundaries, then no one else will. Exhausted people often say stuff like:

- ❀ I can't believe they keep piling on the work when I am already overloaded.
- ❀ He never helps around the house. I have to do it all, all the time.
- ❀ My client was so disrespectful, that last-minute cancellation now means I can't make rent this week.

Well. You know, what we accept is what we endorse. *We get what we allow.* If we give someone else the power to set the agenda over our time and energy, we are going to be run ragged. Figure out what are acceptable energy boundaries for you. For example:

- I work 8 a.m. to 5 p.m. five days a week. I will work diligently throughout those hours and I am prepared to go the extra mile and put in three late nights (until 8 p.m.) per month. That is the boundary for my own personal energy and life situation.
- I will spend four hours cleaning per weekend and prepare meals three nights of the week.
- Cancellations that are within 48 hours must be paid for in full.

Then, state your energy boundary. Calmly and clearly, no need to be passive-aggressive. Just say what it is. Then say what the other person's choices are. Let them choose. Pass the ball back to them. Not every problem, need or desire is something you need to fix at the expense of your own energy boundaries. For example, say:

- Hey, Bob. I'd love to take on that project for you but unfortunately with the projects I am currently running it's not possible to deliver it within your timeframe. Either you can ask my boss Peggy to reassign one of my existing projects to make time for yours, or, you will need to find someone else to help. I suggest Dave. Or you will need to get it outsourced. Which of those do you want to do?
- Hey, honey. I need to talk to you about getting some help around the house. There is too much housework for me to get done each week and still be happy and healthy. Either we need to hire a cleaner once a fortnight, or we need a rota of duties split more equally between us. Which sounds good to you?
- Hey, valued client. I am so sorry you need to cancel at the last minute as I was very much looking forward to our session. I will need to charge you for this session in full as it falls inside the forty-eight-hour cancellation deadline. My time is my income, as stated clearly in my terms and conditions policy. Thank you so much for your understanding. I am keen to continue with our work, so how does one of these times work for you for next week?

ACTION STEP: DEFINE YOUR ENERGY BOUNDARIES

My energy boundaries at work are: ....

....

My energy boundaries at home are: ....

....

My energy boundaries with family are: ....

....

My energy boundaries with friends are: ....

....

My energy boundaries with house cleaning are: ....

....

My energy boundaries with parenting are: ....

....

My energy boundaries for self-care are: ....

....

My energy boundaries for exercise are: ....

....

BE PRESENT

This is a concept that astonished me when I first discovered yoga – the idea of 'being present'. To be happy one must be 'present'. Be 'in the *now*'. Hmmm. Like, thanks for sharing, but what does that actually *mean*?

It turns out it's a really important thing to learn. It's a skill. It's something you can teach yourself to get better at. It's like learning how to drive or play the trumpet. If you set your mind to it, you (yes, even busy, frazzled, tired you!) can learn to be more present. And by being more present your energy levels will increase.

It's actually all quite simple. You don't need to meditate (unless you want to); it's an uncomplicated technique you can use to connect you to your 'now'. And guess what: 'now' is where your energy lives.

The only place we ever truly are is *right now*. The past is gone. The future is yet to come. The place we *exist*, where we can feel, speak and be, is *now*. And only now. The only place we can feel pleasure is *now*. Now is where all the real experience is. The interesting thing is it's a destination that few of us actually visit very often.

Consider the following situations. If you are doing the washing up, the chatter in your head may be something like this:

> 'Well, it's all very well this being in the present stuff, but I'm pretty damn busy, you know. I've got to get the kids' tea in a minute and then get everything sorted out for tomorrow. There's a big presentation at work that I need to prepare for. This being present stuff needs to wait until that's all sorted out.'

Or perhaps:

> 'Well, I've actually tried being present, but the whole meditating thing just doesn't work for me. And I've had such a long day, my boss had a real go at me about that project – mind you, lunch was fun, it was good to catch up with the girls, I really should try to do that more. I can't understand my boss's reaction to that project at all. I thought I had done a good job.'

The first mind chatter shows the person is in the *future*. All the attention is about what's going to happen *next*, in the future. We can get very stuck in this state, how things will be better when *x* has happened or when we have more money or are slimmer or get a new job. It cuts us off from appreciating what we have/are right now because our focus is on what has not happened yet. Our energy is projected *forward*, so we can't feel it *now*. We feel the absence of it. So we feel tired in the now as we scramble towards the future.

The second mind chatter example is focused on the *past*. It's all about stuff that has *already* happened. It can be a place where we build stories of worry about what happened and how it didn't turn out as we wanted. Again, it cuts us off from fully experiencing the present moment, and it leaves our energy *behind*. So, again, we are tired in the *now*; all we feel is the absence of energy. All the energy is tied up in the past.

The future and the past are great places to visit, but not to live. It's how we gain valuable perspective and life lessons, it's how we remember and evoke great memories. It's also how we plan and build anticipation and move our life forward towards our dreams.

Most people, however, have a real tendency to live life more dominant in one mental place: past, present or future. I know I had an almost pathological future focus, worrying about what was going to happen at work the next day so much I couldn't sleep. I wasn't really ever enjoying what I was doing when I was doing it, as I was always thinking that if I could just sort that thing out, or get that thing done, life would be much better. I also spent a fair chunk of time rehashing stuff I could have done differently, different decisions I could have made that would have meant life would not be how it was then. In fact, if you had drawn a pie chart of where I spent my mental energy it would have looked like this:

My Headspace with Adrenal Fatigue

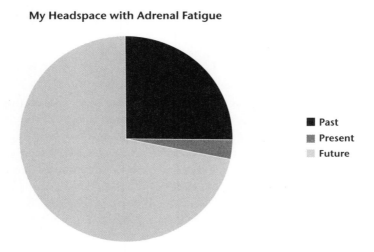

Here's the thing: our energy is in the *present*. And it can only exist in the present. The more time we can spend mentally in the present, the better we are going to feel. In the above example, the present was doing the washing up! If I had been aware, even for a few moments, of my hands in the warm, soapy water, the feel of the plates as they slipped between my hands, the sensation of the weight in my feet as I stood at the sink, I would have been in the present. My mind would have been with my body while I was actually doing the thing at the time. I would be connected with my energy in the present.

Living in the future or the past leaches not just energy but also enjoyment out of the present. If you are talking with your children while also checking Facebook, the interaction with your children will be half-hearted, the interaction on Facebook also perfunctory. If you are out for dinner with your partner but your mind is fully in the office, focused on the presentation you are giving the next day, then you are not present with your partner. You do not engage and connect to the same level because you are not 100 per cent there. Your body is there but your mind is in the future.

Does that seem fair? Being in the future or the past robs us and those around us of truly meaningful interactions in the moment. Your body is in one place but your mind is elsewhere. Connecting to the present is as simple as *your mind and body being in the same place at the same time*. Wherever your body is is your now. *This* is your present.

At the start of the yoga classes I teach, I say to my students 'let your mind meet your body, here, in this room'. I encourage them to be there for class not just in body but also in mind. We miss out on mental, emotional and spiritual benefits if all we do is just go through the physical motions. To really get the full advantage from our yoga practice we need to consciously choose to be as present as we can. To soak up the full experience our mind needs to meet our body, and be in the same place at the same time.

It's hard, of course. We need persistence and discipline. The mind needs to be gently guided back to the present as it wanders away. Below is a great technique to do just that: to help you get connected with the present. To let your mind meet your body in the same room.

Scrunch your shoulders up to your ears, tense, tense, tense, then do a big exhale and release them to the floor. Let the tension go and then observe the thoughts in your mind. Are you in the future or in the past? Are you worrying about what's past or what is yet to come? Choose to release those thoughts for the moment and allow your focus to come to the present moment.

Let your mind meet your body in the present moment in that room. Be aware of what's real for you right now. Know that in the present moment you have everything you need, and all is well.

> Below are a number of ways to connect to the present. Choose the one that is the easiest for you. You can find all of these (including the meditations above and below) in the recorded audios in the full programme at www.louisethompson.com.

ACTION STEP 1: INITIAL RELAXATION

- ❈ Make sure you are somewhere warm and quiet, and preferably not too bright. Lie down and support your head with a cushion. Be comfortable.
- ❈ Start to breathe just through your nose. In through the nose, out through the nose. In through the nose, out through the nose. Feel your breath, feel it at the tip of your nose, feel how it is a little cooler as you breathe in, a little bit warmer as you breathe out.
- ❈ Start to slow and deepen your breath. Feel the belly gently rise as you inhale and gently fall as you exhale. Belly gently rises on the inhale. Gently falls on the exhale. Feel the breath slowing and deepening.
- ❈ This is your experience right now. The experience of your breath, the sensation of your belly rising and falling with each breath.
- ❈ When you pay attention to your body in this way, you are bringing your awareness to what is real for you right now. You are bringing your mind to the present. Your mind is focused on your experience right now.
- ❈ If the mind is wandering into the past or the future, gently bring it back. Inhale, belly gently rises; exhale, belly gently falls. Inhale, belly gently rises; exhale, belly gently falls.
- ❈ Be fully aware of the other sensations in your body right now. Feel the weight of your body against the floor. Feel

how you are supported by the earth beneath you. With each exhale let your body gently sink a little deeper into the floor. Your mind remains focused on your breath. Feel the belly gently rise as you inhale. Gently fall as you exhale. Belly gently rises on the inhale. Gently falls on the exhale. Your breath is slow and deep.

※ Know that you are connected to the present moment. In the present moment all is well. We have everything we need. Allow the muscles on your face to gently smile as you acknowledge the present moment moving through you.

※ Feel the floor beneath you. Your body relaxing, sinking into the floor. Feel the weight of the body on the floor beneath you. Feel your heels on the floor, your calves, your thighs, buttocks, shoulder blades, back of the hands and arms, the back of your skull, all relaxing and sinking towards the floor.

※ You are in the present. You are fully aware of the sensations of relaxation you feel right now. Your mind is meeting your body. They are together in the present. All is well.

※ Stay with your breath. Feel the temperature of the air around you. Where it is cooler, where it is warmer. Feel the weight of the body sinking into the floor. The gentle rise and fall of the belly as you breathe.

※ Appreciate the energy and the possibility in the present moment. Know you have everything you need, and that all is well.

※ Choose to take this energy and intention with you through your day.

Try the meditation audio from www.louisethompson.com. It's a great way to start your day before the worries of the day (future) creep in. Set your alarm eight minutes earlier and listen to it on your iPod in bed. Start the day connected to the present moment and set that intention as you get up for breakfast and move through your day.

ACTION STEP 2: ENERGY COMMITMENT

Be honest with yourself. How much of your headspace is given up to being in the present, and how much in the past or future? Fill in this pie chart to show your headspace.

Your Headspace Right Now

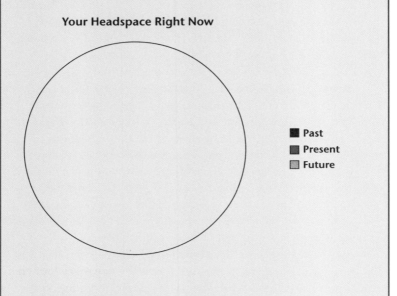

■ Past
■ Present
□ Future

Give a percentage. Draw it on this pie chart.

Commit to increasing your percentage of present-moment time. When you are with loved ones, be truly *with* them in mind as well as body. Turn off your phone. Focus on the sensations in your body that you can feel right now. When you are at the bank, be at the bank. When you are playing with the kids, play with the kids.

Be present. That's where your energy lives.

KNOW THYSELF

In my first few years in the corporate world there was a real emphasis at each appraisal on identifying the individual's weaknesses and then working with them to improve them. I have really moved on from that view. I think that working to improve your weaknesses is, frankly, a royal waste of time. Life is short, and I think time and effort is much better invested in recognising our strengths, honouring them and setting life up to reflect and build upon where we are strong.

Obviously, the first step here is identifying your strengths. I use two types of profiling. The Myers-Briggs Type Indicator system is a great overview on how you tick. I also recommend the Kolbe concept of conative profiling for an overview on action style and behavioural preference. I highly recommend that you check out both these options. How can you make life choices that honour who you are if you don't know who you are?

If you have already had this profiling done at work, I advise you do it again. Here's why. Workplaces have a personality type. This is the prevalent culture of the organisation. We know employers are looking for certain things so we answer accordingly. I think very few people actually give an accurate and true personality reading at work. Even if the bias is subconscious, I believe there is bias nonetheless to make us conform to the prevalent cultural personality profile.

I want you to have a really clear idea of who you really are, regardless of workplace fit. This is super-important.

We all have a very definite personality preference in terms of how we process information, how we make decisions, where we get our energy from, how we communicate, how we like life to be organised. But we are smart and we can be flexible when the situation demands it, and operate in a manner that is the opposite of our natural preference. This is fine as a short-term strategy to operate 'out of type', but on a long-term basis it can spell disaster. For instance, I have a significant proportion of clients who are beautiful introverts. Naturally quieter and more reserved, they prefer smaller groups and solitary pursuits. Many of them feel under pressure to be more chatty, to speak up more often, to be the life and soul of the party. Introverts get their energy from the inside, so actually this is 'out of type' for them and they quickly find it exhausting. Embracing their true strength of introversion and honouring that with time to themselves, staying at social events for shorter periods and responding in writing honour their preferred style and are 'in type' behaviours which create energy.

Here's the thing. People who operate most of the time outside their natural personality preference and action style become more depleted in their energy reserves because they are not honouring who they really are for most of their waking hours.

There are sixteen distinct personality types in Myers-Briggs. Each one is as valid as any other. Knowing what you are and setting life up to honour that is a really fascinating, empowering and crucial step in fully owning your best life and health.

ACTION STEP 1: MYERS-BRIGGS PROFILE

Check out Myers-Briggs Type Indicator online or find a qualified Myers-Briggs practitioner near you. Think through where in life you are operating out of type. At work, for instance? Or do you have a spouse with a very different personality type to you? Figure this out, and work harder at honouring your true type rather than flexing at will to fit with someone else's culture/type. Work out when, where and how often to compromise, and when, where and how you can make life choices that honour who you really are.

ACTION STEP 2: THE KOLBE CONCEPT

Check out the Kolbe concept and the four Action Modes. Are you a Quick Start, Follow Thru, Implementor or Fact Finder? I can't tell you how much difference this knowledge will make to you knowing your dominant action styles and setting up your life to honour that.

There are numerous Myers-Briggs options for testing available online, and the Kolbe system is available at www.kolbe.com. I really think that these investments are well worth it. When you know your strengths, it is much easier to make choices that honour them.

HAVE A FAVOURITE WASTE OF TIME

Some people have a real thing about any kind of downtime being 'wasted time'. I think it's a new and growing phenomenon that's leading to a whole heap of stress. I must confess to being susceptible to this cult of productivity myself. I notice it when I am stuck in traffic or when the computer isn't working as quickly as I would like it to. This stressful thought keeps rearing its ugly head: 'This is *such* a waste of time', usually accompanied by its good friend: 'This should be quicker/easier/more efficient.'

These thoughts lead me directly to a place of stress. Bad for the head, bad for the body.

It's occurred to me that I haven't always felt this way. When I was younger I didn't put this pressure on myself for everything to have an outcome. Just enjoying or doing something for its own sake was enough. At school and university my friends and I elevated wasting time to an art form in its own right! And those are the bits I look back on with the most fondness. The endless games of cards and mucking around (car surfing, anyone?) and our favourite, the Finals Revision Avoider, pitch and putt. I had so many favourite wastes of time! And yet I seem to now feel so uncomfortable with even the most limited moments of unproductivity. What is that about?

As the world has become increasingly immediate and increasingly measureable I think it has encouraged us to lead our lives in the same way. An expectation that all time and every effort invested should show some sort of meaningful outcome. But should it?

I think the stress that the concept of 'wasted time' generates is due to a perception that time is inherently limited. That leads to a perception that all time needs to count with an outcome, which generates stress. Is the point of time well spent to get things accomplished, or is it to have fun and experience the maximum amount of joy? As adults in this increasingly technologically enabled, measurable and immediate world, I think we have lost the ability to play and to see play as an important part of what makes life fun and ourselves happy.

Look at how children play. When children play it's as a means to an end in itself, because they see time as unlimited and therefore no outcome is required. So how can it possibly be wasted if it's unlimited?

I think there is a lot we can learn from that attitude. This is what I have learned around the concept of 'wasted time':

1. **Just because it produces some sort of outcome doesn't mean that it's important.**
2. **Just because it's quantifiable doesn't mean I should do it.**

3. If the only joy in the doing is the crossing off on the list when it's done, then I should consider not doing it or getting someone else to do it for me.
4. Some of the best, most fun and memorable times in my life had no definable outcome.
5. Unproductive time is a fact of life. We are not built to be 'on' all the time.
6. Unproductive time is thinking and daydreaming and processing time. That is productive in itself.
7. Play and fun are important.
8. Resting and chilling *are* an activity in their own right. The outcome is being chilled. That's something the body requires for health. It's really important time.
9. Enjoyment is just as valid a goal as achievement.
10. I need to play more.

To live a truly balanced life, I think we should all have a favourite waste of time. So, I challenge myself, and you, to reconnect with play just for the sake of itself. For example, I've joined a mosaic class one morning a week. I am really enjoying it; there is something very satisfying about fitting all the tiny shards of ceramic together for no reason at all – other than the simple pleasure of doing it. It's a bit fiddly and a bit messy. I like that as well as the quiet companionship of the other women in the class. Sometimes I feel guilty about all the work I 'should' be doing and worry that it's 'wasted time', but then I remember: I'm a life coach, I teach people about life–work balance . . . this is me practicing what I preach, and I relax and focus on the little fiddly tiles again, and the couple of hours simply flies by! It's been good for the mind and the soul.

You may like to take up archery, quilting, writing, baking, golf . . . there are all sorts of playful activities. Looking at what you used to enjoy as a child is an excellent place to start looking for a new playful activity or two to introduce into your life. More energy means reconnecting and allowing yourself to have a favourite waste of time.

ACTION STEP: WHAT'S YOUR FAVOURITE WASTE OF TIME?

If you find yourself running mental loops about wasting time, it's my bet that you could do with reintroducing a bit of play to your life, too. Think back to something you loved to do as a child (baking, playing footie, making things, etc.) and try to introduce a related aspect of *play* into your week with no aspect of outcome attached. Play for its own sake. See that if you are in the moment and enjoying yourself then no time is ever really wasted.

Things I loved to do as a child:

1. ....
2. ....
3. ....
4. ....
5. ....

Pick one you could integrate into your life *now* as non-outcome-focused *play*. Book it in! Go and intentionally waste some time and generate a little more joy in your week.

STOP DEFERRING

Do you have a 'When I Am' story? They are very common. I have to confess I have been very partial to many of my own. One of my favourites was 'When I have paid off the mortgage, I will quit this job and work for myself.' We all have them. These When I Am stories are a really good technique to procrastinate like hell and to keep us separated from our true heart's desires. As you know by now, separating ourselves from what brings us genuine joy sucks up our energy like a top-of-the-range Dyson.

When I Am stories are the eternal carrot of deferred happiness. They don't rule out the happy thing, they just keep it dangling out there for when life is better/easier/wealthier, or we are thinner/happier/have more time. And more often than not that time never comes. It's just a way of making us feel better about not doing the thing that we really want to do.

Frankly, that sucks. Happiness is not for deferring, it is for having. The difficulty is that we are allowing one state to be dependent on the other.

Have a think . . . What When I Am stories are you telling yourself? You may have told them to yourself so many times that you can't even see that they are a story. Do any of these sound familiar?

- ❀ **When I am thin, I will start dating again/dancing again/ wearing skinny jeans.**
- ❀ **When I have paid off the mortgage, I will spend more time with the kids/start my own business/move to Tuscany.**
- ❀ **When I have more time, I will write that book/learn to surf/ join the circus.**

You can list yours here:

When I am/have (a) ....
I will (b) ....

When I am/have (a) ....
I will (b) ....

When I am/have (a) ....
I will (b) ....

When I am/have (a) ....
I will (b) ....

When I am/have (a) ....
I will (b) ....

You then have three choices:

1. **Continue deferring your happiness with your When I Am story, sometimes indefinitely. Not recommended!**
2. **Say 'Sod it! I shall not defer my happiness any further!' And simply make the call, make the decision to do (b) and figure out how to make that happen. Fine. Do it!**
3. **Look at your story a little deeper . . . maybe you *can* have what you want but not in the way you may have expected.**

Let's work on choice 3. Maybe the thing we are looking for is *not* actually dependent on us achieving state (a). Identify what the feeling state is that will accompany reaching goal (c). It could be feeling confident or secure, for example. Use at least three words to describe your feeling state when you reach goal (a).

So, it could look something like this:

❀ **When I am thin (a) I will feel confident, happy and beautiful (c) and I will start dating again (b).**
❀ **When I have paid off the mortgage (a) I will feel secure, strong and in control (c) and I will start my own business (b).**

When I am/have (a) ....
I will feel (c) ....
(c) ....
....
and (c) ....
and I will (b) ....
....
....
....

When I am/have (a) ....
I will feel (c) ....
(c) ....
and (c) ....
and I will (b) ....
....
....

When I am/have (a) ....
I will feel (c) ....
(c) ....
....
and (c) ....
and I will (b) ....
....
....

When I am/have (a) ....
I will feel (c) ....

(c) ....

....

and (c) ....

and I will (b) ....

....

....

....

When I am/have (a) ....

I will feel (c) ....

(c) ....

....

and (c) ....

and I will (b) ....

....

....

Here's the thing. Your heart's desire is not the thing (b), *it is the feeling state* (c). What we are really ever after is *how we will feel* when we get the thing, rather than the actual thing itself.

So take your deferred carrot of happiness and think laterally and see what you can do *right now* to bring some of that feeling state you are after into your life now.

For example, I can introduce feelings of (c), (c) and (c) into my life *right now* by doing (d) (achievable thing).

'When I am thin I will feel confident, happy and beautiful and I will start dating again' becomes 'I can introduce feelings of confidence, happiness and general beautifulness in my life *right now* by booking a new haircut/buying a great pair of jeans/ having a luxurious bubble bath'.

Or

'When I have paid off the mortgage I will feel secure, strong and in control and I will start my own business' becomes 'I can introduce feelings of security, strength and control in my life *right now* by leaving work on time/delegating more/setting up my side hustle business two nights a week to see if I can run my own small business in a risk-free way'. (A side hustle business is one we start alongside our regular job from which we want to escape. This means we can do it with less risk, and grow it and build it until we are sure of its success and make the leap to quit the day job. It's a great strategy, and you can read more at the very smart Pam Slim's popular blog www.escapefromcubiclenation.com.)

I can introduce feelings (c) ....

(c) ....

....

and (c) ....

in my life *right now* by doing/organising/buying/talking to/finding

(d) ....

and (d) ....

....

....

....

I can introduce feelings (c) ....

(c) ....

....

and (c) ....

in my life *right now* by doing/organising/buying/talking to/finding

(d) ....

and (d) ....

....

....

....

....

I can introduce feelings (c) ....

(c) ....

....

and (c) ....

in my life *right now* by doing/organising/buying/talking to/finding

(d) ....

and (d) ....

....

....

....

I can introduce feelings (c) ....

(c) ....

....

and (c) ....

in my life *right now* by doing/organising/buying/talking to/finding
(d) ....
and (d) ....
....
....
I can introduce feelings (c) ....
(c) ....
....
and (c) ....
in my life *right now* by doing/organising/buying/talking to/finding
(d) ....
and (d) ....
....
....

See how that works? When we realise the feeling state is what we are really after we can start bringing that into our lives immediately rather than just endlessly bribing ourselves with the carrot of our 'When I Am' story that might never actually happen because it's saved for 'one day'. We can only live and experience each day in the present, so seize the day, my friends! Deferring your heart's desires helps no one. Take a moment to examine your most common When I Am stories this week and decide not to be separated from the good feelings you are after any longer by introducing a little sprinkling of these feelings today.

MISSING OUT

I have lost count of the number of gigs/parties/events I have missed out on over the years while I am teaching my fabulous yoga students of an evening. I absolutely love what I do, but I do get the odd grump about missing something every now and again. Sometimes I see my friends from corporate days doing a big glitzy thing on Facebook. The sort of industry event with black ties and champagne and fabulous shoes that I would have been at in years gone by, and I feel I am missing out, just a bit, as I potter about in my yoga pants.

I see numerous clients who are upset about missing out on career opportunities or family opportunities or travel opportunities or run-away-and-join-the-circus opportunities. If I had a dollar for every time 'I hate missing out' has been uttered, I would have enough to host my own black tie and champagne event! In fact, I hear that FOMO (fear of missing out) is now actually in the urban dictionary, e.g. 'Even though he was exhausted, John's FOMO got the best of him and he went to the party.'

Here's the thing. We have so many opportunities today that we live in the age of 'missing out'. Which actually is a fantastic thing. Not a bad thing at all. I should be saying 'I missed out!' with joy and not regret. Why? Because missing out means *I had a choice to do something else*. It meant I chose another thing and I am actually so lucky to have that choice.

There are so many women around the world who miss out on things because they have no choice. Things like getting to vote, having financial independence, having a career outside the home that doesn't require a 'male guardian'. In Saudi Arabia, it is still illegal for women to drive, for example. Many do not even have the choice over what they wear.

So, when I drive myself to class (rather than to the party I fancied), I am calling out my FOMO for what it is. And I think you should, too. This is all part of the energy-boosting process of embracing empowered choice. Missing out is a fantastic thing. I've missed out because I made the choice to run my own fabulous, thriving business. To be financially independent. To drive myself to class. On my own. In my yoga pants.

Missing out is confirmation that I have infinite choice in my life and that I am using it. And that is something to be very happy about indeed. Not the fear of missing out, but the joy of missing out. I shall call it JOMO. JOMO is the new FOMO, my friends. You heard it here first.

I wrote a blog post on this and had many comments from, in particular, mums of young kids. Karen said, 'As a stay-at-home mum I sometimes feel like I'm missing out on those fabulous work events, too, and today I felt like I was missing out because a friend told me they were having a beer with Friday lunch . . . those were the days. *But,* and that but is huge, I've chosen not to miss out on my kids growing up, which I think in the long run is way more important than that beer I so feel like on a hot day like today. I have actually made a choice I feel lucky and thrilled to have made, and that's a good thing to know!'

ACTION STEP: MISSING OUT

Consciously start reframing 'missing out' occasions. Try a few right here:

I sometimes feel I am missing out on ....

....

but I am going to choose to reframe that, as I realise I am not missing out at all! I have consciously chosen ....

.... instead!

I sometimes feel I am missing out on ....

....

but I am going to choose to reframe that, as I realise I am not missing out at all! I have consciously chosen ....

....

.... instead!

I sometimes feel I am missing out on ....

....

but I am going to choose to reframe that, as I realise I am not missing out at all! I have consciously chosen ....

....

.... instead!

DANCE IN YOUR OWN SPACE

Remember *Dirty Dancing*? The late Patrick Swayze in his prime. The kooky Jennifer Grey (whatever happened to her?) in that archetypal 1980s movie of froth and fun and burning romance. Oh, the sweet agony of love! Well, you know the scene where he is teaching her to dance? There is a bit where she keeps stepping on him, not holding her arms rigid to create the space between them. He calls her 'Spaghetti Arms'. He tells her to stay in her own dance space, and he'll stay in his. Creating and holding that space between them is an essential boundary for a successful dance. When she responds to this by honouring that dance space in the way she moves with him, they both perform so much better. Then, later, when he moves in for the long-anticipated clinch, tension unbearable, she coquettishly knocks him back, telling him to stay in his own dance space. This definition of dance space is a wonderful metaphor for holding our energy boundaries for a successful dance through life.

Here's the thing about busy people who have no energy. They are doing a heap of stuff for other people. Like Maddy, the young grandmother who was doing the parenting for her daughter's daughter; Harriet, who was making three meals a day, seven days a week for her entirely grown-up family of capable men; Sarah, who was breadwinning and working herself to the bone to support her entirely able husband and sister; and Belinda, who ran herself ragged doing everything for 'the business' at any hour of the day or night. Whatever it took. I see it again and again and again.

Know this. If you take on more responsibility than is actually reasonable, and you make that your role, then eventually everyone around you will expect that. Let's be honest, if someone was happy to get up and feed your child in the middle of the night so you could sleep through, or make and clear up all your meals, or pay your rent, or do all your work so you didn't have to pay to hire someone else . . . well, that's great, isn't it? They must love doing it, if they keep doing it. That's the obvious assumption to make.

Basically, what has happened is you have stepped into someone else's dance space, scooped up their responsibilities, and in a completely non-manipulative way (usually) that suits the other party just fine, too. They think you *like* doing all that stuff! So, they step back. And you *keep* doing it. And the more you do, the more they step back, and the more tired you get.

This may or may not be accompanied by a bit of a whinge: 'I have to get to the supermarket – if I asked Bob to do it, it would never happen', or 'If I don't pick up that project it just won't get done and the business will suffer.' Well, sure. But the status quo is never going to change if there are no consequences for the other party. If there is no pain point to get attention for someone to step up and own their own dance space, they ain't gonna just spontaneously do it.

The fascinating thing is that when you change the status quo, provide the pain point or consequences in a consistently delivered way, then things change faster than you can ever imagine. My clients are blown away by how quickly the people in their lives will step into the void in their dance space, when they themselves leave it.

So make the change, Spaghetti Arms. Get real – where are you actually stepping past the boundary of your own dance space into someone else's? Start by stepping back, but in a smart, transitioned way like Harriet did with her houseful of grown men. She calmly explained why the change needed to happen and exactly what each person would be responsible for. She trained them on the new menu. She ordered the groceries so it would be easy and smooth and a good experience for everyone as they got started. She praised their efforts even when things were a little burned to start with. She didn't expect perfection straight away (of course, they are not going to do it exactly like you, but – you know what – if you want more energy then you need to accept that some things will be done other people's way, and that's just fine). Guide them, praise them, then step back from their dance space and leave that space for them to step into. If you are permanently blocking it, they will never step up or in. *You* need to create the space.

ACTION STEP 1: GET OUT OF THEIR DANCE SPACE

Identify whose dance space you are in and what you are doing for them.

I am in ....
dance space when I ....
....
....
I am in ....
dance space when I ....
....
....

I am in ....
dance space when I ....
....

I am in ....
dance space when I ....
....

I am in ....
dance space when I ....
....

Now what can you *stop* doing to free up your time and energy? What are you doing that you don't need to do, that could (or should) be done by someone else?

- ❀ **Could your husband order the groceries online?**
- ❀ **Could your deputy at work take on some extra responsibility?**
- ❀ **Can you flick a particular project over to another department?**
- ❀ **Can each of the children make their own beds?**

ACTION STEP 2: UTILISE FREED-UP SPACE
Name three things you are going to start doing, now you have this additional space. ....
....
....

Identify it and *do it*. Remember: just because something has always been done one way (i.e. *your way*) it doesn't mean it always has to be so. *Sometimes just the fact that it gets done is enough.* Progress not perfection, remember. Relinquish a little control and reclaim some time and energy.

KNOW YOU HAVE ALL THE TIME YOU NEED

'I'd love to but I don't have enough time!' This really is the mantra of modern living. How many times a day do you find yourself saying just that . . . I'd love to but I don't have time? I really want to do that thing/go to that place/see that person, but I don't have time. Once a day? Twice? If you are anything like me, a dozen or more. 'I don't have time' is a silly Inner Lizard fear and not even real.

In fact, I do have enough time. You have enough time. We all have all the time we need. It's not lack of time that's the problem here. Accepting that is the first step. We are not lacking in time. And that's a fact. What we are lacking in is clear priorities. It's much more accurate and empowering to say I don't have clear priorities rather than I don't have time. Clear priorities are something you can do something about; manufacturing more time is not.

So here is how to have more than enough time. First, set some very clear priorities for yourself for the next twelve months. What do you want to achieve and how do you want your life to be this year? I make three personal goals and three professional goals per year. This should be the maximum, three of each. It gives you some balance between your work and personal life, and it will force you to be ruthless. You can't have twenty-five priorities; choose six at most. One of mine is to be really fit, another is to write an amazing coaching book that will change tired people's lives around the world (this book!). The others include quality time having fun with my gorgeous husband and an amazing travel trip. List yours now. Think big-picture and be ruthless and honest with yourself.

Personal Goal #1 ....

Personal Goal #2 ....

Personal Goal #3 ....

Professional Goal #1 ....

Professional Goal #2 ....

Professional Goal #3 ....

Done? Okay, so, next time the 'I don't have enough time' mantra rears its ugly head, take stock. Don't have enough time for *what*? It then becomes a very simple choice. Now I always choose the task or thing that is in alignment with, and will move me towards, my six life goals for the year. If there's a choice between getting through all my email and going for a swim, I choose to make time for the swim; the email will have to wait. Or if there's a choice between working late on the website or going on a date with my husband, I choose the date every time; the website can wait.

I also look out for what I call 'high-impact' activities. These are tasks that actually move me forward on two or three of my priorities at the same time. Playing tennis with my husband: that's movement towards getting fit and having fun in my marriage. Two priorities for the price of one. When you get really good at this, it's such a laser focus you can sometimes find things that move you towards three or four goals at the same time. Then it becomes, in corporate speak, a no-brainer. Why would you consider doing anything other than that?! That's clearly the right choice to make in terms of how you spend your time.

By setting very clear priorities for myself and consistently choosing in favour of them, I find that I do have more time. And I have less panic about the things that are not getting done, because clearly they cannot be that important if they did not make it to my top six priorities for the year. I worry about them less because they are obviously a seventh or lower priority for me.

Here's a handy checklist:

1. Accept that you do have all the time you need if you have clear priorities.
2. Define three personal and three professional priorities for the year.
3. Choose consistently in favour of these priorities.
4. Enjoy the time spent on priorities, and relax about what doesn't get done as it's obviously less important.
5. Whenever the feeling arises of not having enough time, realise it's not a time issue but a priority issue.

ACTION STEP: PRIORITY-SETTING WORKSHEET

Get clear on your top three personal and top three professional priorities for the year ahead. Choose your six priorities, then *drop the guilt* and make conscious choices in favour of them.

My personal and professional goals

	To be accomplished by (date)		
	Three things I can do in the next month that will move me towards this goal	**Two** things I can do this week that will move me towards this goal	What is the **one** big benefit of this goal? How will I feel when I reach this goal?
Personal goal #1	1 2 3	1 2	1
Personal goal #2	1 2 3	1 2	1
Personal goal #3	1 2 3	1 2	1
Professional goal #1	1 2 3	1 2	1
Professional goal #2	1 2 3	1 2	1
Professional goal #3	1 2 3	1 2	1

I commit to choosing consistently in favour of my goals in order to accomplish them and have the life that I want!

Alternatively, download the handy worksheet and get the free ebook *The Smart, Busy Woman's Guide to Being a Time Ninja* from www.louisethompson.com. These two tools make how to get yourself prioritised for the next six to twelve months super-easy and clear. Print it out and pin it by your desk, on the fridge or wherever you can be constantly reminded that you have absolutely enough time if you choose consistently in favour of your true priorities.

SAY WHAT YOU MEAN

Want to transform your energy at work or home with just four little words? Well, it's easy . . . just Say What You Mean. Be aware of what you need, what works for you and what doesn't and actually voice it. Say. What. You. Mean. It's so simple, yet so many of us struggle with it and hope others will read our mind.

TONI'S STORY

Resentment is an energy killer and it just builds and builds. It's like a slow build-up of toxin in the body that kills us by degrees. Toni is a lovely lady in her fifties, kids grown, who was working hard as she and her husband adjusted to life as just the two of them. She loved her husband, and actually quite liked her job, but she was also a seething mass of resentment. Unpicking her resentment was fascinating. It was a hundred tiny things. For instance, she and her husband would go to a farmers' market each Saturday morning and buy various goodies for a picnic lunch. Toni fumed with resentment that her husband always had the crusty ends of the bread and she didn't. 'But there are two ends of the bread,' I said reasonably, 'Why don't you have one each?' 'Well, he should offer, he should ask me that and he *never does!*' she cried indignantly. She was also resentful that

'We watched yet another sci-fi movie at the weekend. His choice –
I hate sci-fi. He has been doing this for *years*!' When I asked why
she didn't choose the movie sometimes, she said, 'Well, it's his
job to go to the video shop while I make the dinner.' Right. At
work it was a similar story: 'They never get the month-end report
to me on time. I always have to chase it, and it means I end up
having to work late under pressure. Every. Single. Month!' Okay.
'What do you say when they email through the report?' 'Oh . . .
er . . . I say thank you.' Nothing more? Nope. Right.

Clearly, this one wasn't rocket science. In not one of the
instances that was upsetting her had Toni actually told the
other party what she actually needed. She expected them to
'just know'. She never put them right. So they thought there
was no problem and just continued as they were, while she took
this as evidence of their lack of caring, and resentment built. I
encouraged Toni to say to her husband, 'Hey, honey, I'd love to
share the crusty bit of the bread. I'd like us to go halves on that
please' and 'Hey, honey, I'd like to come with you to choose the
DVD this week, I'd really like to get a drama that we would both
enjoy'; and to say to her colleagues, 'Thanks. Please be aware
this is the last month I will be accepting these numbers late.
The impact on my workload with your continual late supply is
not okay for me. Please note that the numbers are required on
the 24th of the month in future. If you have a problem with this,
we will need to meet directly with the CFO. Thanks so much for
your understanding and cooperation, it is greatly appreciated.'

Her amazed and slightly shocked face came into my coaching
room the next week. 'Wow! My husband thought I actually
liked sci-fi!', she laughed. 'Because I never said anything he
had been assuming he was making good choices, so he kept
choosing them. He thought he was doing well! Same with the
bread. He had no idea I wanted any of it, but he was only too
happy to share when I asked. Even the accounts department
apologised! They had no idea how badly they were affecting my
workload. They even took me out to morning tea to apologise!'
Her eyes were full of bewildered amazement. She simply could
not believe how easy it was to get what she needed. Nobody
minded; in fact, more than that, they were all delighted to know
what she needed and to comply. It simply wasn't a drama.

> After that Toni started frequently saying what she needed, clearly and truthfully, and life just started moving her way. Her resentment melted away and energy bounced back into her life, just like that.

It sounds almost too simplistic to be true, but so many people have issues with this concept. It's very easy to get trapped in a destructive cycle where we want what we want and we are resentful if we don't get it, but our wants are unvoiced. They are so blindingly obvious to us that we assume the other party should just know what we need. We can also become expert in expressing that resentment in a passive-aggressive manner, which isn't good for anyone.

Remember: it's not one big choice or change that enables you to live a life of High Energy Happiness; it's a million tiny ones.

Moving yourself up your own To Do list is, for some people, breaking a habit of a lifetime. The main reasons we avoid doing it are because of the following misconceptions:

1. My needs are less important than my children's/spouse's/boss's.
2. He/she should be able to know what I need/would make me happy.
3. If I say what I mean there will be conflict and it will be horrible.

What this boils down to is:

1. Completely, illogically thinking that other people's needs are always more important than your own. How can that be? It makes no sense. Your needs are equally as important as those of any another human being.
2. Expecting your spouse, friends and colleagues to be mind-readers, which, of course, they are not. A sure-fire recipe for disappointment. It's not their job to read your mind; it's your job to voice your mind.
3. Assuming that there will be conflict if you voice your needs. Actually, generally other people welcome the clarity and direction.

If you could do with a little more in your life that really pleases you, try working through four easy steps:

1. **Say.** This is key – you need to actually voice it. Yes, out loud. Take responsibility for your needs and voice what's on your mind. You don't need to be aggressive, just calmly state what's important to you. Stop expecting everyone else to be a mind-reader.

2. **What.** Be specific. How can anyone really help or support you if they don't understand exactly what it is that will make you happy? Instead of something vague like 'I'd like it if I could choose a movie I liked for once', be specific: 'I'd like to choose the movie on Saturday night this week.'

3. **You.** This is often the biggest stumbling block. After so many years of putting the needs of your spouse, children or workplace before your own, it can be hard to actually tune into the fact that: a) you have a need/preference; and b) that it matters. Remember: your needs are equally as important as anyone else's.

4. **Mean.** You don't need to be mean, but you do need to mean it! Let go of the false assumption that Saying What You Mean will always lead to conflict. You will be surprised how little it does. As you get more of what you want in your life, you will find that you are less resentful of the things that don't go your way or that you compromise on.

It's very easy to see in someone else's life the problem they have and why resentment is building. Reading about Toni's situation I am sure you are shouting at the page right now! That's great, but please use this example to look at reducing any resentment in your own life and see where you can voice your needs more clearly.

ACTION STEP: SAY WHAT YOU MEAN
Write a list below of ten ways in which you are going to Say What You Mean this week:

1. I need ....
   ....
2. I would really love some help with ....
   ....

3. I would really appreciate some extra ....
....
4. I want to ....
....
....
5. I will tell ....
....
....
6. I would like to choose ....
....
....
7. I am choosing to ....
....
....
8. Doing ....
is a real priority for me.
9. That's not acceptable, I need ....
....
to happen to resolve this situation.
10. Sorry, the answer to ....
....is no. I have other plans that day.

Start small. Speak up with the accounts department and say when you would like the report and that you think that's a reasonable request; choose the restaurant that you really want to go to; take turns to pick the movie; say no to the party you don't really want to attend. I challenge you to Say What You Mean once a day to start breaking the habit of constantly deferring your own needs. It's a fascinating process. The first few times, you Say What You Mean with utter trepidation, waiting for the sky to fall. But the sky doesn't fall and, spooky, you actually start getting what you ask for much of the time! You'll find people like to please *you* for a change, and before you know it you will be accelerating way past the once-a-day challenge without prompting. Why? Because life becomes easier, more fun and less resentful when you own what you need to make you happy. You'll have more energy. Your partner will be happier because they can stop the guessing game of 'what will keep her happy'. Life becomes a whole lot easier all round.

Will you get what you want every single time? Absolutely not. Compromise is an integral part of a happy and balanced life. But you'll get what you want a lot more than you do when you don't Say What You Mean. Start embracing these four simple little words and the balance of life will start to shift in your favour immediately.

SAY NO AND MEAN IT

When I first got bitten by the yoga bug over a decade ago in London, my life was very out of balance. If something needed doing late or at the weekend, I'd do it, no problem. I was super-committed and ambitious, but my personal life was crumbling.

When I stumbled into that first yoga class (a Beginners Course very like the one I teach today), I felt such an overwhelming and unexpected sense of relief and peace. It scared me actually: I didn't know what that feeling was as it had been so long since I had felt it. But I knew it was something I had to pursue. Pretty soon I was doing yoga three times a week. Even when I moved across London I would schlep all the way from Shepherd's Bush to Clapham and back. I loved Simona's classes so much, I didn't mind the travel hassle. It really was a revelation for me.

It was a revelation for my working hours, too. I developed my own 'naughty step' technique for getting out of work on time no matter what. I realised that when you are working on a newspaper everything is always urgent; there is always something that needs to be done. I also knew that there was now something I wanted more: to practise yoga, to learn more, to improve. So, on Mondays and Thursdays I started leaving the office at 4.55 p.m., which was unheard of for me. The stuff kept landing on my desk, people rocking round expecting me to handle things at that time just as I had for the previous six years. But I still left. I chose the thing I wanted more. I chose in favour of the feeling that I got at the end of class and of improving my new yoga practice.

In those first few weeks I had some heated discussions at work and I chose to let some people down, but the paper came out and the world continued to turn. And then, do you know what, the last-minute requests on Monday and Thursday stopped. Instead, the Head of Production might come over and say, 'Now I know Thursday is your yoga night, but can you look at this tomorrow morning?' or one of my staff would step up and say, 'I'll clear that last page boss, you head on to class.' I hardly missed a class from then on, despite having a senior job in a highly deadline-oriented business. My career continued to go from strength to strength, too. Probably because I was more relaxed and had more balance.

If my former workaholic self can do it, you can do it. You can be there and make that time for yourself each week. It's a case of training the people you work with and live with in much the same way you would teach a toddler what is and is not okay behaviour. My favourite example of this type of training is by the inimitable 'Supernanny', Jo Frost. She gets parachuted into struggling families' homes and restores discipline and harmony with some tough love and some cool parenting tools. When you watch Jo, what hits you, as well as her sunshiny but no-nonsense approach, is her consistency. She is so clear and so consistent in her approach. Irrespective of how much the child (or parent!) throws a tantrum, she holds the line absolutely consistently and that is what delivers the results. It's the same here. The key to getting more free time, or self-care, or whatever it is you need, is in being clear about what you want. Consistently voicing it, and following through regardless of the reaction you get. In short, it's the 'Yogic Naughty Step'.

The Yogic Naughty Step

1. **Voice.** What is it you *want*? Be clear with yourself so you don't get distracted by passing momentary tasks. For example, I want to feel flexible and relaxed by Easter. I want to give myself an hour each week in class. I want long-term health and wellbeing. Diarise it. Commit to yourself.

2. **Choice.** Wait for the inevitable last-minute thing that's just so important that it has to be done *right now* to come up. Assess it calmly. Be aware of the choice that you are making. Choose to be able to stand a moment's discomfort as you say 'No, sorry. That will have to wait until the morning, I have an appointment now.' No need to explain. Choose a moment's discomfort so you can have what you really *want*. If it's really that important, someone else will step up and do it.

3. **Follow-through.** Go do your thing: guilt-free! Do your yoga class, go for that run, have the weekly ball game with the kids. Do whatever your thing is. Next week, when it inevitably

happens again, repeat the same thing: 'No, sorry. That will have to wait until the morning, I have an appointment now.' Consistency is key. Before you know it you will have reclaimed that time, and the last-minute requests will stop. It's a funny thing, but once you consistently respect your time by saying 'no', other people will, too.

An additional idea here to help put this approach into practice is to give a grade, like a DEFCON level, to the stuff that 'just comes up' and threatens to derail your plan. Apply a grade out of 10 (1 being urgent/important/possible negative impact if not actioned quickly, and 10 being not urgent/can be dealt with later or by someone else). Being a good team player means staying to help on a team member's level 3 emergency as a rare exception. Being good to yourself means choosing your own priority instead for anything over level 5.

ACTION STEP: USE THE NAUGHTY STEP

What change do you want to make? Where do you really want to say *no* in life where you have been saying yes?

I have been ....
when really I want to say no. What I want instead is ....
....
....

I have been ....
when really I want to say no. What I want instead is ....
....
....

I have been ....
when really I want to say no. What I want instead is ....
....
....

I have been ....

when really I want to say no. What I want instead is ....

....

....

Pick one example and start implementing the Yogic Naughty Step technique today.

EMBRACE GOOD STRESS

Newsflash: stress has only existed for eighty years. Did you know the word 'stress' was only ever applied to *things* (not people) prior to the 1930s? It referred to a load on, say, a rope or building and was used exclusively in the fields of engineering and physics. Enter stage right an endocrinologist from Vienna called Hans Seyle. Through his experiments with mice he coined the terms 'stress' and 'stressor' within a physiological and biological context. In this context, stress is defined as the body's reaction to a physical, mental or emotional strain (either real or imagined) that is placed upon it. And, thus, stress as we know it today was born. Da-dah!

However, there is a little more to this story. Hans and his mice also came up with a very interesting distinction: the difference between good stress and bad stress. What is fascinating about this is that the definition of good stress seems to have got lost somewhere in the mists of time and the definition of stress today is almost universally perceived as negative.

Good stress actually has its own name: eustress. (Think euphoria, 'eu' is the Greek root for good.) It's the positive stress that helps you bring your A game to the interview or win a race. It's a positive stressor and accompanies fulfilment. Distress was Seyle's term for negative stress or what we commonly call today just 'stress'. Interestingly, physiologically the two things look the same, which is perhaps why the two terms have morphed into one.

So what does this tell us? What I take from this is that *not all stress is bad*. We are built to undertake stress. It's a mechanism brilliantly developed to allow us to rise to the challenge and go the extra mile. If we are to grow as people then we need to stretch ourselves, and that challenge may be scary but it's a good scary: it's eustress. To rock our lives we need to welcome eustress as an important mechanism for growth and conquering life's challenges.

Our distress response is for emergencies only. And yet, semantically at least, it is the most prevalent. Distress is meant to be turned on, and crucially *off*, at the flick of a switch. But distress is our default and we assume that 'being stressed' is a bad thing.

The body was built with the complex neurophysiological cascade of the stress response for a reason. The reason being: life is stressful! The aim is not to avoid stress completely (impossible) but to try to choose the right kind of stress. I think it's a ratio thing. What we can do is change the ratios. If my ratio of eustress to distress is 80:20 then I am going to be much happier than if the ratio is reversed.

Eustress vs Stress

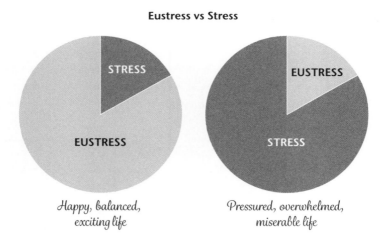

Happy, balanced,
exciting life

Pressured, overwhelmed,
miserable life

Eustress is what it means to be alive! It is feeling the butterflies in your belly when you take on that job that will stretch you, dip your toe back in the water of dating, book the space to have your own exhibition, buy the motorbike you always wanted, have another baby.

Distress is just misery. It is forcing yourself into a job that you hate, going out to dinner with someone you would much rather not see, being roped onto a committee you don't really have time for. It's doing the things that you know, deep down, don't really serve you.

The key here is the true want. If you are moving towards what pleases your true self, then the stress is positive. It might be scary, but it's moving you in the direction that is right for your best life. If you are moving against that and forcing yourself to do something that does not serve your true self out of guilt or obligation, then it is negative stress. I think it boils down into this handy equation:

Something you really want + fear = eustress
(this stretches and grows you towards your true self and best life)

Something you don't really want + fear = distress (this diminishes you, leads you away from your true self and best life)

For example:

Getting married to someone you really want to marry = eustress

Getting married to someone you know deep down is not right = distress

Living an energetic and happy life means living life to the full. That means taking some risks and some challenges along the way! Learning to welcome the right kind of stress – and to not fear it – is an important part of a happy, balanced life.

ACTION STEP: CHECK YOUR RATIOS

Understanding that all stress is not negative is a really important mind shift. Take an inventory of your life here. What is the ratio of eustress and distress in your life? Mark it on the pie chart below.

Your Distress vs Eustress

☐ **Distress**
☐ **Eustress**

> Is this a good ratio for you? Choose to change the ratios if you need to. Turn down a challenge or task that you know causes you distress. Pick up one that creates eustress. Next time you say you are stressed, know that the majority of the time it's in a good way and your body is designed to help you get the most out of a stressful situation. Embrace eustress.

EXIT YOUR COMFORT ZONE

When we are very fatigued, life can become very small indeed. We turn down social engagements because we feel too tired to be bothered to converse, we put off trips, adventures and plans until we have enough energy. Well, if you have been following all the steps in this book you should find you are well on your way now to living a life of energy every day. That means that it's time for life to expand, to grow, to stretch. It's time to expand life to embrace some energy-giving magic.

Want to know where the magic in life happens? I'll tell you where it doesn't happen: it doesn't happen in comfy pants on the sofa! It happens in the 'stretch zone'. The place outside your comfort zone. The place where you feel the flutter of scariness (eustress!), but take a deep breath and do it anyway. The place where things can go wrong, but you still feel compelled to act.

Magic happens when we name a dream that stretches us and then move towards it. I am a big fan of the comfort zone: easy is nice and easy is good and easy is predictable, which is relaxing. But for a truly positive balance in my life I know I need to spend a measured percentage of my time outside that zone, stretching myself even if it's uncomfortable and/or scary, being open for the magic to happen.

Some, or in fact all, of the most magical things in my life happened way outside my comfort zone. This year my 'where the magic happens' goal is to write and publish this book. It scares and excites me all at the same time, putting myself out there. Being disciplined enough to prioritise the time and make it happen. Huge. Scary. Exciting.

I love working with my clients as they move from their comfy pants on the sofa to realising dreams that used to scare them but are now their life: starting their own business, travelling overseas, getting that awesome new job, reclaiming time and energy from their families, making their health a priority, saying *no* to some stuff, saying *yes* to some scary stretch-zone stuff. It really is a magical process to watch unfold. It's all about balance. You need to have some stretch in some areas of your life, but some comfort zones to retreat to in others. Get a ratio of comfy pants to scary pants that works for you.

ACTION STEP: EMBRACE STRETCH

Where can you embrace the stretch zone this year? What would stretch you in terms of your body, your work, your interests, your family, your skills? How big a stretch should it be? Think big. Act big. Be big.

At work: ....

At home: ....

In terms of physical fitness: ....

In terms of friendships: ....

In terms of relationships: ....

In terms of family: ....

In terms of travel: ....

Pick one that seems juicy and delicious, and be brave — work on expanding life in that direction.

STOP PROCRASTINATING

Those nagging tasks that have been in the back of your mind for weeks, months or years take up a lot of energy. They are like a slow leak in a tank of water, slowly, imperceptibly draining resources away. They are one of those apps running unseen on your phone, draining the power away. Time to plug the leak.

First, identify all of those things on which you have been procrastinating. List them right now, whether it is chores around the house, people to call, stuff to make, projects at work, places to be, whatever you have been subtly avoiding.

1. ....

2. ....

3. ....

4. ....
5. ....
6. ....
7. ....
8. ....
9. ....
10. ....

Now let's look at *why* we procrastinate. We need to understand why stuff is on this list before we start addressing it. Below is a story that might help.

After about three years of promising to do it, on one sunny Sunday in February 2012, we held the first Positive Balance Wellbeing Retreat Day for my lovely yoga students. Thirty-four fabulous ladies (and a couple of enlightened gents) joined us for a day of broadening and deepening their wellbeing practices. It was a lot of fun seeing people connect with those they had been in class with for years but never spoken to, and seeing everyone learning new and cool things (spoon-bending, anyone?). I was thrilled with how the day went and the positive feedback we received.

My main thought by the end of the day, however, was 'Why didn't I do this sooner?!' It was a lot of work, for sure, but it was so obviously what people needed (and I had known that) and yet it had taken me *forever* to get around to making it happen. Why?

Good old procrastination, that is why. Many of us put off doing things, even though we know it's something we really want to accomplish. I received a phone call last month from a man who said, 'You know, I have been planning to come to yoga for about fifteen years. I think I should just do it. When does your next Beginners Course start?' Imagine how flexible and strong and chilled that chap would be if he had taken up his yoga habit fifteen years ago?

There are five key 'reasons' (excuses/lies) we tell ourselves when we procrastinate. The interesting thing is that the underlying emotion for all these justifications is exactly the same. Fear. Plain and simple. Inner Lizard fear, based on scariness and scarcity. *Peeling* away the top layer of procrastination and realising that procrastination is simply Inner Lizard fear in disguise can be very liberating. See if you recognise the following five elements of the Procrastination Peeling Principle.

1. I can't do it yet, it won't be perfect

Perfectionism is a killer of great ideas and splendid plans. It literally stops us in our tracks. The website doesn't get launched, just draft after draft, fearful of the reaction we will get when it goes live. The course doesn't get taken through fear of not being able to do it 'well enough'. The house doesn't get painted through fear of making a mistake choosing the 'right' colour.

Solution: make a decision to start something or launch something as it is (even if it is only 80 per cent good enough, not 100 per cent perfect), and use that to get feedback on your performance and then improve from there. Accept that perfectionism kills plans and that 80 per cent of Good Enough is better than 0 per cent of Perfect because it never actually happens. Very few things are set in stone – you can always tweak things as you go.

2. I can't do it yet, I don't have time

If it's something that you want, that you really want, then you have to choose to make the time. Life is busy. Time doesn't magically just create itself in your diary. You need to make space for it. If this is your issue, reread the section 'Know You Have All The Time You Need' (see page 189) or work through my ebook *The Smart, Busy Woman's Guide to Being a Time Ninja.*

If the thing you are procrastinating on is a priority for you, then you need to just *do it.* The rest of life will flow around it. Some other less important stuff will drop off the list. If you are waiting for a 'good time', it will never come. Just take action and let the rest of your life flow around it.

Solution: book that holiday. Go see the bank about house-buying options. Reserve your place on that course. Schedule the retreat day. Just do it and force the flow of your time around it.

3. I can't do it yet, people might not like it

Sure, they might not. No one might buy that thing you are selling/ like your sculpture/approve of you joining the circus. But if it's the thing that you want, that you really want, then your own approval is more important than any external praise. You cannot control other people's reaction to your choices. It's just not your business. They will think whatever they are going to think, and that's up to them.

Solution: trust your own judgement, and as long as *you* like the choice you have made then that's what's ultimately most important.

4. I don't know how to do it, I'll get it wrong
This kind of fear is completely soluble in information. If you don't know how to do something, break it down, figure out the first step, then research how to go about it. Information neutralises fear.

Solution: we have the sum of human knowledge at our fingertips. Jump online and figure it out!

5. I just don't want to do it
Okay, fair enough. *So don't do it!* Unless this outcome is going to land you in jail or put someone in harm's way, then don't do it. Choose another option. Ask yourself, 'Does it need to be me who does it?' Sometimes throwing a small amount of money at a problem you have procrastinated on for years can solve it right there, releasing all that mental space and energy for you to focus on other things.

Solution: if you don't want to do it, either flag it completely or throw some money at the problem to fix it. Hire a guy to tidy the garden, pay the kids to wash the car, or a bookkeeper to do your tax return.

Procrastination Peeling Principle

ACTION STEP 1: MAKE IT HAPPEN

Once you have identified what is driving your procrastination, there are some more tools you can use to keep making things happen:

1. **Make it public**

   Tell everyone you are running the marathon in six months/ going to lose 20kg/going back to university. The public feedback and encouragement will help keep you to your commitment and prevent you from backsliding into procrastination. This was essential for the retreat. Once I had put it in my 'Wellbeing Wednesday' newsletter and on my Facebook page, I could not backslide on that commitment to my students.

2. **Set a timer**

   Parkinson's Law: work expands to fill the available time. Avoid 'project creep', and the project taking over your entire life, by setting timed boundaries. Accept that in the Information Age in which we live, you can never know 'everything'. There is always more info out there, so instead of driving yourself mad with trying to get to this unreachable place of 'complete', set a time limit. For example, I am going to research circus training schools for two hours and then I am going to *make a decision* and move forward and book one. Be strict. Your best work will be in the first section of time anyway. Be okay with not seeing every single possible option, but learn enough to make a decision (even if it is only 80 per cent perfect). Decide and move. Decide and move. Keep the momentum going.

3. **Big project: small steps**

   The project you have been procrastinating on forever is usually a big project; if it was small and easy you would have done it already. So accept it will mean small steps, lots of them, joined together. Break it down, and start stepping forward. Keep putting one foot in front of the other. Just keep inching forward. Research paint samples. Buy the paint. Hire the ladders. Rope in the friends. Order the pizza. Clean the walls. Paint the house one wall at a time.

4. **Improve it**

Some projects that we procrastinate on are not always the most fun projects. We are just not attracted to doing it; for example, clearing out the garage. Make the task 'better' and as 'improved' as you can (e.g. put on some great music, get your teenager to help, order pizza for lunch to be delivered as you work). Be creative. Improve the thing as much as you can. Doing the ironing? Download a book read by your favourite author and listen to it as you iron. Commuting? Travel with a friend and chat on the way in, or learn Spanish on your iPod, or whatever floats your boat. If you choose to do it (and, remember, it is a choice), see if you can make it an improved experience.

5. **Reward yourself – big time**

If all else fails, bribe yourself. Rewards are not just for small children. Treat yourself to a round of golf or a family meal when it's done. Something that gets you excited. Whatever is a big enough reward to break the inertia of procrastination.

ACTION STEP 2: DEAL WITH THE LIST

Go back through the list you made of things that you have been procrastinating over (page 205). Cross off anything that you really don't want to do or can delegate to someone else either as a paid job or a swap of time/tasks. Then figure out which of the fear-based reasons have been holding you back on the other items. Identify the appropriate technique for dealing with it, and deal with it! Tackle energy-sucking procrastination today!

CULTIVATE AN ATTITUDE OF GRATITUDE

Cultivating an Attitude of Gratitude is a cornerstone habit of an energetic life. It's a basic law-of-attraction thing. The feeling state we put out is what we attract back to us. So, if we put out a lack of energy, fun or money because our Inner Lizard is running the show, then that is what we will attract right back.

So if you continually feel (remember, feeling states are driven by the thoughts you choose to think) that you lack energy, time, love or money, that means you are actually *repelling* energy, time, love or money from your life. What you are attracting is the lack, the absence of those things. Like attracts like. Examples of energy-repelling thoughts are:

- I am worried I won't have the energy to get through the afternoon.
- I am so tired right now.
- I am so exhausted.
- We just can't afford it.
- I have no time.

Conversely, if you are generating feelings (from your thoughts) about the abundance of energy, time, love or money in your life, that means you are *attracting* more energy, time, love or money into your life. What you are attracting is the presence of those things. Like attracts like.

So, when it comes to a life of energy, gratitude becomes an incredible tool to attract more of what you want into your life. The more grateful you are, and the more focused you are on the amount of time you *do* have, the energy that you *do* feel, the money that you *do* have, the more of those things you will attract into your life. So, to attract more energy and good stuff, you need to focus your thoughts on the good things in your life. For example:

- I feel good right now.
- My body is energetic and recovering brilliantly.
- I love the $5 treat I bought this week.
- I have plenty of time to get done what I choose to make happen.

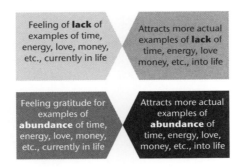

You don't even need to believe in the law of attraction for this to work. You just need to practise it.

ACTION STEP: GRATITUDE JOURNAL

Start a gratitude journal. I love to do mine before bed each night. I list five things that I am grateful for that day. It can be a big thing, like an amazing party I went to, or that I had a great run, or a small thing like the garden looked beautiful in the rain. Try not to repeat yourself. Challenge yourself to come up with five new things each evening. This will get your gratitude muscles working and flexing daily.

SEE REST AS WORK

As discussed in the section on Reframing Rest (see page 149), resting is an essential part of recovery. It is the wisest of guides to lead you back to health and energy. If you think 'But I'm not *doing* anything right now', then remember that continual doing is what got you to this place of fatigue in the first place. Continual doing is highly overrated. Besides, you *are* doing something: you are resting! That's your work right now and it's very important. Rest. Nap. Recharge.

As your body recovers and you have more energy to do things, you may notice a backlash from your mind. Thoughts like:

- ❋ I should be able to do more than this in a day.
- ❋ I have achieved nothing today.
- ❋ When will I be able to work again?
- ❋ I am wasting so much time resting.
- ❋ I shouldn't still need to nap.

These thought processes are deeply unhelpful, and deeply Lizardy, drenched in scarcity. In fact, these thoughts will actually slow your recovery by unconsciously stimulating the fight or flight response. It is much more helpful and healthful to replace these thoughts with the truth:

- ❋ Napping is exactly what I should be doing right now.
- ❋ My body needs rest and I am listening. That is the right thing to do.
- ❋ I am doing something right now. I am *resting*!
- ❋ I accept that napping and resting are an important part of improving my energy levels.
- ❋ I embrace napping. Every nap brings me closer to full health.

And when you are well, understand that rest is a critical component to staying well. Building in time to rest, relax, refresh and revitalise is not a luxury to be done when everything else is sorted, it's an essential component of overall health and balance. Plan for it. Take it without guilt.

If you are beating yourself up about resting to recover, I want you to stop that right now!

What thoughts do you beat yourself up with when you need to rest/ are resting?

1. ....
2. ....
3. ....
4. ....
5. ....

What thoughts are more helpful and healthful to honour your body?

1. ....
2. ....
3. ....
4. ....
5. ....

ACTION STEP: YOUR KIND OF REST

If you are only mildly fatigued, you won't need to be napping but you will still need to rest. That's just what human beings need to do. Rest looks different for different people: for some people it's a long nap, a hot bubble bath or a massage; for others it is something active like Zumba or playing with the kids, or cooking or a yoga class. Whatever is restful for your mind and body is all good. Rest looks different for everyone: what does it look like for you?

What are restful activities for you?

1. ....
2. ....
3. ....
4. ....
5. ....

Make sure you schedule them into your week as a priority. Making time for rest is important. Commit time to rest and recharge yourself today.

DO YOGA

Okay, I am a yoga teacher, so I am bound to say that, right? For sure. This book is a blend of the best Western smarts (life-coaching tools, supplements) and the best of the East (meditation, yoga, yogic breathing). Yoga has endured for thousands of years because *it works*. It's a beautiful, ancient wisdom that nourishes mind, body and soul. It's spiritual growth by stealth.

Yoga is something you need to try. It will put your body into parasympathetic dominance (see page 31), allowing you to restore and recharge. Yoga liberates the flow of prana – your life force, energy – around your body. Open yourself up to what this can do for you. Just one class a week will make a huge difference to your life and energy levels.

Here's a little secret. I don't enjoy every yoga class I go to. I know I should, right? I teach it, I love it, so I should always enjoy it. Wrong. While I believe absolutely in the benefits that yoga brings to life, helping us put a bit of balance into our hectic day-to-day lives, every type of yoga has its own unique style and signature, and every teacher has their own approach. I meet people who tell me, 'Oh, I tried yoga once. I didn't like it.' And I think it's such a shame to judge the whole of yoga on one class. That's like trying just one flavour of ice cream, and on the basis that you don't like raspberry ripple you don't like any ice cream at all. There are so many other flavours to be tried and explored! To give up at raspberry ripple would be to miss out on a lifetime of chocolate, or hokey pokey, or strawberry. Some days I am in the mood for chocolate, and some days it's strawberry. So I will choose a class or personal practice based on what I fancy at the time. Mostly, though, I am a creature of habit with a busy schedule, so I go to my usual class of Sivananda yoga, as I know I am going to get the experience I want from that class. But I will mix it up every now and again. It's really good to try a new style, but I keep returning to Sivananda, which is what speaks to my soul the best (you can read more about it at www.sivananda.org). I love the blend and balance and traditional focus. It's not that it's 'better', but it is the best fit for me.

So don't give up after one class! Shop around until you find a teacher and a style that really resonate with you. Ask your friends what style they love and why. Not every yoga style is for everyone, and not every teacher is a fit for every student. And that's totally okay. But there is a style out there for you. Keep trying until you find the yoga experience that is the most delicious for you.

If you are looking for a class near you, then here are some tips on finding a great one, because not all classes are the same. I can't emphasise how important it is to find a style of class that resonates with you and a teacher you connect with.

1. **How do you want to feel when you leave class?** Get clear upfront. If you don't know what you are shopping for, how will you know when you have found it? List three adjectives that describe how you want to feel after your perfect class. Do you want to feel energised, connected, stretched? Sweaty, shaking and empowered? Balanced, relaxed and peaceful? Get clear upfront so you have a benchmark to assess against.

2. **What else do you ideally want from the experience?** New friends? A sense of community? Hands-on instruction? Hands-off? Lots of props and fewer asanas, or no props and more of a flow? Room for silence in the class or more continual direction? Great showers and organic shower gel? Practice in front of mirrors? Great yoga nidra or no yoga nidra? Variety? Routine? Variety within a routine?

   You won't get everything you want in one place, but it's good to be clear. There are so many different options and nuances. Decide what's a non-negotiable for you. Remember this is your precious and valuable 'me time' so make it count!

3. **Convenience: the best class is the one you actually go to!** There is a huge amount to be said for convenience. Not very spiritual, but there we are, that's reality. In my opinion, when all is said and done, the best yoga class for me is the one I actually go to! And, as the real estate agents would have us believe, location, location, location is all-important. Is the class at a time that you can make a regular and consistent part of your schedule? Can you make the class in a difficult week (when one of the kids is sick, the boss is being a pain, and you need to get a plumber to sort out the hot water cylinder)? Is it local? Is it easy to get to? Can you find a park easily? The best class for you is one that fits your routine enough that you can be there regularly.

4. **Find the right level.** Look for a Beginners Course not a one-off lesson. I run a ten-week Beginners Course, and I believe that's the sort of timescale you need to let your mind and body adapt to all the new things you are asking of it. Doing a course lets you learn in a safe and structured way, and builds

your confidence, strength and flexibility with great technique. I don't let beginners into my Intermediate classes, they have to do the Beginners Course first. I truly believe this is the right approach, but again, find an approach that speaks to you.

5. **Give it time.** You will be asking your body to move in ways it hasn't for, often, *decades*. It's going to feel unusual and odd to move your hips in a way you haven't for many years. Unusual and odd is not pain. Be very clear on the difference. We can work with unusual and odd (just breathe into that sensation and you will find it will start to ease), but we *do not* work with pain. A safe practice is the most important thing, so be aware of this distinction and ask your teacher for an alternate asana if something is genuinely painful for you.

6. **Vibe.** What's the feel in class? Do you get a good vibe from the teacher and fellow students? Do you feel connected? Do you feel welcome? Do you relax? Do you feel encouraged but not judged? Check back in with what you wanted to get out of it, and see if it matches your actual experience. The proof of the pudding, as they say, is in the eating.

ACTION STEP: CHECK OUT CLASSES

Check out your local classes (all the tips you need to pick the right class are above). Alternatively, I have made a set of audios and videos for you to follow at home with a class flow specifically designed to be healing and restorative to your adrenal function and to boost your energy. You can find it in the full programme for download on my website, www.louisethompson.com.

MEDITATE DON'T MEDICATE

It's not going to be news to you that Buddhist monks who practise compassion meditation have shown changes in their brain chemistry (including in the amygdala, the Lizard Brain, of course!), and are the gold standard in living a Zen, calm and peaceful life. We all know that, and yet so few of us actually meditate when it would do us so much good. Why is that?

Well, here's the thing. It's been scientifically proven that of the people who start a meditation practice, 96.4 per cent of them give up within the first month. Okay, I just made that number up, but I bet it's not far wrong. Hardly anyone manages to sustain a practice. Why is that? We know it's good for us, yet we can't make it happen consistently. I'll tell you why: because we are setting the bar too high. We have an image that we aspire to of someone who meditates, serenely sitting perfectly still with a miraculously unlined forehead and beatific smile on her face. Meditating. Still as stone. For *hours*.

I also think meditation has had a bit of a brand issue. It has seemed deeply uncool, too hippyish and really not a doable thing unless your name is Rainbow Patchouli and you have bells on your skirt; that it's not something practical for 'real people' in the 'real world'. But there is a big shift happening out there and meditation is becoming very hip, very cool. I am a big admirer of the work of Gabrielle Bernstein, who is bringing sexy back so far as meditation is concerned. Check out her website at www.gabbyb.tv.

What I believe we need are meditation guidelines for the real world, practical steps that mean you can not only start a meditation practice but actually keep it up and experience the benefits long-term. Here are my nine simple steps to do just that. I'm calling it 'Meditation That Sticks for Real People'.

1. **Expect it to be *easy*, not hard.** We get in life the experience we expect. So, if we expect meditation to be really hard, and difficult and uncomfortable, then that's exactly what we are going to get. If we expect it to be easy and enjoyable, then that's what is much more likely to show up. Getting across New York in rush hour = hard. Sitting quietly and breathing = easy. Release the struggle before you even begin.

2. **Be comfortable.** Frankly, I am a big fan of comfort and I can't emphasise this enough. Inner bliss is always going to be more challenging to achieve if your knees are screaming at you. Be comfortable. If that's sitting cross-legged (or in lotus) in the traditional meditation pose, then good for

you. If that's not comfy, then sit in a chair or on a big pile of cushions, or buy a special little meditation stool that is the perfect height from a Buddhist centre. Whatever it is, you just need to be comfortable enough to not fidget about for 5–10 minutes. Again, decide that this is going to be *easy*. When you watch a movie, how long do you go without moving on the couch? Two hours, that's how long. Exactly.

3. **Lower the bar.** This one is the most important of all, and the reason why the vast majority of meditation practices fail to stick. We set the bar too high: we decide we are going to meditate for at least half an hour a day and we are going to feel amazing and enlightened by the end of the week. That, my friend, is a strategy for absolute and guaranteed failure. Instead, start with the *least* amount of time you think you can sit and meditate for. Not on the best days when you leave work on time and the kids are being angels, but on the worst days when the dog needs to go to the vet and the dry-cleaning needs collecting. How much time would you have to meditate on a day like that? Fifteen minutes? Maybe just ten minutes? Eight minutes? Excellent. Think of the minimum time you would expect on that sort of a day and then halve it. Start your practice with just four minutes a day. That's perfect for starters. It will allow your mind and body to relax into the experience. It will mean you don't struggle mentally or physically. It will mean you are more likely to do it every day and form a habit. It will mean, and this is crucial, that you actually *do it*. You can increase the time later, but for now, start small.

4. **Sort out the practical stuff.** Again you can make this easy. It doesn't need to be some big performance. Pick the time of day that is the best for you. (Traditionally sunrise and sunset are the most auspicious energy-filled times to meditate, but in essence the best time for you is whenever it fits in with your life and your commitments.) Try to make it the same time of day every day as that will help form a habit. Have your cushion handy, light a candle or place a vase of flowers in front of you. Make sure you are somewhere quiet. That's it. Keep it simple.

5. **Stick with a technique that works for you.** There is a multitude of different meditation techniques. There is no right or wrong. They are all methods of trying to stop the incessant mental chatter that characterises our waking hours and still the mind to allow us to relax into that place of inner peace and stillness. You can research various techniques, or go on a course or try one of these simple techniques:

   ○ Try the 'Eat, Pray, Love' technique, as described by Elizabeth Gilbert in her bestselling, world-changing novel of the same name (*Eat, Pray, Love: One Woman's Search for Everything Across Italy, India and Indonesia* is an absolute must-read). Simply sit comfortably and create an 'inner smile'. Feel every bit of you is smiling, from your liver outwards.
   ○ Repeat a mantra. You can try a Sanskrit mantra like 'Om Namo Narayanaya' (your yoga teacher can suggest one for you, or check out the worksheet of Sanskrit mantras on my website) or something grounding and inspirational such as 'I am whole and complete', which is my personal favourite. Alternatively, use your new energy mantra from page 160. With each inhale and exhale, repeat your mantra.
   ○ Follow your breath. Simply focus completely on the movement of your breath. Breathe in through the nostrils, out through the nostrils. Notice how the air is a little warmer on the exhale, a little cooler on the inhale. Stretch your inhale so it is the same length as your exhale. When the mind wanders, gently return it to observing the flow of your breath.

6. **Don't get cross with yourself.** Expect your mind to wander. Don't judge yourself for it. It doesn't mean you are stupid or crap at meditating. It's all part of the process! When your mind wanders, notice, do not get cross with yourself, just notice the wandering mind, then bring it back to your breathing and your mantra. You may need to do it hundreds of times. That's okay. That's learning to meditate. Over time your mind will wander less. Think about it, when you first learned to ride a bike, did you never put your feet on the ground while you were finding your balance? Of course you did. Well, this is the same. Your

mind is learning to find its balance and there is no point being frustrated about it. Just notice it and then gently bring the mind back to your practice.

7. **It's a treat not a chore.** Look forward to your meditation practice. It's a few minutes of silence and peace in your busy, busy day. It's just for you. Relish the thought of pressing the pause button on your life for a few minutes. It's a treat in itself, but it's also nice to reward yourself while you form this new habit to positively reinforce your progress. Every day that you meditate, allow yourself a little treat – take a long, hot bath or read a favourite book – and every fourth day in a row that you meditate give yourself a bigger treat, like a pedicure. By rewarding yourself while you establish the routine and habit of your practice, you are far more likely to make it stick.

8. **Commit to the benefits.** Who wouldn't want to be less anxious, reduce the threat of heart disease, immune- and stress-related illnesses, and bring more clarity into their life? Not only this, but meditating has been scientifically proven to actually make you *happier*. Happiness from sitting still and doing nothing. Bring it on!

9. **It's not an enlightenment competition.** By letting go of the perfect image of the perfect meditation practice, you can start to develop your own real practice that fits your real life. By removing struggle and the tendency to compare and compete, you open yourself up to just being with your own developing experience. It's not an enlightenment competition: it's a personal daily commitment to your own space and wellbeing. Being open to however that experience unfolds for you is the most valuable part of the journey.

So we know meditation is going to be good for us. It's just sticking with it long enough to feel the benefits that is the issue for most people. With the above tips you should be able to create a thriving and rewarding practice that nourishes your body and soul. And there you have it. No mountain tops. No austerity. No struggle. Meditation That Sticks for Real People.

> **ACTION STEP: MEDITATE**
>
> Try out one of the techniques above and see what works best for you. Try some meditation audios; it can be an easy way to access meditation as you are guided through the process. I have recorded some for you in the full programme on my website, www.louisethompson.com.

ENLIST INSPIRED ACTION

A whole lot of energy is expended when we *push* ourselves towards choices in life that do not really serve our true selves. The job that actually gives us a sick feeling of doom when we think about it on a Sunday night, the boyfriend who makes us cringe, the supposed friend who launches one passive-aggressive attack after another. Life feels like a fight, a struggle, a grind.

In comparison, when we are heading in the direction of our right life it all seems easy, things flow, much less effort is required. The job feels easy, we have more fun. The conversations flow. Minds meet. The next steps feel obvious. Right.

We can live life the hard way or the easy way, it seems to me.

I definitely used to do it the hard way. Push, push, push. I was mainly *pushed by fear* (yep, that's that pesky Lizard Brain again!) – fear that I wasn't good enough at work, that someone might overtake me, or that I would never find anyone to settle down with while my peers pushed out baby after baby. Life being pushed by fear is not fun. But I think it is the default for many these days.

The alternative is a life that *draws you forward with love*. This is what is called Inspired Action. It's what you feel called to do.

It looks like this:

Pushed by fear → Forced action that moves us forward. It feels hard, an effort, a fight, a struggle, a grind.

Pulled by love → Inspired action that effortlessly draws us forward. It feels easy, effortless, pleasurable, flowing.

ACTION STEP: PUSH AND PULL

Think about your job, home, health, friends, relationship, family, hobbies and downtime. Where are you taking action out of fear (push) and where are you taking action from love (pull)?

I am taking action in my life from a fearful place of *push* when I
....

I am taking action in my life from a fearful place of *push* when I
....

I am taking action in my life from a fearful place of *push* when I
....

I am taking action in my life from a fearful place of *push* when I
....

I am taking action in my life from a fearful place of *push* when I
....

I am taking Inspired Action and being *pulled* forward by love in my life
when I ....
....

I am taking Inspired Action and being *pulled* forward by love in my life
when I ....
....

I am taking Inspired Action and being *pulled* forward by love in my life
when I ....
....

I am taking Inspired Action and being *pulled* forward by love in my life
when I ....
....

I am taking Inspired Action and being *pulled* forward by love in my life
when I ....
....

Start to consciously choose more of the activities, people and opportunities where you are coming from a place of Inspired Action. Choose to let your life move forward pulled by love. Seek it out and choose it.

THE MAGIC OF SYNCHRONICITY

Here's another thing about hooking up to the energy of The Universe. When you start getting on your right path in life, which if you are following the Action Steps in this book you will be, then The Universe lets you know that you are headed the right way by bringing you gifts in terms of the people and things you need. These magical things appear in the form of coincidences and chance. It feels easy, like things are just clicking into place. Being aware of this indefinable magic happening increases the attraction and brings more good stuff to you!

When clients start working with this programme, claiming back their time and energy, putting more play into their lives and being truer to themselves, this magical turning point always, but always, happens. They meet someone at a party who has the perfect contact for their new business; their horrible boss resigns unexpectedly, opening up a promotion; a house sale falls through to deliver them their dream home; the most awesomely suited flatmate appears out of nowhere.

Awareness of the magic and energy of synchronicity is vital. I want you to get conscious of what you are attracting into your life right now. Then it is all about *commitment*. The Universe doesn't move until you move. You need to commit. *If you move, The Universe will move.* But it needs to see your commitment first. Register the web address. Put the flatshare ad on the notice board. Make the appointment to talk about a promotion. Action is required. Take a step or two in the direction of your right life. Once you do that, The Universe moves, too.

From an energy perspective this is so important. You can relax, knowing not everything is down to you, that there is a force for good on your side once you start moving the right way. Magic in action. Who doesn't want a bit of that in their life?

ACTION STEP: MAGIC IN ACTION

Who am I attracting in my life right now? Who is showing up? What is showing up?

....

....

....

What are the common themes and characteristics of these things?

....

....

What other coincidences have I noticed? What is The Universe bringing me in my life right now?

....

....

What else would I like to attract into my life right now? What would I love to magically happen/work out? Who would I love to meet?

....

....

What one step forward could I make in this direction?

....

....

CLEAN IT UP

Most of this book is concerned with getting your health and energy restored by cleaning up what is going on inside your mind. Working on thoughts and beliefs that have brought you to a place of exhaustion, and changing them. It's all about focusing on finding the answers inside of you.

This section and the following two are exceptions. They are focusing on the external. Your house, your living environment, your body. The reason we are doing that is not because the answer to fatigue is to be found in the external, but because how you manage your external living space is a reflection of your inner world. As the phrase goes, 'messy bed, messy head'. It's so true.

I always listen carefully when a client describes their house and how they live; it's a spookily accurate mirror for their lives. 'Tell me about your house, Jayne,' I said. 'Oh,' she sighed, 'it's overwhelmed with clutter, everything in it is worn-out and tired. I hate living in it, it's so dark and pokey.' Right. Overwhelmed, worn-out and tired. She hates living in it. 'Tell me how you *feel* right now, Jayne?' 'Tired, and . . . oh,' she said as the penny dropped, 'overwhelmed, worn-out and tired.'

As you go through this journey to High Energy Happiness (by becoming aware of your beliefs, thoughts and emotions, examining them and making sure they support a life of energy and vitality), you can support this inner work directly by ensuring your living environment is on the same path. Cool right? It might even mean you get to go shopping!

Walk through your house. See where there are piles of clutter or things are worn-out or in disrepair. Throw out anything that is old/tired/broken, or get it mended. Don't just leave it in a pile for another day. Look at what needs cleaning and what needs replacing. Look at what you have two or three of and donate the surplus to charity. Look at every object in your home and ask: Is this still useful? Does this really please me? Unless the answer is a strong yes to one or both of those questions, get rid of it. Sell it or donate it.

Make it easy on yourself. Start with the smallest room in the house – usually the bathroom. Throw away all those half-used toiletries that have been there for years. The manky old mascaras. The old nail polish you never wear in that hideous purple colour. Get rid of it. Keep only what you use and only what you love. Replace the mouldy shower curtain. Introduce a new toothbrush mug in a colour that pleases you. See the transformation. See how you feel different each time you enter your new clutter-free bathroom. Feel the little lift in energy you get.

Once you are done with the bathroom, start on the next smallest room or the room that bothers you most. Don't just move clutter between rooms, make a decision on it and either keep, donate, bin or sell it.

There are some excellent decluttering resources out there, from personal organisers who will come to your house to books and websites that will give you great information and tips. Gretchen Rubin's bestselling book *The Happiness Project*, which I highly recommend, is a great read, and is chock-full of great tips and tricks. If you need extra support, then get it (and check out the website, www.happinessproject.com). Or ask a tidy and organised friend to come and help you. My best advice is to just *start*.

When your living space is cluttered and full of old, worn-out and unpleasing objects, it sucks your energy. Release the clutter to regain your energy. Bring in new things; they don't have to be expensive, but they *do* have to please or delight you in some way. Go shopping. It doesn't have to cost a lot. A new $10 vase you adore can change the vibe of a whole room, once it's decluttered. Bring some new energy into the house now that you have released these old and outdated beliefs, represented by old and outdated objects and clutter.

No procrastination allowed! If you are too tired to do this stage, then enlist a friend to do it for you. Lie on the bed saying yes and no to items as they declutter your wardrobe. Accept that although that pant suit was really expensive it's just not in fashion any more and you are not going to wear it again. Donate it. Donate it with a good, giving energy from a place of abundance. Release it out to The Universe where it will be something that someone really needs and appreciates. Know that with every item you release you are gaining back a bit of energy and clarity for yourself.

ACTION STEP: START NOW

Write three adjectives that describe your house right now.
My house is . . .

1. ....
2. ....
3. ....

Write three adjectives that you would *like* to describe your house. Jayne, for instance, wanted serene, peaceful and calm.

I'd like my house to feel/be . . .

1. ....
2. ....
3. ....

What is the smallest room in the house where you could start?
....

Good. Now don't be overwhelmed. Set a timer for ten minutes. Make a start. Do ten minutes of decluttering in that room *right now*. Ask yourself: is this item useful? Does it really please me? Be ruthless!

Start the process of releasing your energy back into your environment. Go!

LOOK SHINY

Once you have started making your living space resemble the internal clear-up that is happening in your mental space, we will move on.

The next step is to mirror it in how *you* look! Oh, yes. This stuff is important. You are changing, on the inside. You *feel* different. You *believe* different. You *think* different. You need to *look* different!

ACTION STEP 1: HAIRDRESSERS

Book an appointment, or go to the hairdresser of a friend whose hair looks great. Go for something a little different. A change in style. Get a fringe cut. Or change the colour. Or go short. Or whatever. But do something. This is the *new you*, you need to look like her.

ACTION STEP 2: BEAUTY PARLOUR

Do whatever your budget will afford, I say. Ask for a voucher for your birthday. Call a girlfriend/sister/your mum and make it a fun girls' trip. Get plucked and buffed and waxed to within an inch of your life. Tidy, shaped eyebrows make such a difference to how your face looks, and are all the better to show off your new hairdo. Get a full manicure and pedicure or a facial. Or organise a girls' night in where you paint each other's nails and apply face masks. Whatever your budget allows.

ACTION STEP 3: SERIOUS CLOSET OVERHAUL

Right. I know you half-heartedly threw away a few old clothes when you cleared out the house in the last chapter. But you didn't really go for it with the closet, did you? Be honest now.

This time I mean it! Go get some large rubbish bags. Now, get *everything* out on the bed. The whole closet. Empty. All the drawers. All of them. Then wipe down the closet and drawers so they're nice and clean.

Nothing goes back into the closet unless it meets these criteria:

1. **You love it.**
2. **It looks awesome on you and you feel good in it.**
3. **You do not already have three identical things. (No one wears their fourth-favourite-or-less pair of black pants. Fact.)**

4. It fits you (that's you now, not your fantasy skinny self).
5. It is clean and in a good state of 'I can wear it right now' repair.

Start *ruthlessly* dividing clothes into the following categories:

1. It looks awesome on you, it fits you now, is clean and in a good state of repair. (Okay, you may put that away.)
2. Duplicates, unflattering, outdated, out of fashion. (Put in a rubbish bag for charity/giveaway or to sell.)
3. Old, worn, tired garments. (Throw it away. Now. Yes, in the bin.)
4. Mending/dry-cleaners. (Have a bag set aside for this, and actually take it.)

Methodically work through. It can be a really good idea to do this with someone, either a stylist who does wardrobe reviews, or a stylish and, above all, honest friend. A slightly bossy school ma'am attitude delivered with love would be a bonus.

Get it done. It's going to give you so much energy when you see your clean, fresh closet of clothes you actually like.

ACTION STEP 4: GO SHOPPING! FOR REAL!

Exciting. Ask a fashionable friend (or stylist) to help you assess what you are missing in your newly slimmed-down wardrobe. Think capsule wardrobe and think quality. You don't want to fill up all the beautiful space you have created with just any old garments. Your aim is, as the magnificent Gok Wan says, to 'buy less and wear more'. Stuck on what flatters you? Again, ask a friend who you think looks great or hire a stylist for a few hours to give you some tips you will use for life. Check out the books and Gok's website for inspiration (www.gokwan.com).

Obviously, it goes without saying that you should get yourself a fabulous pair of shoes or boots that are highly impractical but make you feel a million dollars. That's not a luxury, ladies: it's a necessity.

ACTION STEP 5: PAINT IT UP

Book in at your local department store for a makeover; these are usually complementary if you make a purchase afterwards. Select who does your makeover carefully: if the shop assistant is wearing full-on warpaint, then look around to see who has a look you like. Natural-looking makeovers are great. Like you, but better.

ACTION STEP 6: TA-DAH!

Look at you! That's a whole heap better than the tired and washed-out girl I met in chapter one. Go spread some energy, joy and prettiness!

Look on the outside to see how you are now feeling on the inside.

GO ON A FRIEND DIET

Now you have had a clear-out in your house and your closet, it's time to expand that practice. Making physical space in your life allows new, fresh energy to enter. Well, we need to do the same kind of thing to your relationships, too.

It's just a basic fact of life that some people's company is restful or calming: it can light you up. On the other hand, it can drain you utterly, sucking the life blood right out of you! I know I used to have a few people in my life who, whenever I met up with them, would make me feel like I was losing the will to live, right there over the peppermint tea and the carrot cake.

Here's the important thing to know: it is not a *judgement* on that person. It does not mean they are a bad/evil/nasty/unlovable person. In fact, it is quite possible to love a person but have them suck your energy at the same time. It's not a judgement on them, and it's not a judgement on you to be a better person or nicer to them. It's an emotionally neutral reading of your energy level that contact with them provokes. It's just a fact. It's like a voltage reading on the electricity meter. That's not a judgement on whether the power providers are good/bad people, it's just a voltage reading. It's just a number. It's really important to get your head around that point so you can move forward with this exercise without guilt.

List the people you associate with most and then rate from −5 to +5 according to the amount of energy you feel when you are in contact with that person. For example, my soul-sister friend Claire Turnbull is super-high energy for me. Always. Whatever sort of day I have had, whatever I have on my mind, whenever we meet up I feel infused with energy. I feel bright and perky and that I can take on the world. Yay! I had another friend, whom I will call Jody. Whenever I used to meet her I would feel my life and energy disappearing as I was sitting there, as wave after endless wave of endless gossipy stories rolled over me. Frankly, it felt like time was moving in slow motion and Jody just wiped me out. So, I would say for me, Claire is a +5 and Jody is a −4 on the energy scale. They are both lovely women, it's not a judgement on who they are. It's simply an observation of how my body and energy levels react.

Once you have this figured out, it's time to go on a High Energy Diet of your social relationships.

If you want a life of sizzling and sustainable energy, and I know you do, then you need to associate predominantly with people who make you feel energetic.

ACTION STEP 1: LOOK AT THE PEOPLE IN YOUR LIFE

List all the people in your life on the graph over the page. Don't forget to include people like ex-husbands, etc., who are still in your life. Imagine how you feel when you see them or speak with them on the phone. Do you feel infused with energy, absolutely drained or somewhere in between? For each person, score your energy reaction on the chart. Remember this isn't a judgement on them, it's just a score on how your *body* reacts. You can absolutely love your gran, but she can drain your energy, too. It's not a judgement on Gran, it's a score from your body, an objective energy-level reading.

	-5	-4	-3	-2	-1	0	1	2	3	4	5
Partner											
Ex-partner/s											
Family members											
Mum											
Dad											
Siblings											
Pets (really)											
Friends											
Boss											
Colleagues											
Other people											

ACTION STEP 2: GO ON A FRIEND DIET

It's a tough one, I know, but it's time for a Friend Diet. Understanding that you have to make a few hard choices in order to regain full energy is really important. Remember that it is all about choice.

- **Scores of –1 or below.** Do you really need to keep this person in your life? Can you let the friendship just 'drift' away into nothingness? You are just not a fit any more and *that's okay*! If you choose to keep in contact with that person, can you reduce the energy intensiveness of it? Can you change a lunch into a coffee instead? Can you make a coffee a phone call? Can you make a phone call an email? How can you downgrade the energy you invest? If it's a really low score, like –5, then do you need to have a tough conversation where you are honest and truthful and say you need a break from the relationship because it drains you?
- **Scores of 0 to +3.** Can these people replace some of the people you are going to reduce contact with? How can you add in some high-energy activities (whether it's knitting together or kayaking together) that will improve the score?
- **Scores of +4 or more.** How can you spend *more* time with these people? How can you refocus your priorities to include more contact time?

If there is no one in the high-scoring category, think of who you want to attract into your life right now. What characteristics do you find high energy in someone? Is it the ability to sit quietly together in companionable silence, to share business growth stories, to share drama-free childcare? Get clear and start looking for those people. With your energy now coming from such a clean place, you will more than likely start attracting who you need!

Chapter 6
Energy for Life

You can have the life you want. Remember that vital
energy is the foundation for a truly happy life. Make the
changes that resonate with you and move confidently
forwards to the happy and engaged life you deserve!

NEW IDENTITY

When you start moving from fatigue to wellness and embracing your new energetic life, it's important to start letting go of the old identity of a tired person. You would think this is easy, but, interestingly, many people find it hard. They have spent so long living with fatigue that it's become their constant companion, a security blanket that doesn't leave their side. It becomes part of their identity: 'My name is Caroline and I am fatigued.' This can be reinforced by the people around them, who see them as synonymous with the label of tired.

In order to move on we need to relinquish this old identity. To no longer see ourselves as defined by our energy levels. To see who we are clearly, and honour that instead. A fully rounded picture of who we are.

Some people cannot shrug off the cloak of fatigue fast enough. And it's a joy to see. A whole session will go by without them mentioning they are tired or how their energy is. It simply stops being a factor. They just don't think about it any more. That's when I know they are on their way to a life filled with vitality. It happens when they stop measuring it and stop defining themselves by it. I love being able to ask, 'Did you notice anything different about our session today?' They never guess. 'Not once have you referred to your energy levels or how tired you are or are not. You have stopped defining your life by your energy levels. You are just living your life. Go, you!' They are usually pretty stunned to see that just by working their way through the programme the cloak of fatigue that masked their beautiful shiny selves has fallen away. And they can see how much of a breakthrough that is. I love it.

Stopping talking about energy levels or any other symptoms is key to this transformation. So, you know, just stop! Go cold turkey. Be mindful that every time you define yourself by the energy level you do or don't have you are sapping your energy. Your energy just is. Accept it. And then forget about it. Your focus needs to be on your life: what do you want in it, what would be fun to do today, who would you love to chat to today, what would you like to get accomplished today, how are you going to honour your body and your true emotions today? What would you love to do? What are your favourite characteristics? What do people love about you? Put the focus elsewhere and release the old identity of 'fatigued' to embrace the new one.

ACTION STEP 1: YOUR POSITIVE FOCUS

When an acquaintance asks you how you are, do not parrot out the same old, 'Oh, you know, okay, busy, not too bad, bit tired.' Answer with a bright, confident, 'I'm terrific, thank you! How are you doing?' Be that woman. Be 'I'm terrific, thank you!' Let that define you. Which woman do you think is the one people want to work with and hang out with? Is it 'Oh, you know, not too bad' or 'I'm terrific, thank you!'? This self-definition is key, because you will be asked ten, twenty, more, times a day how you are. Have an energetic answer. This defines you not just in your eyes but in those of others.

ACTION STEP 2: THEIR POSITIVE FOCUS

Ask your nearest and dearest to stop asking you about any symptoms of burn-out or being run down. If there is something they need to know, you will tell them, but you would much rather you all talked about something other than your energy level.

RELAPSE RABBIT HOLES

As you start to recover, or are fully recovered and zinging with energy, there could be the odd time when you think 'Oh, God! It's back – the fatigue. I feel really tired today. Argh!' It's very easy to panic. Take a breath and ask yourself what you have been doing the past few days. Chances are it will sound like this: 'Well, I have been feeling so great, we went away for the weekend and played tennis, so fun. Then we went out sailing, such a great day, but I feel so tired today.' Right. So, here's the thing. It's not relapse. It's normal! Anyone would feel tired after a day out on the water and playing tennis for hours! That's entirely normal. It's really important not to disappear down the rabbit hole of relapse. Please don't freak out. Embrace the sensations in your body as normal, the normal sensations of anyone who has not been that active for a while being active again. It's a *good thing*.

Equally, everyone gets the odd bug, or cough or cold, or virus. Having been sensitised to looking at every single symptom in so much detail when you were searching for answers to your tiredness, it's easy to freak out every time you get a cold. But here's the thing. Everyone gets a cold now and again. Yes, it feels crappy. That's what a cold feels like! That's *normal*! Do not, repeat not, disappear down the rabbit hole of relapse by making something that's perfectly normal (a sore body after tennis, feeling achy when you have a cold) something abnormal or significant. It's not. It's just life. It's just part of the human experience of having a body. Go back and reread this book if you need to. Sit down and write down your thoughts – examine them. Repeat your energy mantra. Do not let your Lizard spin out of control because you have a flu bug. It's just a flu bug. Everyone feels awful.

I believe there are two types of tiredness we can experience: good tired and bad tired. I wanted to share the following to give you a clear distinction between what is normal and what is not. It applies to us all, every single day.

Good tired is:
- the warm, achy tiredness you feel after making time for yourself to have a run or a swim
- falling asleep on the sofa after a hard game of tennis or playing with the kids
- that glowy tiredness you feel after a day on the water
- that satisfied weariness you get after giving that presentation or completing a project dear to your heart
- how you feel after staying up late talking with great friends
- the deep relaxation you feel at the end of your yoga class
- taking on a project that you are so excited about you can't sleep
- relishing a quiet moment while your newborn sleeps soundly
- an achy brain from the challenge of learning something new.

Good tired is *good*. Good tired moves you towards your destiny. Good tired is what brings you joy. Good tired is what keeps your body healthy while nourishing your mind and soul. Good tired is how you make a difference in this world.

Bad tired is:

- ※ the eye-watering tiredness you feel while driving to a job you hate with dread in your stomach
- ※ the tiredness you feel when you need a triple-shot latte just to get you through that next meeting
- ※ how you feel when you network and socialise with people you feel you 'have to' impress
- ※ how you feel when you force yourself to a spin class you don't enjoy to punish your body for how much it weighs
- ※ yawning while checking your work email compulsively out-of-hours
- ※ staying late at work for the fourth time this week, because the business's needs come before your own
- ※ being exhausted but unable to sleep because your brain is so busy worrying about stuff
- ※ reaching for the wine as a pick-me-up, not as a pleasure to be savoured
- ※ the despair you feel while saying 'yes' when you want to say 'hell, no'.

Bad tired is trying to do it all. Bad tired shows you are out of balance. Bad tired is bad for your body and your soul. Bad tired moves you away from your destiny. Bad tired says it's time to reassess where you choose to spend your time and energy.

You can choose. Your life, your body, your energy, your time. Being tired is actually one of life's great privileges. It's good to be tired! Being tired lets you know you are alive. But only you can choose whether you are defeated by bad tired or filled to the brim with good tired.

ACTION STEP: DON'T PANIC

If you feel you are at all verging on the edge of relapse, then first of all don't panic! Remember:

1. Feeling tired after doing stuff is *normal*.
2. We all get bugs and viruses every now and again. We all feel terrible when we get the flu. That's also *normal*.

3. Learn to discern between good tired and bad tired. Use bad tired as a cue to refresh on the tools you have learned in this book. Did you just read them and not actually *do* them? Did you put them into action? This programme will work if you do, so take a few incidents of bad tired as an opportunity to revise and refresh on the tools you have learned and *apply* them diligently. Recommit.

4. Pay attention to your thoughts. Remember your energy goes where your thoughts go. Monitor those thoughts and replace them with your energy mantra whenever appropriate.

5. Make sure you have your Lizard on a short leash. Did you buy a physical representation of your Inner Lizard to help with that psychological separation? If not, do it *now*. Talk to your Lizard, take back control.

6. Mind, body and soul are all equally important not just for healing but for living a healthy, balanced life. Check in once again with your Life Satisfaction Scores (see page 111) and see where you need to tweak things.

7. Is there some situation you are avoiding being honest about, either to others or even yourself? Remember this sucks energy like nothing else, so get clean and honest. Do some private journalling and get in alignment with your truth.

CHANGE THAT LASTS

I don't believe in New Year's resolutions, but I do believe in resolutions.

I believe we all have the capacity to start over at any time; to wipe the slate and to choose different things for ourselves whenever we make that commitment. And that can happen on 1 January, 23 May or 15 September at 1.02 a.m. The time is irrelevant. What is important is the *commitment* to the intention and the *energy* from which it is made.

This is a perfect time to recap on the Ten Truth Flashes of High Energy Happiness.

Truth Flash #1: You have to *prioritise* your energy levels. Only you can do that. There is nothing more important than this right now. It's your most important work in the world and is your foundation for a well-lived, happy life.

Truth Flash #2: Your body is an amazing miracle, it is a healing machine. It is your *job* to create the optimum conditions for it to *heal* itself.

Truth Flash #3: You must to be prepared to choose to *think* differently and *do* differently in order to *feel* differently. It's not a passive programme; it works if you work!

Truth Flash #4: There is a zero-tolerance policy for whinging, moaning and generally feeling sorry for yourself. It brings others down, it brings you down. It brings your energy down. There is no room for a pity party here or in life!

Truth Flash #5: Consistency is key. How do people reach the top of Everest? One step at a time in the right direction. The same principle applies here. Choose consistently in favour of what you want. And what you want is to feel energetic and happy, right?

Truth Flash #6: Your physical body and your true emotional state are your *highest priority*. Now. Always. Forever. Put your own oxygen mask on first.

Truth Flash #7: You don't 'catch' continual tiredness, you give it to yourself. The great news about this is that you can take *responsibility* to heal yourself, too. It's a gift from which to learn and shape an awesome, energetic life.

Truth Flash #8: *Emotions* are messengers from our true, authentic self and they are not to be feared. Emotions are *energy in our body*. And we need to feel them and process them in the body.

Truth Flash #9: The only thing you *have* to do is breathe, and everything after that is a choice. 'Have to' is a limiting thought pattern that keeps you stuck.

Truth Flash #10: *Outrageous energy* **is available to us all. We just need to be aware and consistently choose in favour of it. It's not a magic trick, it's a process.**

You can have the life you want. Remember that vital energy is the foundation for a truly happy life. Make the changes that resonate with you, and move confidently forwards to the happy and engaged life you deserve!

So, my lovely, as our journey here comes to an end I'd like to leave you with a few thoughts.

I believe feeling constantly tired is the silent epidemic of the era in which we live. Life has become increasingly set up to subtly push us in this direction, unless we become hyper-aware of our thoughts, actions and habits. The ever-increasing number of coffee shops and energy drinks, which actually *deplete* our energy rather than restore it, mask our tiredness. The expectation level of being connected, contactable and 'on' at all times diminishes the all-important rest time we are programmed to need. The aspirational world in which we live, filled with messages of what is 'good enough' and 'perfect', encourages us to be all things to all people. The perfect wife, the perfect mother, the perfect employee, the perfect friend. It's unsustainable. We were just not built for this. When we give into this relentless tide, and we are all things to all people, we are in danger of being nothing to ourselves.

Changing this creep of institutionalised tiredness all starts with us as individuals. We need to put our own energy boundaries in place and honour them consistently. We can start a movement here, a movement of energy and happiness. Each tiny change we make that empowers us and moves us towards our most energetic and vital life is a step forward for us all. If we put this pressure on ourselves, it also means we can take it off ourselves.

It is important to know that burn-out does not mean you cannot handle the pressure or cope with modern life. It's a message from your body to stop and reassess. I used to think that anyone who felt like this was weak, and a bit of a loser. Not so! Fatigue can happen to anyone and it can creep up without you even noticing. When I finally collapsed it was the perfect storm of stressful events, so cumulative that it whipped the ground out from under my feet. For you it might be a series of stressful events over years, or one big life-changing tsunami of stress. However it unfolds, it's important to know that you can change the status quo. You can fix it.

Many of my clients eventually come to the conclusion, as I did myself, that becoming severely fatigued was actually an incredible gift. For me, it forced a period of re-examination of what I was choosing to put into my life, my body and my mind. It forced self-awareness and it forced me to step up and take responsibility for my health and my life. It changed the course of my life. It changed how I interact with others. I learned discernment and I learned to enforce my own boundaries on my energy and my time. My life is immeasurably richer, happier and more authentically happy than it was before. This is echoed by so many of my clients. Do they want to repeat the experience of adrenal fatigue? Hell, no! Are they grateful it happened? Interestingly, yes. Burn-out or 'tired all the time' can be the most incredible catalyst for transformational life change. No one wants back the life they had before. They all want to be the person they are *now*, out the other side with a whole new set of beliefs and thought patterns that support the awesome person they are in the life they live today. I can't image the different path my life would have taken had this period of burn-out not happened to me. I like to think it happened not *to me*, but *for me*. I encourage you to follow in our footsteps and see exhaustion as a bizarre gift that can deliver the opportunity to make changes and reassess what is truly important to you.

The change starts with YOU. Put your own oxygen mask on first. And be gentle with yourself. You are precious, unique and loved. You are good enough exactly as you are. Come share your own inspirational journey with us over at www.louisethompson.com.

Go well, be well.

GRATITUDE

I am blessed to be surrounded with more than my fair share of extraordinary people, all of whom have helped to shape my experience and therefore this book. You wonderful people, I salute you!

Huge thanks firstly to Dr James Wilson, without whose pioneering work in the hugely under-diagnosed field of adrenal fatigue I would probably still be a tired shell of a woman today. Dr Wilson's work and his supplements made the most incredible difference to my life and happiness. Not only is he the smartest man you could ever meet, but the most generous, too. I am thrilled that he has written the foreword for this book, and hugely value his support throughout my journey.

Martha Beck and the Martha Beck tribe of coaches and coach buddies have also been an incredible support. Martha's work and my training in her coaching techniques were also foundational in my route to wellness, and I will always be grateful for the work she has put out into the world. Martha, you rock! Come to New Zealand on your travels because the tribe here is growing every day.

To my darling mum, dad, brother Martin and the rest of the family, who have always supported me from near and afar with a lifetime of love and belief that I could do something special with my life, love always. I hope I make you proud. I love you and miss you more than I can say.

Special thanks to Claire Turnbull for being the most high-energy friend and wellbeing co-conspirator. Also for all the work on our recipe book, *Eat for Energy: Simple Strategies to Energise Your Diet*. Girlfriend, the day our paths crossed was one of the best examples of serendipity EVER! Love working with you.

Many thanks to the lovely Jo Elwin at the *New Zealand Herald* for the opportunity to write my weekly newspaper column each Monday, and spread the message of wellbeing more widely. Toni, Rawdon, Suz and the team at TVNZ's *Breakfast*, thank you for making me so welcome and bringing life coaching out of the closet and onto the couch.

Debra, Kate and the team at Penguin. What can I say? You have taken a columnist and turned her into an author. It's been beyond exciting. Thank you for holding my hand, guiding the way and truly understanding why this energy message needs to be heard. I am blessed to be a Penguin author and shall represent your brand with pride.

High-fives to Theresa, Eric, Adam and the crew at Nutrisearch Ltd for the enormous faith and support along the way, and for getting supplements to my clients with such efficiency; to Dave and Andrea for making such professional videos and audios to complete this programme, and creating such an interactive journey to wellness that people can get from the website (www.louisethompson.com) to follow at home; to Ben and the Digital Hothouse boys for building such a kick-ass new website; and Claire at Creative People for making it look so damn pretty.

To my Positive Balance yoga students who have faithfully attended classes since we launched in 2005: seeing you all progress has been such a pleasure, and the way you have been my cheerleaders with my writing has been amazing. My jouney into becoming a wellbeing professional started with you. Your faith and loyalty have become the foundation of a great thing that none of us could have imagined from early beginnings on a yoga mat in a cold church hall! I thank each one of you. Team Positive Balance, who make it all run with such ease and grace: Tracey, Aroha, Dale and Justine, when I say I couldn't do it without you, you know it's not lip service – I really couldn't do it without you! I am honoured and grateful to have you on Team PB.

My good friends both here and overseas (too many to mention, but you know who you are!) and my new Thompson family, thank you for the inspiration, friendship and support. Please know you make a huge difference to my happiness levels every single day.

I wrote much of this book in the beautiful Cook Islands. Happily, it seems to be the place I write the most easily, and I will be forever indebted to Melanie Cooper, tropical wedding photographer extraordinaire, and her exuberant, loveable hound Lulu who provided me a writing haven on a number of occasions to get this book finished.

My amazing, gorgeous husband, Forsyth, gets the biggest thanks of all. Without his unfailing love and support I doubt I would ever have discovered my way back to wellness and such a happy, energetic life. Thank you for helping me get better, my love, and for believing in me and my work as much (or even more) than I do myself. Thank you for being so cool about my writing sabbaticals that have looked suspiciously like sunshiny holidays, and for never doubting for a second that I could do this. Thank you, also, for being a very patient technical support helpdesk, and meeting every freaked-out cry of 'It's broken!' with good humour, good grace and smart fixes. I am beyond lucky to have you as my husband. You are the true love of my life.

Thank you to all my amazing, extraordinary clients. Thank you for telling me to write this, to spread my work more widely. Thank you for choosing me to help you to a life of energy and happiness. Thank you for trusting me, for embracing the tools, for following the programme, for doing the work, for sharing the tears and the laughter as you have regained your health. Seeing you rock your health, body, relationships, money, career and lives has been better than I ever imagined. Thank you for being the beta-readers for the draft of this book, and for all your feedback to get it as close as possible to the in-person coaching experience you had with me. A million thanks to each and every one of you.

Last, but not least, I offer my thanks to you, the reader. Thank you for picking this book up, and for making it the first step on your journey to the life of High Energy Happiness you more than deserve. You can have the life you want, and it all starts here.

APPENDIX

ADRENAL FATIGUE QUESTIONNAIRE

This questionnaire[1] was originally created and used by Dr James L. Wilson in his practice and later published on page 61 in his book, *Adrenal Fatigue: The 21st Century Stress Syndrome*. Dr Wilson's permission has been given to use this questionnaire in this book. It is designed as an aid to determining a patient's level of adrenal fatigue. Although Dr Wilson and many other physicians have found the questionnaire extremely helpful, no formal reliability or validity tests have been completed to confirm its accuracy, and the author assumes no responsibility for its use or accuracy. No commercial use of this questionnaire is permitted without prior written consent by the author, Dr Wilson.

I have not felt well since (date) ....
when (describe event, if any) ....
....
....
....

Instructions: please enter the appropriate response number to each of the following statements.

0 = Never/rarely
1 = Occasionally/slightly
2 = Moderate in intensity or frequency
3 = Intense/severe or frequent

PREDISPOSING FACTORS

	PAST	NOW	
1.	....	....	I have experienced long periods of stress that have affected my wellbeing.
2.	....	....	I have had one or more severely stressful events that have affected my wellbeing.
3.	....	....	I have driven myself to exhaustion.
4.	....	....	I overwork with little play or relaxation for extended periods.
5.	....	....	I have had extended, severe or recurring respiratory infections.

---

6. .... I have taken long-term or intense steroid therapy (corticosteroids).
7. .... I tend to gain weight, especially around the middle (spare tire).
8. .... I have a history of alcoholism and/or drug abuse.
9. .... I have environmental sensitivities.
10. .... I have diabetes (type 2, adult onset, NIDDM).
11. .... I suffer from post-traumatic distress syndrome.
12. .... I suffer from anorexia.*
13. .... I have one or more other chronic illnesses or diseases.
.... **TOTAL**

KEY SIGNS AND SYMPTOMS

PAST   NOW

1. .... My ability to handle stress and pressure has decreased.
2. .... I am less productive at work.
3. .... I seem to have decreased in cognitive ability. I don't think as clearly as I used to.
4. .... My thinking is confused when hurried or under pressure.
5. .... I tend to avoid emotional situations.
6. .... I tend to shake or am nervous when under pressure.
7. .... I suffer from nervous stomach indigestion when tense.
8. .... I have many unexplained fears/anxieties.
9. .... My sex drive is noticeably less than it used to be.
10. .... I get lightheaded or dizzy when rising rapidly from a sitting or lying position.
11. .... I have feelings of graying or blacking out.
12. .... I am chronically fatigued; a tiredness that is not usually relieved by sleep.*
13. .... I feel unwell much of the time.
14. .... I notice that my ankles are sometimes swollen. The swelling is worse in the evening.
15. .... I usually need to lie down or rest after sessions of psychological or emotional pressure/stress.
16. .... My muscles sometimes feel weaker than they should.
17. .... My hands and legs get restless. I experience meaningless body movements.
18. .... I have become allergic or have increased frequency/severity of allergic reactions.
19. .... When I scratch my skin, a white line remains for a minute or more.
20. .... Small irregular dark brown spots have appeared on my forehead, face, neck and shoulders.
21. .... I sometimes feel weak all over.*
22. .... I have unexplained and frequent headaches.
23. .... I am frequently cold.

24. .... I have decreased tolerance for cold.*
25. .... I have low blood pressure.*
26. .... I often become hungry, confused, shaky or somewhat
paralysed under stress.
27. .... I have lost weight without reason while feeling very tired
and listless.
28. .... I have feelings of hopelessness or despair.
29. .... I have decreased tolerance. People irritate me more.
30. .... The lymph nodes in my neck are frequently swollen
(swollen glands).
31. .... I have times of nausea and vomiting for no apparent reason.*
.... **TOTAL**

ENERGY PATTERNS
PAST NOW
1. .... I often have to force myself in order to keep going.
Everything seems like a chore.
2. .... I am easily fatigued.
3. .... I have difficulty getting up in the morning (don't really
wake up until about 10 a.m.).
4. .... I suddenly run out of energy.
5. .... I usually feel much better and fully awake after the noon
meal.
6. .... I often have an afternoon low between 3 p.m. and 5 p.m.
7. .... I get low energy, moody or foggy if I do not eat regularly.
8. .... I usually feel my best after 6 p.m.
9. .... I am often tired by 9 p.m. to 10 p.m., but resist going to bed.
10. .... I like to sleep late in the morning.
11. .... My best, most refreshing sleep often comes between 7 a.m.
and 9 a.m.
12. .... I often do my best work late at night (early in the morning).
13. .... If I don't go to bed by 11 p.m., I get a second burst of
energy around 11 p.m., often lasting until 1 a.m. to 2 a.m.
.... **TOTAL**

FREQUENTLY OBSERVED EVENTS
PAST NOW
1. .... I get coughs/colds that stay around for several weeks.
2. .... I have frequent or recurring bronchitis, pneumonia or
other respiratory infections.
I get asthma, colds and other respiratory involvements two
or more times per year.
3. .... I frequently get rashes, dermatitis or other skin conditions.
4. .... I have rheumatoid arthritis.

5. .... I have allergies to several things in the environment.
6. .... I have multiple chemical sensitivities.
7. .... I have chronic fatigue syndrome.
8. .... I get pain in the muscles on the sides of my neck.
9. .... I have insomnia or difficulty sleeping.
10. .... I have fibromyalgia.
11. .... I suffer from asthma.
12. .... I suffer from hay fever.
13. .... I suffer from nervous breakdowns.
14. .... I get pain in the muscles of my upper back and lower neck for no apparent reason.
15. .... My allergies are becoming worse (more severe, frequent or diverse).
16. .... The fat pads on the palms of my hands and/or tips of my fingers are often red.
17. .... I bruise more easily than I used to.
18. .... I have a tenderness in my back near my spine at the bottom of my rib cage when pressed.
19. .... I have swelling under my eyes upon rising that goes away after I have been up for a couple of hours.
    .... **TOTAL**

The next two questions are for women only:
1. .... I have increasing symptoms of premenstrual syndrome (PMS) such as cramps, bloating, moodiness, irritability, emotional instability, headaches, tiredness and/or intolerance before my period (only some of these need be present).
2. .... My periods are generally heavy but they often stop, or almost stop, on the fourth day, only to start up profusely on the fifth or sixth day.
    .... **TOTAL**

FOOD PATTERNS
PAST   NOW
1. .... I need coffee or some other stimulant to get going in the morning.
2. .... I often crave food high in fat and feel better with high-fat foods.
3. .... I use high-fat foods to drive myself.
4. .... I often use high-fat foods and caffeine-containing drinks (coffee, colas, chocolate) to drive myself.
5. .... I often crave salt and/or foods high in salt. I like salty foods.
6. .... I feel worse if I eat high-potassium foods (like bananas, figs, raw potatoes), especially if I eat them in the morning.

7. .... I crave high-protein foods (meats, cheeses).
.... I crave sweet foods (pies, cakes, pastries, doughnuts, dried fruits, candies, desserts).
8. .... I feel worse if I miss or skip a meal.
.... **TOTAL**

AGGRAVATING FACTORS

PAST NOW

1. .... I have constant stress in my life or work.
2. .... My dietary habits tend to be sporadic and unplanned.
3. .... I do not exercise regularly.
4. .... My relationships at work and/or home are unhappy.
5. .... My life contains insufficient enjoyable activities.
6. .... I have little control over how I spend my time.
7. .... I restrict my salt intake.
8. .... I have gum and/or tooth infections or abscesses.
9. .... I have meals at irregular times.
10. .... I eat lots of fruit.
.... **TOTAL**

RELIEVING FACTORS

PAST NOW

1. .... I feel better almost right away once a stressful situation is resolved.
2. .... Regular meals decrease the severity of my symptoms.
3. .... I often feel better after spending a night out with friends.
4. .... I often feel better if I lie down.
5. .... Other relieving factor: ....
.... **TOTAL**

Scoring and interpretation of the questionnaire

A lot of information can be obtained from this questionnaire. Follow the instructions below carefully to score your questionnaire correctly. Then proceed to the interpretation section.

Total number of questions answered

1. First count the total number of questions in each section that you answered with any number other than zero. Enter the 'past' and 'now' totals separately, entering each in appropriate boxes for each section of the 'Total number of questions answered' scoring chart over the page. For example, if you answered a total of 21 questions in the 'past' column and 27 questions in the 'now' column of the 'Key signs and symptoms' with a 1, 2 or 3, your

total number of questions answered score for the 'past' column would be '21' and for the 'now' column would be '27'. Note that there are no entries for the first section of the questionnaire entitled 'Predisposing factors'. This section is dealt with separately and is not included in the summary below. Therefore, your first entry into the summary boxes will be for the 'Key signs and symptoms' section.

2. After you have finished entering the number of questions answered in both columns for each section, sum all the numbers for each column and the total in the 'Grand total – total number of questions answered' boxes on the bottom row of the scoring chart.

3. All the boxes in the 'Total number of questions answered' chart should now be filled.

Then go on to the next part of the scoring.

TOTAL NUMBER OF QUESTIONS ANSWERED WITH ABOVE 0		
	TOTAL ANSWERED	
NAME OF SECTION	PAST	NOW
Key signs and symptoms (Number of questions = 31)		
Energy patterns (Number of questions = 13)		
Frequently observed events (Number of questions = 20 for men, 22 for women)		
Food patterns (Number of questions = 9)		
Aggravating factors (Number of questions = 10)		
Relieving factors (Number of questions = 4)		
Grand total – total number of questions answered with above 0		

Total points

This part of the scoring adds up the actual numbers (0, 1, 2 or 3) you put beside the questions when you were answering the questionnaire. Add these numbers for each column in each section and enter them into the appropriate boxes in the following chart. Then, sum each column to get the Total points scores. Enter these totals in the Total Points = SEVERITY boxes to complete this part of the scoring.

TOTAL POINTS		
	TOTAL ANSWERED	
NAME OF SECTION	PAST	NOW
Key signs and symptoms (Total points possible = 93)		
Energy patterns (Total points possible = 39)		
Frequently observed events (Total points possible = 60 for men, 66 for women)		
Food patterns (Total points possible = 27)		
Aggravating factors (Total points possible = 30)		
Relieving factors (Total points possible = 12)		
Total points = SEVERITY		
Grand total – total number of questions answered with above 0		
Severity index = total points divided by total questions answered above 0		
Asterisk total – total points on questions marked with *		

Interpreting the questionnaire

The questionnaire is a valuable tool for determining IF you have adrenal fatigue and, if you do, the SEVERITY of your syndrome. Of course, the accuracy of its interpretation depends upon you completing every section as accurately and honestly as possible. Because there is such diversity in how individuals experience adrenal fatigue, a wide variety of signs and symptoms have been included. Some people have only the minimal number of symptoms, but the symptoms they do have are severe. Others experience a great number of symptoms, but most of their symptoms are relatively mild. This is why there are two kinds of scores to indicate adrenal fatigue.

Total number of questions answered with a number above 0

This gives you a general 'yes' or 'no' answer to the question, 'Do I have adrenal fatigue?' First look at your 'Grand total – total number of questions answered with above 0' scores in the first scoring chart. The purpose of this score is to see the total number of signs and symptoms of adrenal fatigue you have. There is a total of 87 questions for men and 89 questions for women in the questionnaire. If you responded with a number **above 0** to **more than 26** (men) or **32** (women) of the questions (regardless of which severity response number you gave the question), you have some degree of adrenal fatigue. The greater the number of questions that you have responded affirmatively to, the greater your adrenal fatigue. If you responded affirmatively to **less than 20** of the questions, it is unlikely adrenal fatigue is your problem. People who do not have adrenal fatigue may still experience a few of these indicators in their lives, but not many of them. If your symptoms do not include fatigue or decreased ability to handle stress, then you are probably not suffering from adrenal fatigue.

Total points

The total points are used to determine the degree of severity of your adrenal fatigue. If you ranked every question as 3 (the worst) your total points would be 261 for men and 267 for women. If you scored **under 40**, you either have only slight adrenal fatigue or none at all. If you scored **between 44 and 87** for men or **45 and 88** for women, then overall you have a mild degree of adrenal fatigue. This does not mean that some individual symptoms are not severe, but overall your symptom picture reflects mildly fatigued adrenals. If you scored **between 88 and 130** for men or **89 and 132** for women, your adrenal fatigue is moderate. If you scored **above 130** for men or **above 132** for women, then consider yourself to be suffering from severe adrenal fatigue. Now compare the total points of the different sections with each other. This allows you to see if one or two sections stand out as having more signs and symptoms than the others. If you have a predominating group of symptoms, they will be the most useful ones for you to watch as indicators as you improve. Seeing which sections stand out will also be helpful in developing your own recovery program.

Severity index

The severity index is calculated by simply dividing the total points by the total number of questions you answered in the affirmative. It gives an indication of how severely you experience the signs and symptoms, with **1.0–1.6** being mild, **1.7–2.3** being moderate and **2.4 plus** being severe. This number is especially useful for those who suffer from only a few of these signs and symptoms, but are considerably debilitated by them.

Past vs now

Now compare the total points in the 'past' column to the total points in the 'now' column. The difference indicates the direction your adrenal health is taking. If the number in the 'past' column is greater than the number in the 'now' column, then you are slowly recovering from hypoadrenia. It is a good sign you are recovering. If the number in the 'now' column is greater than the number in the 'past' column, your adrenal glands are on a downhill course and you need to take immediate action to prevent further decline and to recover.

Asterisk total

Finally, add the actual numbers you put beside the questions marked by asterisks (*) for the 'now' column. If this total is **more than 9**, you are likely suffering from a relatively severe form of adrenal fatigue. If this total is **more than 12**, and you answer **yes** to **more than 2** of the questions below, you have many of the indications of true Addison's disease and should consult a physician.

Answer the following questions only if you scored more than 12 on the questions marked with an asterisk (*).

ADDITIONAL SYMPTOMS (THAT ARE PRESENT NOW)

The areas on my body listed below have become bluish-black in colour.

.... Inside of lips, mouth.
.... Vagina.
.... Around nipples.

.... I have frequent unexplained diarrhoea.
.... I have increased darkening around the bony areas, at folds in my skin, scars and the creases in my joints.
.... I have light-coloured patches on my skin where the skin has lost its usual colour.
.... I easily become dehydrated.
.... I have fainting spells.

Interpretation of the 'predisposing factors' section

This section helps determine which factors led to the development of your adrenal fatigue. There may have been only one factor or there may have been several, but the number does not matter. One severely stressful incident can be all it takes for someone to develop adrenal fatigue, although typically it is more. This list is not exhaustive, but the items listed in this section are the most common factors that lead to adrenal fatigue. Use this section to better understand how your adrenal fatigue developed. Seeing how it started often makes clearer what actions you can take to successfully recover from it.

Disclaimer

The ideas and suggestions contained in this questionnaire are not intended as a substitute for consulting with your physician. All matters regarding your health require medical supervision. Neither the author nor the publisher shall be liable or responsible for any loss or damage allegedly arising from any information or suggestion in this questionnaire. To find a local natural health practitioner to discuss this with, visit www.adrenalfatigue.co.nz.

REFERENCES

Recommended Reading

Beck, Martha. *Finding Your Own North Star: Claiming the Life You Were Meant to Live*. London: Piatkus Books, 2001.

Beck, Martha. *Steering by Starlight: The Science and Magic of Finding Your Destiny*. London: Piatkus Books, 2008.

Hanley, Dr Jesse and Deville, Nancy. *Tired of Being Tired: Rescue. Repair. Rejuvenate*. London: Penguin Group, 2004.

Turnbull, Claire. *Lose Weight for Life*. Auckland: Penguin Group (NZ), 2013.

Wilson, Dr James. *Adrenal Fatigue: The 21st Century Stress Syndrome*. Petaluma: Smart Publications, 2010.

Useful Websites

www.louisethompson.com – There are many free and paid-for resources available to support your journey on my website, and I'd love to hear how you are doing! Come chat with me and sign up for the free weekly newsletter 'Wellbeing Wednesday'.

www.positivebalance.co.nz – Lists my yoga classes.

www.adrenalfatigue.co.nz – Will put you in touch with your local naturopath across New Zealand.

www.marthabeck.com/find-a-coach/ – Worldwide options for finding a life coach.

www.goodvibeblog.com – Jeanette Maw's work on making the law of attraction work for you.

www.sivananda.org – Worldwide yoga options.

Come hit me up on twitter @flexhappy